D0908307

Interviews with
Latin American Writers

Interviews with Latin American Writers

Marie-Lise Gazarian Gautier

Dalkey Archive Press

Library of Congress Cataloging in Publication Data
Interviews with Latin American writers / Marie-Lise Gazarian Gautier. —
1st ed.
1. Authors, Latin American—20th century—Interviews. 2. Latin American
literature—20th century—History and criticism.
I. Gazarian Gautier, Marie-Lise.
PQ7081.3.I58   1989   869—dc19   88-25052
ISBN: 0-916583-32-5

First Edition

PHOTO CREDITS: The photographs of Guillermo Cabrera Infante, José
Donoso, Rosario Ferré, Carlos Fuentes, Isaac Goldemberg, Nicanor Parra,
Elena Poniatowska, Manuel Puig, and Luisa Valenzuela are by Layle Silbert,
copyright © 1982, 1983, 1984, 1985, 1986, 1987, 1988 by Layle Silbert; the
photo of Isabel Allende by Irmeli Jung and of Juan Carlos Onetti by Vincenzo
Flore are used courtesy of the Literature Department of the Americas Society;
the photo of Ernesto Sábato is used courtesy Available Press, a division of
Random House; the photo of Severo Sarduy is by D. Roche and is used
courtesy Editions du Seuil; the photos of Luis Rafael Sánchez and Mario
Vargas Llosa are by Marie-Lise Gazarian Gautier.

Partially funded by grants from The National Endowment for the Arts and
The Illinois Arts Council.

The Dalkey Archive Press
1817 North 79th Avenue
Elmwood Park, IL 60635 USA

In memory of María Mora Molares

and

To Nathalie, my Mother, who, through her gentle ways, taught me how to listen to people's voices and reach out for their inner thoughts.

Contents

Introduction

Over the past ten years I have interviewed more than one hundred prominent writers from both Spain and Latin America. Some of these interviews were held in the privacy of their homes or amidst the turmoil of a hotel lobby or airport; others were conducted in front of a television camera and the critical eye of the public; still others grew out of transatlantic or transcontinental telephone calls.

This book, the first of a two-volume set of interviews with Spanish-speaking writers, represents innumerable hours of dialogue with fifteen Latin American authors. The second volume, to appear in the near future, will contain interviews with writers from Spain. In both volumes will be heard the multiple voice of the Spanish language.

The interview is one of the most revealing and authentic approaches to literature. It allows the reader to penetrate into the creative mind and find out at firsthand what are the components of the craft of writing and the workings of the writer. Some feel a challenge as they face the "blank page," others are startled by the flow of words. Rosario Ferré, one of Puerto Rico's leading writers, said in this respect: "Unlike other writers, I do not have this great fear of the 'blank page.' In fact, it is completely the opposite for me: I am frightened of the page which, even before I start writing, overflows with words. I have to control them in order to avoid their invasion of the page." Guillermo Cabrera Infante, the Cuban novelist who now lives in London, spoke of the meaning of the page filled with words: "I can then play with them, transform them, parody them, and find their relation to phrases from earlier times." And another Cuban, Severo Sarduy, made the striking remark that the page, after it experiences a series of corrections, "looks like an enormous scar or tattoo. In some way, writing is like tattooing."

Watching an interview or reading its transcript is the next best thing to knowing writers personally and certainly the most illuminating companion to their works. The interview is without a doubt what comes closest to a conversation between friends or to a therapeutic session with a confidant or an analyst. In a conversation, both people have equal rights at questioning, answering and pausing. In an interview, both parties are bound by a series of questions which bring about a series of answers. One must ask, the other answer; one must challenge, the other respond to that challenge. In many cases, both partners in that interactive game are equally motivated; they may come out of their intellectual exchange exhausted, but fulfilled.

Of course, the interview taped in a television studio in front of blinding spotlights and cameras may not always be as relaxed as the one held at home, when both people are leaning back in comfortable armchairs and sipping a cup of tea. It must follow a somewhat rigid and formal pattern, unlike everyday dialogue. I recall that with each televised interview I continuously had to keep an eye on the cue cards to know whether we had five minutes or five seconds left. On the other hand, the television interview may have the effect of a stimulant (not always available in one's home) and can bring out the performer in the participant. When I finished my three-part interview with Carlos Fuentes, for instance, the crew and the directors in the control room stood up and applauded the Mexican writer because they were galvanized by his sharp wit.

In a private and pleasant conversation between friends, no one is really limited by time; in an interview, the clock usually rules the game. I must add, however, that I sometimes experienced the contrary. When I interviewed Isaac Goldemberg, Nicanor Parra, Luisa Valenzuela or Luis Rafael Sánchez, we never once looked at our watches and we felt totally relaxed and enjoyed our meeting. Actually there was something magnetic about it. It seemed as though neither of us wanted the conversation to come to an end.

With all the writers except Ernesto Sábato, our conversations had been taped. The recorder stood at all times as a faithful companion and working tool between writer and interviewer. In Sábato's case, it was not so. We met twice for long spans of time and he was most kind in allowing me those hours. He wanted to find out about me, watch my reactions, and, of course, see the questions I planned to ask him. In a way, he was seeking equal rights: to interview me as much as I would interview him. I can say that we virtually interviewed one another, but at no time did he allow me to tape our conversations. He took my questions along with him to Argentina and promised to send an interview written in his own style and fashion, which he did. Basing his dialogue on my questions, he elaborated in the leisure of his home an interview that resembles a movie script, where both characters interact, talk, laugh and move about. I have tried to preserve as much as possible of its flavor in the translation.

In some interviews, on the other hand, I did have to submit myself to time constraints. I can recall the many instances when I had to coax some of the writers and plead with them for extra time. For example, I drove Manuel Puig to Kennedy Airport after he had spent a hectic day of lecturing in New York so I could have the chance to interview him. The interview took place while he was waiting for his plane to leave for Rio. Strangely enough, this was the same airport where he had once worked when he lived in New York. Needless to say, I was left with an unfinished conversation which I had to continue over a long telephone call to Brazil.

This brings me to another vehicle I have used for interviewing, the telephone, which encompasses an incredible range of possibilities. I reached Juan Carlos Onetti and Severo Sarduy in their homes in Madrid and in Senlis, near Paris, respectively, and held long dialogues with them. Onetti told me that he was very shy and that he had spent the entire night waiting for my call. At first it was hard to communicate; we both felt the need to see a face that would go along with the voice. But the magic of

words took care of that and I was won over by his straightfor-
wardness and his sense of humor. Severo Sarduy, as a typically
extrovert Cuban, did not need to see his interviewer. He talked
with a Caribbean exuberance that made me forget that we were
more than three thousand miles apart and that we had never met.
Before reaching Elena Poniatowska at her home in Mexico, I
felt somewhat apprehensive. She was, after all, the winner of a
journalistic prize for the art of interviewing. I kept wondering
how it would feel to interview an interviewer. Once we started
our conversation, however, my worries were dispelled and we
went on as if we were two old friends and colleagues, used to
doing the same type of work. Of course, I would have loved to
see her face, to know the setting in which she lived, the objects
that surrounded her. But in all earnestness, I can say that I have
come to know her through that telephone conversation.

Some people have compared the interview to a game of chess
where words, like pawns, are manipulated by two players. I
would like to compare it to a game of Ping-Pong. The ball
bounces back and forth and challenges the players into a
dynamic encounter. This brings to mind the reaction of the
Chilean poet Nicanor Parra, whom I met for a second session
after the interview had been done and transcribed. After a careful reading of the text to see what he would include or exclude,
he exclaimed, without changing anything, "I like it, it flows!"
Interestingly, he told me that he visualized poetry as a conversation with questions and answers, similar to those of an interview.

Questions may trigger a burst of spontaneous and unpretentious remarks, as in the case of Isabel Allende, who kept on
saying that she knew nothing about literature. Or, on the
contrary, they may bring about a series of tricks which the
interviewee plays on the interviewer. Another Chilean, the
novelist José Donoso, for instance, enjoyed evading my
questions or refuting them, just for the sake of responding to
them in his own time and at his own pace, hoping to catch me off
guard.

In an interview, the rhythm of the encounter between the two players largely depends on their ability to serve and to return the serve. If one of the players hesitates, the ball drops to the floor and the conversation grows silent. Silence is the worst enemy of the interview. A few seconds of it during a television or radio interview may be nearly fatal. Fortunately, I never had to experience that moment of dead silence. None of the writers answered my questions with a curt "yes" or "no." They all possessed the bewitching qualities of a storyteller. Since words are their primary tools, they felt the urge to speak, although some were more private and required greater prompting on my part. Mario Vargas Llosa, whose recent novel does refer to a storyteller, told me about the importance of the anecdote in the making of a novel.

Now that I can reflect on the enthralling experience of the hours spent in the company of the Latin American writers I interviewed for this first volume, I have come to realize that they speak the way they write. Like magicians, they played with words and cast me under a spell. Luisa Valenzuela, for instance, told me that language was to her like a house, the home in which she felt most comfortable. Each brick was a particular word and had to be laid in an exact position so as to retain the whole structure. Luis Rafael Sánchez stressed the need for giving a sense of permanence to street language: "I wanted to make a compilation of this fleeting and fragile language, I wanted to give it Puerto Rican citizenship." Isabel Allende confided that for her the novel was a magic trunk, where everything fits: poetry, essays, testimonies, fantasies. Reality for all of these writers was not the simple obvious reality people are accustomed to; it infringes on what most of us refer to as the realm of the unreal, the "magic realism," typical of Latin Americans, which we call fantasy.

Most of my questions were geared to each author's work. However, some questions were asked of all of them: "Why do you write?" "What do words mean to you?" "What is your relationship with your characters?" "In what genre do you feel most at ease?" "Do you wear a mask?" Some said they wrote to expel personal ghosts and obsessions; some wrote out of the sheer pleasure of manipulating the language; some, to tell the story of those whose voices had been silenced; some, in an attempt to redeem humanity and recreate a new world; and some, to lift the veil of censorship and to disclose the plurality of voices that makes up the Latin American continent. Writing was to them as vital a function as eating or breathing. When asked what shape they would give their writings, some saw them as a whirlpool or a hurricane, others gave them the well-defined shape of a book.

What do these authors have in common? They share a similar concern for creativity, calling upon all forms of art: music, dance, painting, film; they seek freedom to discover and disclose its many expressions; they rewrite history and create multidimensional levels of interpretation; they unravel the secrets of the mind and play at witchcraft and magic; they bring together the religions of the East and the West.

All the writers responded to the challenge of the interview in a fashion that best characterized them. Some seemed to hide behind a somewhat didactic, perhaps defensive mask; others, in a confidential tone, were ready to reveal their inner thoughts; others enjoyed making startling remarks, mixed with a gossiplike quality; yet others partook of all these seemingly contradictory elements. When asked whether masks could be removed, the Peruvian writer Isaac Goldemberg shared with me the disturbing revelation that the stripping down of layers of masks to unveil our bare identity could only be attained in a subconscious state: "We can't even take them off when we are alone. From the moment we wake up to the moment we go to sleep, we are completely masked. Perhaps when we sleep is the only time we can really remove our masks." On the other hand, Juan Carlos Onetti insisted he was not wearing one.

As the interviewer, I kept a low profile so as to bring out to its fullest the captivating magic behind each of the authors. But at the same time I was propelled through their wizardry into creating along with them, as if I were another character in their works. I witnessed glimpses of the process of writing in action, the need to go over one's work in a perpetual quest and a sense of wonderment or despair in front of the finished product.

Fifteen authors have spoken. Their thoughts have been assembled into a mosaic of impressions. The questions and answers we tossed back and forth across the table in a dynamic repartee are now set in print. These enlightening remarks on vital issues will no doubt help in deciphering their works and bring us closer to solving the intricate maze of creativity. I hope that the reader will enjoy sharing the reactions of these authors as much as I did when I interviewed them.

*   *   *

Throughout this work, books that have been translated from Spanish into English are referred to by their English titles. Those that have not been translated are identified by their original titles. In the headnotes that precede each interview, however, both the Spanish and English titles of each book have been given whenever a translation was available, together with the respective dates of publication. For the titles of those works for which no English version was available, I have provided my own translation in parentheses. The interviews with José Donoso, Carlos Fuentes, and Manuel Puig were conducted in English; those with Isabel Allende, Rosario Ferré, Juan Carlos Onetti, Nicanor Parra, Elena Poniatowska, Ernesto Sábato, Luis Rafael Sánchez, Severo Sarduy and Mario Vargas Llosa were conducted in Spanish. The interviews with Guillermo Cabrera Infante, Isaac Goldemberg and Luisa Valenzuela were conducted partly in English and partly in Spanish.

I would like to express my deep gratitude to each and every one of the writers who so willingly shared his or her time and thoughts with me. Almost all the interviews were conducted for the specific purpose of being included in this book. Four of them, however, were part of two televised series I hosted, the nationwide Summer Semester Series "Contemporary Hispanic Fiction" and "The Hispanic Writers of Greater New York." I would, therefore, like to thank WCBS–TV and WABC–TV, respectively, as well as St. John's University Television Center, for coproducing these series, and the Center's former Director, Winston L. Kirby, for his interest in promoting Spanish and Latin American literature. I am most grateful to the members of my family for their constant advice and encouragement, especially my mother and brothers. I would also like to acknowledge the strong support of my friends and colleagues. Special credit should be given to the Americas Society, Random House, Editions du Seuil and especially Layle Silbert, whose many photographs enrich this book. Deep thanks are also due to Anil Singh-Molares for his translation and valuable assistance throughout the preparation of this work.

Isabel Allende

Isabel Allende

Isabel Allende, a writer who has emerged from the group of novelists brought about by the Chilean coup in 1973, was born in Lima, Peru, on August 2, 1942. After the overthrow of her uncle Salvador Allende, the late President of Chile, she moved to Caracas, Venezuela. In 1988, she remarried and now lives in Marin County, California.

When she was a child, her father left home, and her mother became the center of her life. Isabel tells us that, while other children would play with dolls, her mother gave her a notebook in which to write her thoughts and allowed her to use a special wall in her bedroom to draw whatever she felt like. These two actions seemed to awake in the future novelist the amazing power for dreaming and weaving stories reflected in her characters. Words became for her a means to accuse, but also a way to grow wings, so as to fly over the horrors of dictatorship into the horizons of democracy. The powerful presence of her grandparents also left a deep imprint on her, particularly the magic qualities her grandmother possessed as a storyteller, which she seems to have inherited.

The *New York Times Book Review* said of Isabel Allende that she is "the first woman to join what has heretofore been an exclusive male club of Latin American novelists." Her voice stands out as a spectacular outcry of the "magically real." Like the Argentine novelist Luisa Valenzuela, she has inherited the spellbound qualities of the "Boom," the literary explosion of the 1960s, when a group of young Latin American writers brought new dimensions and vitality to the Spanish language. Her characters, mostly women, move between the supernatural and the everyday life with extraordinary ease. Eva Luna, for instance, when she feels the need to be protected by her mother who died long ago, conjures her spirit to bring her back to life. The daughter takes her mother by the hand and walks away with her.

Isabel Allende left school at the age of sixteen to join the Santiago Office of the Food and Agriculture Organization of the United Nations. Since the age of seventeen, she has been a journalist. While in Santiago, she worked for a radical women's magazine, had her own television interview show, and also wrote children's stories. Today she combines journalism with the writing of novels and short stories.

Her most famous works are: *La casa de los espíritus,* 1982 (*The House of the Spirits,* 1985); *De amor y de sombra,* 1984 (*Of Love and Shadows,* 1987); *Eva Luna,* 1987 (*Eva Luna,* 1988). Her novels have been translated into twenty-one languages.

Meeting Isabel Allende and listening to her is a rewarding experience. She tells her story in an unpretentious way, insisting on the fact that she knows nothing about literature. We fall under her charm and we can see why her characters talk the way they do: with persuasion and magic, and in a natural and straightforward manner.

INTERVIEWER: What books did you read as a child?

ALLENDE: I read Emilio Salgari, Jules Verne, Charles Dickens, and all the detective novels I could lay my hands on. I also used to read pocketbook "historical novels" on the Roman Empire—I loved anything that had violence in it. When I was about nine years old, the man who would become my stepfather, and was then courting my mother, gave me the complete works of Shakespeare in a single volume made of thin Bible paper. I used to make cardboard figures out of each of Shakespeare's characters. I read his works as adventure novels; I wasn't aware that they were literature.

INTERVIEWER: What works have influenced you the most?

ALLENDE: If I have to acknowledge real influences that affected me deeply, they would be those works that I read as a child, such as adventure novels, because I longed for things to happen, for blood to be shed and for the characters to get

married and have children. The influence of Pablo Neruda
began to be felt after I left Chile. I took along a suitcase, photographs of my family, a small bag filled with soil and one volume
of the complete works of Pablo Neruda. Every time I felt the
need to recover my country, I read Neruda because he is Chile,
he is the voice of Chile. It is a beautiful metaphor that he died
following the military coup. With his death, the voice of the
people and the voice of freedom grew silent.

INTERVIEWER: You speak a lot about Pablo Neruda, but has
Gabriela Mistral had no impact on you?

ALLENDE: Gabriela Mistral's poetry is masterful and I first
understood it when I recorded one of her albums and I had to
read her work with great care. I identify with some of her
poems, but I cannot relate to her tendency to indulge in suffering. This can be explained by the upbringing of women of her
time and the literary mores of that period. Since I am always
fighting against pain and suffering, I cannot identify with her on
that count. By contrast, Pablo Neruda is a poet of emotion and
sensuality. Although he is lacking Gabriela Mistral's mystical
bent, I feel very close to his way of approaching, smelling,
touching, tasting, and walking the world. I like this very much.

INTERVIEWER: What about French writers?

ALLENDE: I feel close to the work of Henri Troyat, a White
Russian who emigrated to France. His literature, like mine, is
stamped by the loss of a world and the dream to recover it. He
wrote long sagas and I have read all his work.

INTERVIEWER: What did your uncle, President Salvador
Allende, stand for?

ALLENDE: Allende was proposing very deep reforms. He
had a dream. He was a socialist, a Marxist, the first socialist
Marxist president ever to be elected by a democratic free elec-
tion. He wanted to institute these reforms within the bounds of
Chile's constitution. We continued to enjoy all the civil rights we
had before: freedom of the press, speech, education and religion.
Within the constitutional framework, he tried to redistribute the

land and that meant taking it from rich landowners who owned half the country. He also attempted to regain control of Chile's copper mines from the North Americans, and do many other things that were very important to our economy and for our dignity as a country. It was a fascinating process and a beautiful dream. Before that, Chile had been a democracy, but without social justice. How can you have a social democracy if there is such great inequality that a few people have all the opportunities and all the wealth while the great majority does not?

INTERVIEWER: Why is Latin American literature always concerned with politics?

ALLENDE: I would say that Latin American literature was born with the first Spaniards who arrived in America, discovered the New World, and started writing the Chronicles of the Indies. In the letters they sent to the King and Queen of Spain and to their own families, they recounted what they saw. They came to conquer, they invented a utopia and spoke with effusive praise of this new continent. Since then, Latin American literature has been marked by political and social restlessness. A major political upheaval resulted from the almost complete destruction of a world on which a foreign culture, religion, and race were imposed. This produced a wave of feelings and emotions that have always been present in our culture and which have affected its political aspects. For five hundred years, we have been exploited and colonized, first by Spain and Portugal, then by other European countries, and nowadays by the United States. The latter is a more subtle form of colonization, but colonization nonetheless. It is impossible for writers to separate themselves from this reality. How could I write without being aware that I come from a society rooted in inequality? I don't think this is solely a Latin American trait, however. It is a characteristic of certain times and certain places throughout the world. All the literature that was written after the Second World War was marked by war: all Jewish literature is marked by the Holocaust, and much of the literature that is being written today has been marked by the Vietnam War. These have been crucial moments in the history of nations.

INTERVIEWER: What relationship do you see between exile and literature?

ALLENDE: Exile is something that has marked our literature significantly. My generation was kicked out of Chile for political reasons. If we had stayed, they would have killed us. The literature prior to ours reflected another form of exile: people who could not stand mediocrity—intellectual and otherwise—in their countries, left them. In my case, I would not have written novels had I not left; I would have continued as a journalist. I communicated through journalism and I had no need to write literature. But when I left Chile, I couldn't keep working as a reporter, so I turned to literature.

INTERVIEWER: In *Of Love and Shadows,* you speak of Irene as follows: "She was saying goodbye to her country. Next to her heart, beneath her clothing, she carried a small bag with soil from her garden that Rosa had sent so she could plant forget-me-nots on the other side of the sea." What is it like for you and your characters to live in exile?

ALLENDE: For me, exile has been a brutal and painful experience, but it has also been very beneficial. I have become strong, and I didn't know I had that strength within me. One learns more from pain and failure than from happiness and success. But it is also true that in fifteen years of exile I have not been able to shake off all my feelings of nostalgia for Chile . . .

INTERVIEWER: Has the transition from journalism to writing novels been a difficult one?

ALLENDE: I didn't choose to make that transition. If I had remained in Chile, I would not have written novels. What happened was that when I left Chile, I could not find work as a journalist because journalism is a profession that is very difficult to carry from country to country, except as a correspondent. A journalist is a person who interprets society, its laws, its way of behaving, and its language, and then writes about these things with the subtlety of everyday expressions appropriate to that culture. When I went to Venezuela, I tried to work as a journalist and the only job I could find was to write satirical articles for a newspaper. I couldn't make a living with that. So I worked at many other things for a few years during which I remained silent. Perhaps the fact that I could not work as a journalist left me no resort but to write books. I started writing purely by accident, after I had returned from working a twelve-hour shift at a school, on the first day of classes following vacation break. It was the eighth of January. When I got home, I received a phone call from Santiago saying that my grandfather was very sick and he was going to die. It's not really that he was sick so much as that he was old; he was almost one hundred years old. One day he sat on his rocking chair and decided not to eat or drink anymore. He wouldn't allow a doctor to see him either because he wanted to die, and my family respected his decision. So when they called me, I sat down and began writing him a letter. I knew that the letter would never reach him and that I would never send it. Deep down, I knew I was writing that letter for myself but I didn't yet realize it was going to be a book. I sat down at my typewriter and wrote the first sentence of the book without any idea of what it meant; it was as if someone dictated it to me. It went like this: "Barrabás came to the family by sea." Barrabás was our very large dog. When people ask me about the meaning of the dog in *The House of the Spirits,* I reply that he symbolizes nothing. Some critics, however, say the dog symbolizes Pinochet, while others maintain that he represents Clara's innocence because he appears in her life when she is a child, and he remains with her thoughout her childhood. When Clara falls in love and gets married with her white dress on, Barrabás is murdered in a pool of blood, which critics view as symbolic of the sexual act. I think there are things that writers are not aware of having put in their books, and it is the task of you people to discover them.

INTERVIEWER: Has journalism helped you in the writing of

your novels?

ALLENDE: Yes, I use the techniques of journalism, such as interviews, research, the concise use of space, synthesis, suspense, etc.

INTERVIEWER: You have said of your mother: "She gave me a notebook to jot down life at an age when other girls played with dolls. She also allowed me to paint whatever I wanted on one of the walls of my room." What did you write in that notebook and what did you paint on that wall?

ALLENDE: I painted landscapes, friends and animals, and wrote about fear, sex, injustice, inequality, violence and loneliness. That's pretty much what I am still doing in my books.

INTERVIEWER: What do you write about?

ALLENDE: What does anyone write about? The things that happen and matter to you. The three novels I have written, as well as my short stories, are marked by two obsessions that are present in Latin American literature: violence and love.

INTERVIEWER: Why do you juxtapose rape and love in your work?

ALLENDE: That's a very strange question. In the literature of the so-called Boom, there is one constant: there is always a house of prostitution involved. Curiously, rape has become a dominant theme in the works of Latin American authors of the 1980s. I think there is a symbolic element in this. When I left my country in 1975, half of Latin America was ruled by dictators. We endured years of human rights violations when people were murdered, mutilated, tortured, exiled, or made to "disappear." I think rape represents the worst humiliation and the worst transgression against a person, and this theme has become prevalent in the stories, novels, and movies that are being done nowadays. It is as if in the collective unconscious the rape of a woman has come to symbolize the rape of all of us as a species, continent, and race. At the end of *The House of the Spirits,* Alba has been raped and is awaiting the birth of a child, and she doesn't know whether it is the baby of her love Miguel, or the offspring of all rapes, and she doesn't care. What she is interested in is that it is her child, it is a being that is going to be born and which is the product of accumulated and shared suffering. But it is a being that is also born out of love. The point of all this is that without forgetting the horrors of the past and by forgiving them, we can build a new society based on love.

INTERVIEWER: Why do you write?

ALLENDE: I come from a family of storytellers, an oral tradition, and that helps a lot. As women, we were kept silent in public, but we had a private voice. And now, because others have made it easier for me, I write about the lives of my people. It is the voice, not of the winners, but of the little people, us, my mother, my grandmother, not my grandfather who wrote history with big capital letters. I never write with a message in mind. I want to tell a story that in some way resembles life and reality. I write to communicate, to survive, to make the world more understandable and bearable, so that people may be moved by the things that matter to me, to firmly establish the need for a collective endeavor to build a world where there is room for love, solidarity, laughter, the pleasure of the senses, the growth of the spirit, and imagination. I write because if I didn't I would die.

INTERVIEWER: Your prose has a poetical musicality. Do you write poetry?

ALLENDE: No, I don't. How I envy poets! In seven words they say more than I do in six hundred pages.

INTERVIEWER: How did you develop your capacity to wonder and astound?

ALLENDE: The world has no explanation. I think what we know is less than what we don't know, and that even those things that we do know, we don't know fully, so we can't control them. The capacity to wonder is always there because it is enough to look at the world to realize that it is unexplainable and ruled by invisible forces. Why do men fight wars? Why does a person fall in love with one particular individual and not another? Why do people hate all of a sudden? These passions have no explanation.

Why do we move? Many times we don't even know why we have to stand up or sit down. Everything that happens in the world and in life makes me wonder.

INTERVIEWER: How is a novel born?

ALLENDE: From deeply felt emotions I have carried around with me for a long time. *The House of the Spirits,* for instance, was born from nostalgia; *Of Love and Shadows* from impotence and anger; and *Eva Luna* from the pleasure of being a woman and telling stories. In my first novel, I didn't have to construct anything artificially; everything was within me, I didn't need to invent the landscape, the smell of peach trees or anything. My latest novel, *Eva Luna,* takes place in the Caribbean; it is a story that could have happened in Venezuela. Despite having lived there for thirteen years, I had to do extensive research, read practically every paper published in this century, travel all over the country and speak to people to make *Eva Luna* real. When I say in that book, "it smelled like a mango," I had to buy a mango and smell it first, because even though I eat mangoes every day, they are not a part of me. *Eva Luna* was written after a lot of hard work and thirteen years of living in Venezuela.

INTERVIEWER: Do you think *The House of the Spirits* would exist were it not for *One Hundred Years of Solitude?*

ALLENDE: Yes, I acknowledge that *One Hundred Years,* like the works of Borges, Cortázar, Donoso, Neruda, Amado, among others, opened the road for me.

INTERVIEWER: Do you see some resemblance between your work and that of José Donoso?

ALLENDE: No, except for the fact that we are both Chileans and our country has influenced us. But our ghosts and obsessions are different, we belong to different generations, and our sexes have affected both our works.

INTERVIEWER: In *Of Love and Shadows* you describe the atrocities that occurred at the mine as if your words had the same visual power as Francisco's camera. How did you manage to capture that horrible world of the dictatorship with your words, and what does the written word mean to you?

ALLENDE: I researched for two years before writing that book. Each fact I detail in it is based on reality. I have lived under a dictatorship; that's why I can speak and write about it. The written word is an act of human solidarity. I write so that people will love each other more . . .

INTERVIEWER: Do you see the novel as a testimony or a documentary?

ALLENDE: The novel is a magic trunk where everything fits: poetry, essays, testimonies, fantasies, documentaries, everything! Through it we can give a fictional order to chaos and find the key to the labyrinth of history. A novel is like a window open to an infinite landscape where the written word records memories which cannot be blown by the wind.

INTERVIEWER: Your work is a criticism of the bourgeoisie and a reevaluation of history. Do you see writing as a process of weaving and unweaving? Do you want to rewrite the world?

ALLENDE: I want to tell a secret story, that of the silent voices who cannot speak. I want to change the world, not just rewrite it.

INTERVIEWER: How do you manage to transform the reader into a witness?

ALLENDE: I don't know if I achieve that, but isn't that the aim of writing? A book is the work of two people: the writer and the reader. So every book is really several books, and each reader is a witness to the reality the author suggests.

INTERVIEWER: Could we call your narrators witnesses, commentators, or participants in Chilean reality?

ALLENDE: Participants, I think.

INTERVIEWER: Who are your narrators and why are they gifted at telling stories and living them?

ALLENDE: They say that every character is the author. Perhaps that's true and I am within each of my protagonists. Storytelling and writing are like a private orgy: they allow me to create and recreate the world according to my own rules and to fulfill all my dreams on the page. I like to do it from my perspective as a woman who challenges the patriarchal order, mocks authority, the law, repressive morals, and the thousand ways they have devised to trap our bodies and our souls.

INTERVIEWER: Who is your favorite female character: Clara, Irene, Consuelo or Eva Luna? Who among your male characters?

ALLENDE: I love all of them: Alba, Irene, Eva Luna, Jaime, Francisco Leal, Professor Leal, Riad Halabí, but especially Clara. Clara is my grandmother. Clara del Valle is exactly the same as my grandmother, although I exaggerated her a little. For instance, my grandmother couldn't play the piano with the cover down. But it is true that she was a spiritualist and a clairvoyant. I come from a family of very crazy people; I haven't had to invent anything. My grandmother was the craziest of the whole family, she was wonderful, she lived apart from all material things in a spiritual world, experimenting with a table with three legs to speak with the souls of the dead. My grandfather was a pragmatic Basque who totally disagreed with the experiences of my grandmother because he said they had no scientific grounding. Later on, when I was five or six years old, my grandmother discovered that it wasn't the souls of the dead who were moving the legs of the table but rather extraterrestrials, Martians. My grandfather felt that this had a scientific basis. The fact that all the names in *The House of the Spirits* mean the same thing— Clara, Blanca, Alba—is like saying that Clara is the great spiritual mother of us all. She is not concerned with braiding the hair of her daughters, or with whether they are going to get married or not. On the other hand, Blanca is the great earthly mother, she fulfills all the household tasks. Alba is the great intellectual mother.

INTERVIEWER: In two of your novels, you give leading roles to effeminate men. Is it easier for you to write about women and about those men who most resemble them?

ALLENDE: No. I don't like to categorize people by their

sexual roles. Women can have "masculine" characteristics (action, courage, rage, ambition), while men can be tender and compassionate. This complexity makes them more interesting in both real life and literature. I also don't have any prejudices against "effeminate" men.

INTERVIEWER: Why do many of your characters speak in the first person?

ALLENDE: Because it can't be done in any other way. I know absolutely nothing about literature, and I am not interested. When one knows too much, one can no longer write. But one knows intuitively when something isn't working. When I finished *The House of the Spirits,* I read the text and it felt magical, but the fuel was missing. I read the novel many times without knowing what was wrong. And then I realized that the character of Esteban Trueba was based on my grandfather, he was exactly like him. But my grandfather would never have told anyone, least of all his granddaughter, about his sufferings. My grandfather, unlike my character, would have never spoken about his intimate love for his wife, the violent moment in which he chopped Pedro Tercero's hand off, the time he humiliated himself in front of the prostitute to beg her to save his granddaughter. So how can Alba, who is writing the book, know all these things? It was too easy and artificial that she should know them. So at the end of the novel, Alba says: "I have written this book based on the diaries of my grandmother." With my grandmother something very different happened: she is the only one who speaks in the first person. Initially, the whole book was written in the third person; I told the story.

INTERVIEWER: Eva Luna says: "The books, silent by day, open up at night to let the characters out so that they may wander the rooms and live their own adventures." Do you share your experiences with your characters? Who dominates whom?

ALLENDE: Yes, I share them. At the beginning, I think I dominate my characters, but then they fulfill their own destinies and I cannot impose my will on them.

INTERVIEWER: You have said more than once that "it is difficult for me to write my biographical information without repeating many things that appear in *The House of the Spirits.*" Where does autobiography leave off and the characters begin?

ALLENDE: Almost all my characters are based on real-life people. A few are the product of my imagination, like Riad Halabí in *Eva Luna.* There is a part of my biography (and that of my family and friends) in *The House of the Spirits* and *Of Love and Shadows.* There are no autobiographical elements in *Eva Luna,* but I think I identify completely with two emotions in that novel: being a woman and being able to tell stories.

INTERVIEWER: Is the family of the Truebas related to that of the Buendías?

ALLENDE: The Trueba family is a lot like my own family.

INTERVIEWER: Where is the magical world and where is reality?

ALLENDE: I don't know. The dividing line between them is constantly being erased for me. I no longer know whether my life is a novel or whether my novels are like life.

INTERVIEWER: Is fantasy a way for you to escape reality, or is it a tool to discover reality?

ALLENDE: It is a means of embellishing it. I don't try to escape from reality but rather to understand its complexity, not just explain it. How pretentious of me! I want to enrich reality and paint it with bright colors, as Eva Luna says so clearly.

INTERVIEWER: When do you know you have reached the last stage in writing a novel and that it is time to turn it over to the publisher?

ALLENDE: You have to set a deadline for yourself. In this respect, I got my training in journalism, because there you always have to race against the clock; it is an unalterable deadline. I have learned to work with a certain discipline and to turn over articles at a given time on a given day. And I write like a possessed person until that time. When I think a work is finished, I hand it to my mother—she is my only reader. She then returns it to me with scribbles all over and we begin discussing what doesn't work, and I rewrite the novel. Later I separate myself from the book and let it rest.

INTERVIEWER: How do you feel upon ending a novel?

ALLENDE: Twenty minutes of sadness because I am breaking up with the characters. Then I feel euphoria at the prospect of starting a new project.

INTERVIEWER: If you had to give a geometrical shape to your novels, what would it be?

ALLENDE: A whirlpool, a hurricane!

INTERVIEWER: What do you plan to write when democracy returns to Chile?

ALLENDE: I don't know what I will write when democracy returns to Chile, but I know that I would not have written any novels had it not been for the 1973 military coup because I was forced to leave the country as a result. The loss of that world and my roots and a feeling of nostalgia led me to write *The House of the Spirits.* My second book is based on a crime committed during the military coup, while the third was written in the Caribbean. I would not have gone to Venezuela were it not for that coup; I would still be in Santiago. The political future of Chile is a democracy, without a doubt. Pinochet is not eternal; immortality is going to fail him at any moment.

INTERVIEWER: Why are women in your family so strong?

ALLENDE: It is true that I have a greater knowledge of women because I am one, because I have worked with women all my life and because I come from a family where women are very strong. My great-grandmother, my grandmother, my mother, my daughter, and I all communicate with each other telepathically, even after death. My grandmother died thirty-seven years ago but she still speaks to me. My mother who lives in Chile also speaks to me telepathically because calling by phone is very expensive. So there is very much of a female focus in my work because of my understanding of women. But I am also interested in the perspective of men because I think it is impossible to imagine a world where we are divided. I believe that machismo and sexism harm both women and men. Of course, we women were victims first, but men are also victims. I think that sex, eroticism, and love are extraordinary forces in human beings. A man who does not consider a woman as an equal cannot live life fully. His life will always be incomplete.

INTERVIEWER: Do you think you have had to struggle harder as a writer because you are a woman?

ALLENDE: I would have liked to have been a man because they lead much more comfortable lives. But due to the absence of one ridiculous little chromosome, life has been made much harder for us. At least I come from a continent where women have had to make twice the effort to obtain half the recognition in any field. And there are some areas where women have not been accepted at all, the world of ideas. A woman is allowed to be an artist, dancer, singer, actress, musician or painter, but she is not permitted to handle ideas. Fundamentally, literature is a concept, it is ideas. You can adduce all the arguments you want, but behind them there are still ideas. Gaining acceptance into the world of ideas has been the hardest task for women.

INTERVIEWER: Do you consider yourself a feminist writer and do you believe women have their own language?

ALLENDE: I am a different person since I read Germaine Greer's *The Female Eunuch* because she expressed what I felt with a great deal of humor. All my life I had experienced feelings of anger, impotence and injustice without knowing why. Suddenly I felt someone understood me and I could finally cope with my emotions. This marked not only my writing but my life. I read Simone de Beauvoir when I was twenty-six. My generation began to read her before I did. I became acquainted with her works when I was a journalist for an avant-garde feminist newspaper. Yes, I consider myself a feminist and I think that any intelligent woman has to be one. What does it mean to be a feminist? For me, feminism is a fight that men and women must wage for a more educated world, one in which the basic inequality between the sexes will be eliminated. We have to change the patriarchal, hierarchical, authoritarian, repressive societies that have been marked by the religions and the laws that we have had to live with for thousands of years. This goes a lot deeper than not wearing a bra, or the sexual and cultural revolutions. It is a revolution that must go to the heart of the world, and that all of us must fight, women and men alike. Both sexes are on a ship without a course, and we must give it a new direction. On the other hand, I don't believe in equality on the more mundane level; I don't want to be equal to a man, I want to be much better than he and I want him to be far better himself. So I am concerned with the struggle to better ourselves as a species. We have to separate this from other struggles. At the beginning of this century, a lot of people said that women's inequality stemmed from a political system which, as it changed and revolutions were won, would improve the lot of women. This is a lie! Revolutions don't change the basic sexual inequality that was established in prehistoric times and which is still present today. Venezuela has some of the more advanced laws as far as women are concerned. They have just changed Venezuela's constitution to give women all the rights that men have. Half of the university students in that country are women, and Venezuelan women occupy important positions such as bank managers and executives, although not yet the presidency of the nation. This contrasts with the macho appearance of Venezuelan society. Chilean society, on the other hand, appears more matriarchal and liberated, but not according to the letter of the law. Women have now learned to develop a voice using male tricks. But I don't think that one can talk of female or male literature as if literature had a sex.

INTERVIEWER: It has been said that Luisa Valenzuela is heir to the Boom. Could we say the same of you, or do you prefer to be seen in some other way?

ALLENDE: I can't classify myself. That's the job of the

critics. I don't know anything about literature, the Boom or the post-Boom. I don't think that those labels are important for an author, at least not for me.

INTERVIEWER: Do you consider your voice that of the Latin American continent?

ALLENDE: I don't pretend to be anyone's voice. I have been very lucky to be published in Europe, and I say lucky because there are women who have been writing in Latin America since the seventeenth century, like Sor Juana Inés de la Cruz. The problem is that few people ever talk about them. Their work is rarely taught at the universities, there is no literary criticism on them, and they are not published, translated or distributed. In Latin America, no one wanted to read my novels, so I sent them by mail to Spain, and that's where they were published. As a result, they were promoted and became known. I think European publishers are opening their doors to many Latin American women authors, even those who have been writing long before me but have not yet been published. I am just one of them. I am bold enough to believe that I have a gift for telling stories, as other people do for singing. This gift came from the heavens! So I must use it to benefit those who don't have a voice. That's why when I speak I always refer to the political and social aspects. How can one not talk about war, violence, poverty, and inequality when people who suffer from these afflictions don't have a voice to speak? I have also been lucky to have been translated into other languages.

INTERVIEWER: What do you think of the future of Latin America?

ALLENDE: It is very difficult to speak of the continent as if it were a bag into which we have all been thrown. Every country, but even more so every social class, has its own reality. If I talk about the middle class in Chile or Colombia, I am certain that there are reforms to resolve basic problems. If one speaks about the poorer classes in El Salvador, Guatemala, Nicaragua, Chile, and Peru, however, there are many years of abuse and anger that must be turned inside out and changed. It is neither just nor natural that some people have everything while the great majority has nothing. The privilege of the few when many are starving is an obscene thing.

INTERVIEWER: Eva Luna said: "I pretended that a ray of moonlight struck my back and I developed the wings of a bird, two large feathery wings that allowed me to take flight." Listening to you speak is like seeing your wings, and reading your work is another form of witnessing that flight.

ALLENDE: When I write, I fly to another dimension. Like Eva Luna, I try to live life as I would like it to be, as in a novel. I am always half flying, like Marc Chagall's violinists.

INTERVIEWER: The area of Monte Grande in the Valley of Elqui was Gabriela Mistral's favorite. What is your favorite spot?

ALLENDE: All of Latin America. I seek epic dimensions. I am fascinated by our history and our magnificent geography, and I identify with the mix of breeds, the mestizo people that we all are. But on a deeper level, which in truth determines my existence and my writing, my favorite spot is to be in the arms of those I care for deeply.

INTERVIEWER: Who is Isabel Allende?

ALLENDE: A happy person, because I always had a lot of love and I have not yet lost the hope that the world can be changed.

Guillermo Cabrera Infante

Guillermo Cabrera Infante

Guillermo Cabrera Infante was born in Gíbara, in the Province of Oriente, Cuba, in 1929. One of the best-known writers of the "Boom," his name nevertheless does not appear in the 1980 *Dictionary of Cuban Literature,* published by the Institute of Literature and Linguistics of the Cuban Academy of Sciences.

Cabrera Infante is the founder of the Cinemateca de Cuba, the Cuban Film Library, which he directed from 1951 to 1956. In 1954, under the pen name G. Caín, he began writing film reviews for the weekly magazine *Carteles,* for which he later served as editor-in-chief between 1957 and 1960. In 1959, he became director of the literary magazine *Lunes de Revolución* until it was banned by the government in 1961.

In 1962, Cabrera Infante entered the diplomatic service as Cuba's Cultural Attaché to Belgium. In 1965, however, he chose political exile and moved to London, where he has been living ever since with his wife, the former actress Miriam Gómez, whom he married in 1961.

Cabrera Infante is known for his puns and his experiments with the language. With a keen sense of humor, which he hides behind a straight face, he views writing as a game: "For me, literature is a complex game, both mental and concrete, which is acted out in a physical manner on the page." He categorically rejects the term "novelist," and insists on the fact that he is a writer of fragmentary tales which reflect the history of Cuba and the life of prerevolutionary Havana.

Among his many works are *Así en la paz como en la guerra* (In War and Peace), 1960; *Un oficio del siglo veinte* (A Twentieth-Century Job), 1963; *Tres tristes tigres,* 1965 (*Three Trapped Tigers,* 1971), for which he received the 1964 Biblioteca Breve Prize of Barcelona and the 1970 French Prize for Best Foreign Book; *Vista del amanecer en el trópico,* 1974 (*View of Dawn in the Tropics,* 1978); *O,* 1975; *Exorcismos de esti(l)o* (Exorcisms and Exercises in Style), 1976; *Arcadia todas las noches* (Arcadia Every Night),

1978; *La Habana para un infante difunto,* 1979 (*Infante's Inferno,* 1984); and *Holy Smoke,* 1985. This last work is Cabrera Infante's first book written in English, which makes him a Cuban-born British writer. He has repeatedly said, "I am the only British writer who writes in Spanish." This work is another play on words, as it recounts the history of cigars and cigar smokers. Writing began for Cabrera Infante as a joke, but it has become akin to a drug which possesses him, the writer now says.

A new unexpurgated Spanish edition of *Three Trapped Tigers* is scheduled for publication in Venezuela in 1989. It will restore the twenty-two sections that were censored from the first edition.

The following two interviews were held in 1980 and 1984, in New York.

Part 1

INTERVIEWER: In the *New York Times Book Review,* David Gallagher said of *Three Trapped Tigers:* "I doubt a funnier book has been written in Spanish since *Don Quixote.* It is also one of the most inventive novels that has come out of Latin America." Do you agree with this?

CABRERA INFANTE: I do agree. What I do not agree with is the title of your TV series, "Contemporary Hispanic Fiction," because of the adjective "Hispanic." A few malicious people have accused the United States of being fascist, which it is not, but it is "faddist." In the 1970s, the fad was to call black Americans "Afro-Americans." Nowadays, it is fashionable to call people who come from Cuba, Puerto Rico or Colombia "Hispanic." Like "Latin" before, it seems to be just another tag. I do not consider myself a Hispanic writer. I do not live in the U.S. and I am not a member of a minority group which comes from Cuba, Puerto Rico or South America. I live in

London and I am a British subject, although I do write in Spanish, of course.

INTERVIEWER: What would you call this series, if it were up to you to choose a title?

CABRERA INFANTE: It is very difficult to call a series like this any one thing. The usage of "Hispanic" in this country is not the same as in its original Spanish. It is like calling an American Jew "Hebraic," a Russian or Polish American "Slavic," or an Italian "Italic," which sounds really silly. But to turn to your question, David Gallagher very generously called my book the funniest written in Spanish since *Don Quixote.* When he made that statement, there were no really funny books in Spanish. Spanish and Latin American literature had always considered writing a very serious matter. Let me tell you about a famous Argentine novelist who went to the University of California at Los Angeles. He was asked by a student there, "What do you think of *Three Trapped Tigers?*" He pondered the question for almost a minute and finally said, "That is not a serious book." So, you see where my book stands among very serious men writing very serious books.

INTERVIEWER: *Three Trapped Tigers* is five hundred pages of humor. The reader gets the impression that you enjoy what you are doing, that writing for you is a kind of game, almost like playing chess, and that you would like to take part in that game. Do you have the reader in mind when you write?

CABRERA INFANTE: A very wise author once said that a writer writes for himself, and then publishes for money. I write for myself and publish just for the reader. But I do not have the reader in mind when I write. No true writer does that. You are just in the middle of a struggle with words which are really very stubborn things, with a blank page, with the damn thing that you use to write with, a pen or a typewriter, and you forget all about the reader when you are doing that.

INTERVIEWER: It seems to me that you want your reader to enter the characters' world or, on the contrary, to react violently against that world.

CABRERA INFANTE: The relationship between reader and characters is very difficult. It is even more peculiar than the relationship between the writer and his characters. For instance, in *Three Trapped Tigers* the main character is called Bustrófedon and he is a kind of ghost who has come back from the dead to play with words. It is very difficult for a reader to identify with such a man, but in spite of everything I have received many letters asking about this particular character and not about the other characters, who were more real than Bustrófedon was. There was even one character based on a real-life singer.

INTERVIEWER: As an author, you like to play games with your characters and your readers, but above all you play with words.

CABRERA INFANTE: That is true, the characters are really swamped by words and so is the reader.

INTERVIEWER: You are a master at pun making. Andrew Sarris, the film critic of the *Village Voice,* has called your work "a perpetual fireworks of puns." Can you comment on that?

CABRERA INFANTE: I do like puns because I like humor. As you know, one man's humor is another man's facetiae, but that is not true for me. Every kind of humor is acceptable; it is there for the writer to work with and for the reader to enjoy. Puns are a form of humor with words. When you have several words that could mean the same thing, but you have several meanings in mind, then you have a pun in a single word. For instance, Spanish is a very difficult language in which to make puns because it is a very square and formal language. You have distinct sounds for everything. In English, on the other hand, it is quite easy to make puns. James Joyce's *Finnegans Wake* is a pun from the title to the very last word.

INTERVIEWER: Do you carry this vital aspect of playing with words into the translation of your works?

CABRERA INFANTE: Yes, of course. *Three Trapped Tigers*

was 445 pages long in Spanish and 480 in the English translation, which is really a version of the original book. The translation has a few extra pages because of all the games I played, by myself and with my translator.

INTERVIEWER: Is that why you said in another interview, "Writers rush in where translators fear to tread"?

CABRERA INFANTE: I think writers rush in where everybody is very frightened to tread. Writers rush in where publishers fear to tread and where translators fear to tread. Let me give you one example. I was working with the French translator of *Three Trapped Tigers* and he was constantly saying, "We can't do that, that is not French." Finally I told him angrily, "Listen, this book is not in Spanish, you can't do that in Spanish, but I did, so I assume you can do it as well in French." From then on, we had no problems because he understood what the book was all about. I had the same initial difficulties with the English translation.

INTERVIEWER: What language do you find most adaptable to your style of writing?

CABRERA INFANTE: English, because of my familiarity with it. It is a very different language from Spanish.

INTERVIEWER: You claim that you write in Cuban, not Spanish.

CABRERA INFANTE: But that was true only of *Three Trapped Tigers,* and I have since stopped this practice. It was a bad habit. With my book *Exorcismos de esti(l)o,* I took the Cuban language further than I could, and that's when I stopped. Another novel of mine, *Infante's Inferno,* is written in a variety of standard Spanish which might even be called mid-Atlantic Spanish.

INTERVIEWER: You like to use colloquial expressions that are typical of Cuba, especially of the Havana nightlife. Why does it have such an appeal for you?

CABRERA INFANTE: I believe that writers, unless they consider themselves terribly exquisite, are at heart people who live

by night, a little bit outside society, moving between delin-
quency and conformity. It is from this atmosphere that the
language for *Three Trapped Tigers* is derived.

INTERVIEWER: Would you say that by playing with words
you have committed an act of terrorism against the Spanish
language in order to destroy and then recreate a new language?

CABRERA INFANTE: It was indeed an act of destruction and
then creation. I have done a little bit of that in *Infante's Inferno*
but not as much as in *Three Trapped Tigers,* where I was out to
terrorize Spanish readers and Spanish writers.

INTERVIEWER: In your writing there is the definite influence
of journalism and film. You started working as a journalist and
you were the founder and director of the Cuban Film Institute.
Do you see the influence of these two crafts in your works?

CABRERA INFANTE: I do not see the influence of journalism.
I was never a true journalist, I was a movie critic. I wrote for a
weekly magazine and then edited a literary magazine, but I did
not really feel comfortable with the profession of journalism
itself. I feel dependent on films, particularly American ones,
because I was taken by my mother when I was twenty-nine
days old to see my first picture.

INTERVIEWER: But you do not remember that picture.

CABRERA INFANTE: I do not remember that picture, but it
was certainly registered by the brain. I have no doubt about
that. I was able to read a movie before I was able to read a book.
Watching a movie from beginning to end is like reading, because
even though what you see are images, they are telling you a
story. So it is like reading, and I did this very frequently as an
infant and a very small child. There were influences in my life
that were more important than journalism, such as comic strips
and radio. I was an avid radio fan when I was a boy, as well as a
great lover of comic strips. Even the name of my surrogate in
Three Trapped Tigers, Sylvester, comes from a fascinating
comic strip from my youth called *The Spirit.* The Spirit used to
live under a tomb in the Saint Sylvester Cemetery in a place

called Metropolis.

INTERVIEWER: Who are the writers who have had the greatest impact on you?

CABRERA INFANTE: First I must mention writers like Petronius, with his *Satyricon,* which I read as pornography. Later, in high school in Havana, I discovered Homer. I read the *Odyssey* because it was the story of a man who returned home after being absent for more than twenty years and was recognized only by his dog. Having always been a great lover of dogs, I was absolutely fascinated by the story of this dog recognizing his master and then dying, because he was a very old dog.

INTERVIEWER: Do you see your own influence on other writers?

CABRERA INFANTE: Not really, I do not think that what I do influences others easily.

INTERVIEWER: You use techniques such as collage, fragmentation, humor and nostalgia, which are part of the *roman comique* and the picaresque novel. Could you describe your own style of writing?

CABRERA INFANTE: I don't have any style. I am against the notion of style in itself. You are referring to one book, *Three Trapped Tigers.* In other works, like *View of Dawn in the Tropics,* there are different approaches and different styles. Each book I write has a distinct style. *Infante's Inferno* is written from an entirely different perspective than that of *Three Trapped Tigers.*

INTERVIEWER: Do you consider yourself a novelist?

CABRERA INFANTE: No, I am a writer of fragments. I describe my works as books, but my publishers in Spain, in the United States and elsewhere insist on calling them novels. I don't know why. Even *View of Dawn in the Tropics* is termed a novel, although it is a series of fragments about Cuban history.

INTERVIEWER: In your opinion, what makes up a novel?

CABRERA INFANTE: That is a very difficult question. Many people have tried to pin down what a novel really is. The traditional concept of a novel is embodied by a writer like Charles Dickens. That is what I define as a novel: something that has a beginning, a middle and an end, with characters and a plot that sustain interest from the first sentence to the last. But that is not what I do at all.

INTERVIEWER: Since 1965 you have lived outside your country, almost in self-imposed exile. Are you not afraid of losing touch with your language?

CABRERA INFANTE: I must tell you that the exile was not self-imposed. I left my country because I was forced to, and I do not think that I am going to lose my language because I live in England. Just the opposite. One day, I discovered that there were too many Anglicisms in my Spanish, so I said, "Well, consider yourself the only British writer who writes in Spanish." And that's how I solved it.

INTERVIEWER: What is the effect of censorship on a novel?

CABRERA INFANTE: I can only talk about myself. I know that many writers have had to write under censorship and yet produced good novels; for instance, Cervantes wrote *Don Quixote* under Catholic censorship. Authors have been writing under censorship for centuries. It is only now that we can write without restrictions in places such as England, the United States, Spain and several South American countries. That is why my book, *Infante's Inferno,* a very erotic work, was published in Spain—this would have been inconceivable ten years ago.

INTERVIEWER: Perhaps because of exile or because of your own approach to literature, memory plays an important role in your writing. *Three Trapped Tigers* and *Infante's Inferno* are memories of a double exile—a recollection of prerevolutionary Cuba, and your youth, lost and regained through your writing. Could you say something about this?

CABRERA INFANTE: I think all writing is done through memory. Memory is the great translator of reality, the great interpreter of past life, the great recollector of dreams. It is of paramount importance to any writer.

INTERVIEWER: Is *Infante's Inferno* an autobiography? Does it contain very personal elements?

CABRERA INFANTE: No, certainly not. Somerset Maugham, describing a novel he once wrote, said he was very sorry he had used the first person singular because everyone mistook his book for a kind of memoir, which it was not. I used snippets of my life in *Infante's Inferno,* just as I resort to fragments from the works of other authors, past, present and future. It is not really autobiographical at all.

INTERVIEWER: How did you arrive at the title for this book?

CABRERA INFANTE: I do not believe in inspiration, but I must have a title in order to work, otherwise I am lost. I started out with "Las confesiones de agosto" (The Confessions of August), which is dreadful, but I needed something. One day, after I had finished the first draft, the title *Infante's Inferno* came to me all of a sudden and I said, "That is a perfect title, I do not need any other." Then I proceeded to rewrite the entire draft with that title in mind, as if it were a new book.

INTERVIEWER: You have said that your work should be read aloud, that it is a "gallery of voices." There is also the influence of music in your books. Could you say something about its rhythmic quality, its beat, its tempo?

CABRERA INFANTE: But that is true only of *Three Trapped Tigers. View of Dawn in the Tropics* is history, and history cannot be read aloud, of course. In *Three Trapped Tigers,* however, what I intended to do was to work with music by other means, such as literature. I use musical patterns there in one of the sections of the book dealing with the life of a bolero singer in Havana.

INTERVIEWER: But even in *Infante's Inferno,* for instance, there is the influence of Ravel's music.

CABRERA INFANTE: Yes, that is true. But only because I use many references to musical terms, as I do with ballet. In this novel, however, I never intended, as I did in *Three Trapped*

Tigers, to apply musical patterns to the writing.

INTERVIEWER: In *View of Dawn in the Tropics,* you say about Cuba: "And it will always be there, that long, sad, unfortunate island will be there after the last Indian, after the last Spaniard, after the last African, after the last American and after the last Cuban. It will survive all disaster, eternally washed over by the Gulf Stream: beautiful and green, undying, eternal." What is Cuba for you?

CABRERA INFANTE: It is difficult to say. It is a country that once was. It is not a country that I really recognize anymore. I think that I've tried many times to get Cuba in my writings, especially Havana, which was once a great and fascinating city.

Part 2

INTERVIEWER: Guillermo, you once said, "For me, literature is a game, a complex game, both mental and concrete, which is acted out in a physical manner on the page." Do you conceive of the art of writing as a jigsaw puzzle?

CABRERA INFANTE: No, absolutely not, writing doesn't have to be like a jigsaw puzzle, it can be a very linear undertaking. For instance, there are very complex games like chess, or very simple ones like Ping-Pong or tennis. What I do believe is that there is always a relationship between writing and reading, a constant interplay between the writer on the one hand and the reader on the other. The page is like a reference point, like the net in tennis, a concrete area to which all the rules of the game can be applied.

INTERVIEWER: So then, what does the page mean for you?

CABRERA INFANTE: Too much has been said on this since the end of the nineteenth century, when Mallarmé unfortunately decided to speak about the blank page. All of a sudden, writers seemed to discover that there really was an empty page before they wrote. Then they all began to complain about that virgin page, the trauma of the blank page, the suffering involved with an empty page, that page which must be filled. All of this has always seemed absolutely wanton and absurd to me, without basis or foundation. When I write, the first blank page, or any blank page, means nothing to me. What means something is a page that has been filled with words. I can then play with them, transform them, parody them, and find their relation to phrases from earlier times, whether they are instances of ordinary street language which any Cuban or Spaniard might use, or examples of extraordinary literature. Sometimes, the words to a song can be truly fabulous and a form of poetry in their own right.

INTERVIEWER: Music has influenced you greatly, am I right?

CABRERA INFANTE: Yes, greatly. My first memories, for example, are about movies and music—specifically, the words of Cuban songs, like the boleros, from the thirties and the forties, a whole gamut of South American songs, Mexican songs, and North American music. These have always been very important to me. In fact, I have said that I like one line from a song by the Chilean Lucho Gatica more than all of Neruda's poetry. I won't say I like it more than all the poetry of Gabriela Mistral so as not to offend your sensibilities. That masterful line, which Gatica used to sing in 1957, is from a song called "La barca" (The Boat), and it went something like this: "Ya mi barca tiene que partir. Voy a navegar por otros mares de locura" (My boat is about to leave. I must sail through other seas of madness). This is an extraordinary poetic find, and I have used this phrase repeatedly, it is something of a leitmotiv with me, unlike any of Neruda's verses.

INTERVIEWER: Why did you abandon your medical career?

CABRERA INFANTE: I didn't abandon a medical career—I never even started it.

INTERVIEWER: But you wanted to be a doctor?

CABRERA INFANTE: I wanted to be a doctor because my parents were set that I should have a university degree. So I chose a field that I thought would be the most interesting for me, and it wasn't philosophy or law or economics that I picked, but rather medicine. In this respect, I was extraordinarily lucky to have been taken to the medical school by a friend after my high-school graduation. He immediately showed me the pathology section, where on five tables lay five corpses.

INTERVIEWER: And that's where your career ended . . .

CABRERA INFANTE: Yes, the corpses looked horrendous, and what was worse was that they smelled like sin. The combination of rotting flesh and formaldehyde in which the corpses were preserved was truly foul. To boot, on the fifth table a group of students surrounded a doctor who was in the process of cutting open a dead man's stomach. That's when I said to myself, "If this is what I have to do for two years in order to become a doctor, I don't want to be one." I am glad to this day that I avoided that because doctors are among the most traumatized people in life. Having to deal with death and disease like that has to be extremely painful and depressing.

INTERVIEWER: In 1952, you were arrested and fined for publishing a story which, in your own words, contained "English profanities." Would you like to tell us a little about that episode of your life?

CABRERA INFANTE: That episode, like many episodes in one's life, seemed tragic at the time it happened, and comical afterward. What happened was that I published a story in the magazine *Bohemia,* which was the most important Cuban magazine, and the editor, who was my mentor and protector, took out all the naughty Spanish words, but not the English ones. The reason for all those indelicate words was that the story dealt with a group of gangsters who set out to kill an individual in Havana. In their midst was an American tourist who waited with anticipation for the killing and who hummed a very obscene tune, which I am not going to repeat now because some people in New York speak English. Since neither the publisher nor the editor-in-chief knew English, however, that obscene tune remained in the story. During the first year of the dictatorship of Batista, 1952, there was a man who was particularly interested in damaging the magazine for political reasons, so he complained to the Government that *Bohemia* was printing stories with dirty English words. When the director of the magazine was asked about this, he replied that he had no idea what those words meant and that all responsibility for the story lay with me. So they came to my house, arrested me, and locked me up for a few days. I have written about the events which then took place in a story called "Obsceno," which was published in my book *O.* As they led me to the police station, the detectives who had arrested me, plainclothes policemen, behaved with such extreme obscenity toward the women on the street that my story paled by comparison. I was finally fined 500 pesos, the equivalent of $500 in those days, a tremendous sum for me back then, but which, thanks to my lawyer and my editor, I didn't have to pay. What was strange about the trial was that I was tried by a very solemn judge in a very noisy and chaotic courthouse replete with prostitutes and characters of that sort running to and fro. All of a sudden, the secretary announced that the next trial would take place behind closed doors. The courtroom hushed, because for a trial to take place behind closed doors meant that the charges were so serious that they could not be made public in front of the audience present that morning. I was led to a decrepit little room where I met with the judge, his secretary and my lawyer. The judge read me a lengthy brief questioning my motives for publishing stories with dirty words in the full knowledge that such obscenity was reaching Cuban homes. That's where that incident ended, although I suffered its consequences afterward. Among other things, I had to stop studying journalism for a period of two years.

INTERVIEWER: Why did you begin writing under the pseudonym of G. Caín?

CABRERA INFANTE: After that story was published, the magazine's director, who had found himself in a tight spot for having permitted the tale to be published, wanted nothing to do with me. After a period of six months, my mentor, Antonio Ortega, who was the editor-in-chief of the magazine, told me, "Why don't you write something for *Bohemia?* You don't have to use your name, just invent a pseudonym." I wanted my pseudonym to be as close to my name as possible, so I took the "G" of Guillermo as the initial, and then I combined the first two letters of each of my last names, and "Caín" is what came out. I then wrote an article on the twenty-fifth anniversary of the creation of Mickey Mouse, which was highly praised by the magazine, although the editor-in-chief did not reveal my name, of course. I published two more articles in *Bohemia,* and when my mentor was finally made director of *Carteles,* he put me in charge of the film section of that magazine. I kept on using my pseudonym, however, to make sure that there would be no backlash against me.

INTERVIEWER: How long did you continue publishing with that pseudonym?

CABRERA INFANTE: For the film reviews, from 1954 until 1960, at which time *Carteles* was closed down by the Government.

INTERVIEWER: You have qualified *Three Trapped Tigers* as a "gallery of voices." What drove you to write a novel which was meant to be heard, where you combined jokes, plays on words, and tongue twisters? Your friend, the critic Emir Rodríguez Monegal, even went so far as to say that you "turned the phrase inside out as if it were a glove."

CABRERA INFANTE: The thing about a gallery of voices was really a guide I gave to those critics who, unlike you, only read the front and back covers of a book. If you look closely, there is no book more visual than *Three Trapped Tigers,* in that it is filled with blank pages, dark pages, it has stars made of words, the famous magical cube made of numbers, and there is even a page which is a mirror. It is an absolutely graphic work, with the movies as its theme, in a way, because the characters behave as if they were actors in a movie; one of them speaks of nothing else, and the other is a photographer. So it is not a book made exclusively to be heard; it is meant to be seen and heard. These are the two most important components of literature: hearing and seeing from the writer's perspective, and seeing and speaking from the reader's point of view. It is a difficult book to read, in any case. For instance, I suggest at the beginning of the book that certain pages should be read aloud, but I don't think many people benefit from that advice because they would have to know what inflections to give, and I am really the only one in a position to know and interpret things like that. There is also a very arbitrary disposition of punctuation—there are commas where there shouldn't be and periods that have been placed whimsically in the middle of a line. So there is an entire series of relations between the author and the written page that were not stylistically oral.

INTERVIEWER: How did you manage to crack the secret language of the night of prerevolutionary Havana?

CABRERA INFANTE: That was one of my goals. . . . Raymond Chandler has a dictum that said a writer should be very careful about using slang because either it is passé by the time the book gets printed or it is completely impenetrable. The only way for the writer to protect himself from those two hazards is to create his own slang. This is what I did with the *Three Tigers*. I created a new language for Havana from Belgium and Spain, where I wrote the book. It began when I read a transcription of a meeting of contemporary Cuban politicians, workers, and peasants in Havana. This transcript ran about 1,500 pages, and I of course did not read them all because they were atrociously boring, but there it was, without any pretension to literature. It was then I realized that there was absolutely no relation between that transcription and my work, and that, in fact, there was no relation between my writing and the language used by Cubans today. Someone told me that the way Cubans speak has changed dramatically in twenty years. That may be possible, but I wonder if they did at some time speak like the characters of *Three Tigers*.

INTERVIEWER: It means that your book represents a language that you invented, but which, at the same time, does really exist.

CABRERA INFANTE: It means that no matter what you write, be it a biography, an autobiography, a detective novel, or a conversation on the street, it all becomes fiction as soon as you write it down.

INTERVIEWER: How do you reconcile a sense of humor with a sense of the poetic?

CABRERA INFANTE: I don't think I have much sense of the poetic.

INTERVIEWER: But there are poetical moments in your writing.

CABRERA INFANTE: There may be such moments through evocation, which is very important, and I resort to nostalgia a lot. *Infante's Inferno* is a book full of memories of Havana. Those memories are manipulated to such an extent that even those people who participated in them are unaware of it. There is a constant manipulation of my own nostalgia, and I use it as a wellspring for my literature. I loathe any pretension to writing well, or to there being such a thing as fine writing, or poetical writing. For instance, an old Spanish educator who used to live in Cuba, when he first read my stories at the end of the 1940s, suggested that I look up certain Spanish writers to acquire another sense of the language. So I read those authors, who are not worthy to be mentioned, who wrote with what was known as a golden touch; they wrote well, with a finely structured prose. But I thought they were truly horrendous and that they were completely irrelevant to what I was trying to achieve.

INTERVIEWER: Since 1965 you have lived away from your country. Do you consider yourself a writer in exile?

CABRERA INFANTE: Well, I write in exile because I cannot return to my country, so I have no choice but to see myself as an exiled writer. Consider the fact that there were writers who went voluntarily into exile, like Fitzgerald, Hemingway, Gertrude Stein and other writers who lived in Paris in the twenties, the "lost generation." They all believed themselves to be writers in exile, and I think I have more right to call myself that than they. That's why I never believed in the "exile" of the Latin American authors who lived in Europe at the same time as I did. The difference between myself and them was that I could not go home, whereas they did return to Argentina, Peru, Colombia, Mexico, and so on.

INTERVIEWER: Who are your readers? Do you think about them when you write?

CABRERA INFANTE: I think that like all writers—and if any writer disagrees with this, then he is not a writer—I write primarily for myself. It is when I publish, or begin to think about publishing, that problems arise. When I write, however, I do so for my own pleasure. I have one main reader, Miriam Gómez, my wife. She reads everything I write—I have not finished writing something and she is already reading it. In fact, she is such a demanding critic that she made me eliminate a hundred pages from *Infante's Inferno!* But I don't really write for her either. When I write, I enjoy myself so much that what is being written really needs no reader. It is like a sexual act with one's self—I see the letters on my typewriter, and for me that is the greatest pleasure.

INTERVIEWER: And do you think about your characters? Or are they also unimportant?

CABRERA INFANTE: I don't much believe in the idea of characters. I write with words, that is all. Whether those words are put in the mouth of this or that character does not matter to me.

INTERVIEWER: You dedicated two of your books to Miriam Gómez.

CABRERA INFANTE: *Un oficio del siglo veinte* is also dedicated to her, although in a mocking way, because I decided to dedicate that book to my wife as well, as she had kept all my film reviews, making the writing of the book extremely easy.

So the dedication was to "Miriam Gómez and Marta Calvo without whom this would not have been possible." I was referring to the structure of the book, of course. But since then I have dedicated *Three Trapped Tigers* and *Infante's Inferno* to Miriam, although the dedication of the latter book was more cryptic, as it said "To M., my driving force."

INTERVIEWER: Does she read your books once they are finished, or do you discuss them with her as you are writing them?

CABRERA INFANTE: "Discuss"?

INTERVIEWER: Well, talk about ...

CABRERA INFANTE: You don't know Miriam Gómez if you think I can discuss with her once she has made up her mind that I am not going to publish something! There is no appeal possible—she is like a medieval judge.

INTERVIEWER: So you believe in the Inquisition?

CABRERA INFANTE: Almost. She even reads and censors my letters, and not only the ones that I receive but the ones I send out.

INTERVIEWER: Why do you write?

CABRERA INFANTE: It started as a joke, a parody, and a bet, even though I am not a gambler. When I was in Cuba in 1947, I read fragments of *El Señor Presidente* by Miguel Angel Asturias. I then discussed that work with Carlos Franqui, an old friend of mine who later went into exile in Italy, and told him, "If this is writing, then I am sure I can do it," and he replied, "Yes, it is very easy." So I wrote a story, he read it and pronounced it quite good—today, I disagree with his judgment completely; I think it was a horrendous tale. But he suggested I take it to the magazine *Bohemia,* and that was where I met the person who was to become my mentor, Antonio Ortega, the editor-in-chief of the magazine. He said he would read the story and that I should come back in a week. When I returned, he told me that the tale would be published, and he paid me fifty pesos, the equivalent of fifty dollars. I had never had that kind of money in my life, because I was very poor then, so I kept on writing stories, and they too were published, and I was paid again. I decided that was what I would do because I didn't have to work or study for it—writing stories and having them published would be enough. This then turned into a sort of *modus vivendi,* but without knowing it I became like the person who plays around with drugs, who as he injects himself with morphine thinks that he is not going to form a habit, that it is like a joke and he can quit any time he wants. Of course, that's when I became hooked for life. What had started out as a parody turned into a game first and then into a habit, from which I have not been able to free myself.

INTERVIEWER: In which genre do you feel the most comfortable?

CABRERA INFANTE: I don't know. I have assiduously avoided calling my books novels. That's something I discussed with my publisher, Seix Barral, over a long period of time, although you have to understand the motives of publishers as well. They need to have some way of identifying works for bookstores, so as to allow an easy categorization of differing genres. For instance, a book of essays would go on the same shelf with the works of Ortega, Cela and Unamuno; a book of short stories, meanwhile, would go next to Borges, and novels would thus be placed next to other novels. But my books could never be called novels—if that had been the case, then my first work would have been a novel, and my last one would not. That's a debate that has been raging forever among critics, whether the book is a confession or a memoir. I never interfere, because the idea of using the label of "novel" was never mine. *Vista del amanecer en el trópico,* for instance, was published here by Harper and Row under the name *View of Dawn in the Tropics.* They respected my demand that the book not be labeled a novel, because it is really a history of Cuba told through various vignettes. But then they sold the book as a paperback, and beneath my name was the label "a novel," which I thought was a terrible fraud and deception perpetrated on the readers because they would believe that they were indeed going to read a novel. In reality, they came up against a history of Cuba told through vignettes, with no discernible characters, and even lacking names to identify historical figures.

INTERVIEWER: Could one call you a patriotic chronicler?

CABRERA INFANTE: No, I completely reject those labels. Not that of chronicler, because I wrote film reviews in which the central character was called "the chronicler," who was the person who went to the movies and criticized them. But I do reject the notion of "patriotism" because that word is so grandiose and so exploited that it has become virtually meaningless. Recently, there was a conference of exiled Cuban writers in Washington, and the organizer told me, "I want to tell you that I am doing this for Cuba." I thought this so pretentious that I had to reply, "Well, if that is the case, then I am doing it for Havana," because it was truly a statement worthy of ridicule, even though he was perfectly serious and believed that notions of Cuba and patriotism were more important than words. For me, words are just words, nothing else. So I do not consider myself a chronicler of my fatherland or even a chronicler of Havana. What I tried to do was to debunk the idea of "History," with a capital *H,* because I have always believed that history is like any other book and that it should be treated as such. Substituting the idea of God for the idea of history really leads back to the same thing. Whether you call it "God," "history," "universe," or "chance," or you believe, as the pantheists do, that God is everywhere, does not matter. What I tried to do in that book was to tackle the notion of Cuba as a tropical paradise, because even before Columbus's arrival, atrocious crimes were being committed there, something which has not stopped to this day. This is true of any nation, of course, but I was not interested in any country, I wanted to deal concretely with Cuban history, which is worshipped so excessively in exile and in Cuba itself.

INTERVIEWER: *View of Dawn in the Tropics* is your most controversial work. You dedicated it to Commander Plino Prieto, who was shot in September 1960, and to Commander Alberto Mora, who killed himself in September 1972. What relevance did these two men have within the framework of Cuban politics and what impact did they have on your life?

CABRERA INFANTE: Within the framework of Cuban politics, very little. But they were both friends of mine, especially Alberto Mora, whom I first met when we were both twenty years old in 1950, and our friendship continued throughout Batista's dictatorship, when he engaged in terrorist activities. Plino Prieto was the first director of the Cuban Film Library in 1950. He was crazy about film, but in a very specific sense, because he was only interested in cartoons. He didn't care in the least for anything that had to do with people on film. He loved cartoons and animation, like Walt Disney, with identifiable caricatures, like the stuff the UPA used to do, or the work of abstract Canadian animators. But the life of my two friends was greatly changed when Batista took over after a coup in 1952. They both dedicated themselves to anti-Batista activities, and in this respect, as I show in a vignette, Plino Prieto was a man for whom everything always turned out badly. His life was a series of failures. For example, in 1958 he organized a boat supply of arms to Cuban shores, but the small ship went astray in the Gulf of Mexico, which was subject to strong and unpredictable winds. Prieto had left from Yucatán, I believe, and the boat was adrift for several days. Finally, he managed to land at a secret spot in Cuba, only to see unexpected festivities going on—Batista had fled five days earlier! So, even though Prieto and his crew almost died several times in the crossing, his mission was a complete failure in every respect: consider the effort required to gather money and purchase weapons and a boat, travel with that boat to Cuba, land in complete secrecy, and find out there was absolutely no need for it. Shortly afterward, however, he became a counterrevolutionary and was caught in the Province of Las Villas, where he was summarily shot. Alberto Mora's life was quite different. He was mildly successful because he was in one of the revolutionary groups that attacked the Presidential Palace. That group later became a part of the revolutionary Government, and he himself was the first director of its student wing. Later, he became Minister of Commerce after he associated himself with Che Guevara. When the latter fell from grace in Cuba, Mora ceased to be Minister. He then drifted into increasing obscurity, until the famous Padilla case, when he wrote personally to Fidel Castro to protest the treatment given Padilla, who was jailed and made to confess. As a result of this letter, he was sentenced to hard labor on a farm in the same area where Plino Prieto had been shot. But rather than go there, he decided to kill himself. These two persons were much beloved by me: Alberto was always very generous with me, and I admired Plino from afar, because he was not really a very communicative individual, thoroughly un-Cuban in this respect, and given to telling extremely dry jokes. They were both noteworthy persons, and I thought that they were victimized by the same historical event that they helped bring about. So I remembered them in a very particular manner, and they are the only truly relevant and real characters in my book.

INTERVIEWER: In that book you mention the murder of a police lieutenant by some youngsters, followed by their eventual deaths, and you don't disclose their names. Is there some connection between that story and the deaths of police sergeant Rubén Darío González, and the two students Gustavo Maso and Juan Regeiro, who died on December 12, 1949?

CABRERA INFANTE: The only possible connection is that Juancito Regeiro and Gustavo Maso were fellow students of mine in college. They were part of a gang that is difficult to understand in this country, if one does not think of the Mafia in the eighteenth or nineteenth centuries. They were gangsters because they were armed and violent, and wouldn't give too much thought to killing someone. At the same time, however, they were not like American gangsters—they did not dedicate themselves to robbing banks. They thought of themselves as revolutionaries, and in that sense they were political gangsters. Curiously enough, they belonged to the same group as Fidel Castro, the *Unión Insurreccional Revolucionaria* (*UIR*) (Revolutionary Insurrectionary Union). The police sergeant belonged to the *Movimiento Social Revolucionario* (*MSR*) (Revolutionary Social Movement). As you can see, they insisted on the "revolutionary" aspect constantly. The sergeant's name was Rubén Darío González, although he was everything but a poet. He was an extremely violent man, who had quite possibly killed one or two members of the other band. What truly interested me in this occurrence was its similarity to a parallel scene from a western. Juancito was sixteen and Gustavo was twenty when they walked in through the swinging doors of the bar where Rubén Darío González was seated. There were several people sitting on stools, and the two youths said, "Gentlemen, please step aside, this does not concern you." González had no time to react; he was drinking a beer, he turned his head, and they shot him with .45 caliber guns and killed him. Then they fled and sought refuge with the leader of their band, but since they had committed the murder without permission, their chief wanted nothing to do with the killing, although he was hardly a humanist. So instead of hiding him, he handed them over to the other group. They turned up dead the next day at a place called El laguito, a well-known pond in an aristocratic residential area. They were both very young, and although Juancito Regeiro was most definitely a psychopath, Gustavo Maso was a reasonable boy and a good student. I saw how they degenerated step by step into gangsterism and mindless, destructive violence, which eventually did them in. The incident was widely commented on at the college because we all knew them well.

INTERVIEWER: In the same book, there is also a story in which you tell of the death of a character and say, "He who had to die, died." Could you comment on this?

CABRERA INFANTE: This is a typically violent episode from that capitalist democratic period, 1947 and 1948, involving various so-called revolutionary student groups. It is an extraordinary occurrence because the head of the *Federación de Estudiantes Universitarios* (*FEU*) (Federation of University Students), Manolo Castro, was killed. This assassination is recounted by Hemingway in one of his famous articles. He used it as the beginning of a piece in which he went on to relate how he hunted antelopes in Idaho or something like that. Hemingway said Castro had been a very honest man because he had died with thirty-two cents in his pocket. He was indeed an honest person, but he had also engaged in violent acts. The group who decided to kill him was the same to which Fidel Castro belonged, the UIR. So there is a great probability that one of the men who murdered Manolo Castro was Fidel Castro, because the leader of the UIR had a very macabre sense of humor. For instance, if the UIR had been after someone for years, they would leave a note on the dead body saying, "Justice is slow, but it comes." This was the trademark of the UIR. So the fact that one Castro should kill another probably appealed to the dark sense of humor of the UIR's leader, although it was never conclusively proved that Fidel Castro was one of the killers, only that he knew when the murder was going to occur, and that he was a member of that group. And the reference to "he who had to die" indicates that Manolo Castro had been on the UIR's death list for quite some time.

INTERVIEWER: How do you come up with the titles of your works?

CABRERA INFANTE: Titles are not only important, they are essential for me. I cannot write without a title. The example that comes to mind is the book *Infante's Inferno*. When I first started that work, it was called, as I told you, "Las confesiones de agosto" for obvious reasons, which, however, are not always the most visible. I gave it that name because when I started

writing the book—which incidentally was based on an idea by
Miriam Gómez—it was August of 1976. I wanted to allude to
Saint Augustine's famous *Confessions*. As you know, there
was nothing Christian or exemplary about his early life. I
worked for two years on the book, between 1976 and 1978, and
one day, as if Saint Augustine or Ravel were whispering to me,
the Spanish title, *La Havana para un infante difunto,* came to
me. And that is the title of my book, there is no other. It is a
parody of Ravel's famous title *Pavane pour une infante défunte.*
Ravel was making a joke because as you know *infante défunte*
rhymes very well in French; it is both homophonic and caco-
phonic at the same time. That is to say, the words sound the
same and yet they are shocking together. The word *pavane* was
brought in because it is an archaic musical form, while *infante*
was used because of the fascination foreigners have with that
term, which in Spanish designates the sons of the king who will
not ascend to the throne. When the title came to me, I became
convinced it was perfect, so I set out to rewrite the entire book,
which took me about a year. At the end of this period, I told
Miriam Gómez the title, and she liked it. All my friends agreed
that it was a very comic title. Many of my books have begun
with the title, because naming a work already in progress makes
no sense to me.

INTERVIEWER: From all the books you have written, which
is your favorite?

CABRERA INFANTE: I don't have a favorite book, but I have
a most despised book which I have tried to forget as much as
possible.

INTERVIEWER: Which one is it?

CABRERA INFANTE: *Así en la paz como en la guerra,* my
first book, which is a collection of fifteen short stories, out of
which maybe three are salvageable. The worst thing about the
book is the fact that my attitude when I wrote it was very negative. I was completely under the influence of Sartre, because I
accepted the premise that a book should be a comprehensive

critical act. So not only did I have to include reality, which is an idiotic pretension, but I also had to have criticisms of reality and of the work itself. That book is therefore execrable for me. The next book I wrote, however, which was called *Un oficio del siglo veinte,* is perhaps my favorite work, because it is then that I truly began to write as I wanted to write, and not as I thought I should write.

INTERVIEWER: The Institute of Literature and Linguistics of the Cuban Academy of Sciences published a dictionary on Cuban literature a few years ago. How is it possible that your name does not appear in it?

CABRERA INFANTE: It's very simple. I turned out to be an enemy, and I am going to explain why. My parents were founders of the Cuban Communist Party, and I grew up extremely poor. When we moved to Havana, my father founded the communist newspaper *Hoy.* I began my writing career by doing translations for that paper. I also used to participate in many insurrectionary activities against Batista. Many of Cuba's current literary "heroes" (whose names I am not going to repeat here because it would be giving them free publicity) used to go to Mass every day in those times, and some even worked within Batista's government. By contrast, Alberto Mora hid in our house for six months at one time, and at great risk, since the second in command of Batista's police lived right next door to us. But it was decided that he should stay at our house because this represented a natural sort of camouflage—nobody in his right mind would hide a fugitive next to the house of a chief of police. I did other things as well, like writing for the clandestine newspaper *Revolución* with Franqui. When the revolution came to power, I collaborated with it. I was the first delegate of the cultural section of the Ministry of Education sent by the first revolutionary Minister of Education himself. This past is irrevocable; if anyone had credentials to be a part of today's Cuba it would be I, not Alejo Carpentier or Lezama Lima, because the former lived in Venezuela until the revolution ascended to power and the latter was an official of Batista's cultural division. So they can never say that I left Cuba because I was the son of filthy rich parents who had ten sugar plantations confiscated. That is impossible. The only way to attack me was to completely eliminate me. My books, for instance, were banned in Cuba, but not because I had made counterrevolutionary declarations. They were banned from the very time when they were published abroad. *Three Trapped Tigers* never circulated in Cuba, and I had not criticized Fidel Castro's government at that time. So why did they ban this book? Because there was the possibility that, since I was abroad, I would sooner or later become a counterrevolutionary. There were also certain literary cliques and political interests which contributed to drawing a curtain of silence around me. I first came out against Castro in June 1968, fifteen months after my book had been published, and you cannot imagine how quickly a void was created around me. I ceased appearing in anthologies. I could tell you about a series of anthologies where they mentioned literally anyone, and I didn't appear. So it does not surprise me that I am not mentioned in that book.

INTERVIEWER: In an interview you held in Caracas, you described Fidel Castro as the "Stalin of the Caribbean." Nevertheless, your parents had portraits of Stalin and Jesus in their house in the 1930s. Why these apparent contradictions?

CABRERA INFANTE: I can explain quite simply why we had both a portrait of Stalin and one of Jesus. My mother had been educated at a convent, and she had been converted to communism by my father during Stalin's most rampant period, at the beginning of the 1930s. So she had two gods, God in heaven and god on earth. The comparison between Castro and Stalin is not really so farfetched if you consider that here are two men who eliminated practically all their enemies, amassing all the power for themselves. But in certain respects the comparison is not apt. A better parallel would be with Hitler, for instance in the massive mobilization of people. Specifically, Castro would bring millions of Cubans to the Plaza de la República, while Hitler drew two or three million Germans to Nuremberg or Berlin. They both used loudspeakers, extreme body language, and could employ their voices in a particularly inflammatory, moving manner, in the sense that they could sway their audiences in one direction or the other. They were both great actors, at the peak of their powers when performing before the masses. All these factors make the comparison more plausible. Of course, there is one great difference between them: Fidel Castro never wrote a *Mein Kampf.* He was a surprise Hitler, because he never delivered what he promised: to reinstitute the Constitution of 1940 and return Cuba to a democratic state, with free elections. Hitler, on the other hand, did exactly what he set out in *Mein Kampf,* down to the extermination of the Jews.

INTERVIEWER: Who is Guillermo Cabrera Infante?

CABRERA INFANTE: I would prefer that we leave my strip-tease to a more private place.

José Donoso

José Donoso

José Donoso, one of Chile's foremost writers, was born in Santiago on October 5, 1924, into a family of doctors and lawyers. As a child he studied at the British School in Santiago, and he is thus totally bilingual. After studying at the Instituto Pedagógico of the University of Chile, he received the Doherty Foundation Scholarship to study at Princeton University, obtaining his B.A. there in 1951. He has conducted writers' workshops at the Catholic University of Santiago, Princeton University, Dartmouth College and the University of Iowa. In 1956, he was awarded Chile's Municipal Prize for short stories and the Chile-Italia Prize for journalism. He has received the Guggenheim Fellowship twice, first in 1967, then in 1973.

José Donoso is the author of countless books. His first work, *Coronación*, 1957 (*Coronation*, 1965), won him the William Faulkner Foundation Prize. His works include: *Este Domingo*, 1966 (*This Sunday*, 1967); *El lugar sin límites*, 1967 (*Hell Has No Limits*, 1972); *El obsceno pájaro de la noche*, 1970 (*The Obscene Bird of Night*, 1973); *El Charleston*, 1960 (*Charleston and Other Stories*, 1977); *Historia personal del "Boom,"* 1972 (*The Boom in Spanish American Literature: A Personal History*, 1977); *Tres novelitas burguesas*, 1973 (*Sacred Families: Three Novellas*, 1977); *Casa de campo*, 1978, winner of the Spanish Critics Prize (*A House in the Country*, 1984); *La misteriosa desaparición de la marquesita de Loria* (The Mysterious Disappearance of the Little Marquesa from Loria), 1980; *Poemas de un novelista* (Poems of a Novelist), 1981; *El jardín de al lado* (The Garden Next Door), 1981; *Cuatro para Delfina* (Four Novels for Delfina), 1982; *La desesperanza*, 1986 (*Curfew*, 1988).

José Donoso has lived in Mexico, the United States and Spain. In 1981, after almost eighteen years of absence, he decided to return to Chile with his family to make a home there. He is the recipient of the Woodrow Wilson Fellowship for 1986-87. The *Philadelphia Inquirer* has said of him: "He dazzles, intoxicates and disgusts—

which is why his works have been compared to the painting of Hieronymus Bosch, the films of Luis Buñuel and the writings of Charles Dickens."

Speaking of his own work, Donoso has said, "Walking into a novel is like walking into my house. I feel at ease there, it is enough that I have a handle, a first sentence, a jumping board."

The interviews that follow were done on three successive occasions: the first was held at St. John's University, New York, in 1980; the second at Winthrop College, South Carolina, in 1981; and the third in New York in 1987.

Part 1

INTERVIEWER: Would I be correct in saying that since the 1960s the novel in Latin America has replaced the position that poetry used to enjoy in the first half of the century? In fact, hasn't the novel become the true representative of your continent?

DONOSO: I do not know what Latin America represents, except itself. It is a rather large reality. But the fact is that, when I went to Iowa to teach in 1963-64, I wanted to offer a comparative literature seminar on the Latin American novel in translation, and I was told, "No, why don't you give one on Latin American poetry, it is so much more distinguished." And I said, "No, I want to do one on the Latin American novel, which I think is, at this point, the more interesting thing." So, yes, I think something has happened, and in general the novel has replaced poetry. Many things have happened in Latin America and Latin American literature which could explain that change—if an explanation were possible.

INTERVIEWER: Would you say that the novel reflects politics in some way?

DONOSO: No, that is an easy explanation of meaning through history, which I don't very much believe in. I think a novel is a novel is a novel, a rose is a rose is a rose.

INTERVIEWER: And yet the Cuban revolution had some effect on most of the writers.

DONOSO: Yes, but so has everything. To explain the Latin American novel in terms of the Cuban revolution is obviously not enough. It would be more and it would be less.

INTERVIEWER: You have said, "I feel so identified with the adventure of the internationalization of the novel of the 1960s that in giving my testimony about it I have found myself at times writing parts of my autobiography." Do you think that you could explain in some way the literary explosion which is referred to as the "Boom"? Can it be defined?

DONOSO: "Defined" is a very strict word. It could be described rather than defined. In that piece you quoted, I used the word "internationalization," to become international. It does not only mean that the Latin American novel began to be read abroad, it also points to the very strange fact that most of the big novels of our so-called Boom were written abroad, not written in the authors' own countries. Cortázar wrote *Hopscotch* in Paris. Vargas Llosa wrote *The Time of the Hero* in Paris and *The Green House* in London. I wrote my own books in Spain, Cabrera Infante wrote *Three Trapped Tigers* in Brussels, and so on. The big novels of the 1960s and 1970s were all written outside Latin America.

INTERVIEWER: Is there something special about the fact that most of the writers of that period have written in exile or self-imposed exile?

DONOSO: I think the trip is the thing. It all goes back to Odysseus, to the fact that you go out of your country to become yourself. It is very strange that you should talk of the poetry just before my generation as being so important. That poetry was also the poetry of self-exiled poets. Neruda spent thirty years abroad, Gabriela Mistral forty years abroad, Vicente Huidobro, César Vallejo and Rubén Darío spent most of their lives abroad, as did Octavio Paz, who is still alive.

INTERVIEWER: Do you identify much more with Latin America when you are abroad?

DONOSO: If you are in Latin America you are drawn into action which is not writing. As you know, we Latin Americans have a great tradition of the right to be statesmen, politicians, diplomats, men of letters. What was it Byron said in a letter to Lady Melbourne? I think he said, "I am through with all our dreams, I want the talents of action, of war, of the senate, of politics," and I believe this is true. We have inherited the romantic urge to be useful, to be men of action.

INTERVIEWER: Do you think that most of the writers of the Boom looked more to North America than their predecessors?

DONOSO: Who was it who said, "We are a generation of parasites"? I think all generations are generations of parasites.

INTERVIEWER: So is it breaking away from the previous generation or not?

DONOSO: It is becoming, getting through the Oedipus complex, I think, trying to find one's way.

INTERVIEWER: What would you say are the main characteristics of the novels written during the Boom of the 1960s?

DONOSO: I think the Boom as such is past. It was something that happened. It was not a question of novelists, but a question of novels. During a period of ten years, there was intersection, there was the coincidence of many very important Latin American novels published at short intervals. This is what made the Boom, not the persons.

INTERVIEWER: Vargas Llosa's definition of the writer is that of an exorcist of his own demons, a sorcerer who creates without explaining, but whose work is in itself a question and answer. What is your concept of the writer?

DONOSO: I have a fair number of concepts. Again, I have no

definition. I think that one writes because one wants to know why one writes. I think a novelist is a man who does not want to teach or say something but wants to know something. Writing is not a didactic experience, it is more of an existential experience. One becomes something by writing, one does not show who one is.

INTERVIEWER: In *The Obscene Bird of Night,* would it be true to say that the narrator is at the same time the executioner and the victim?

DONOSO: Yes, I suppose so. But again I think to reduce a novel to something different from itself is perhaps wrong. The novel is a metaphor, you cannot reduce a metaphor to another form of expression, it is the thing itself. One receives a novel, not its meaning.

INTERVIEWER: Your work has similarities with *Frankenstein* and the grotesque, and with the art of caricature of Quevedo and Valle Inclán.

DONOSO: I think if one is too conscious of doing a caricature, one does a caricature of oneself. If one believes that what one is doing is true, then the result may have some relation to caricature. I do not think Valle Inclán creates caricatures, I think he does another thing altogether.

INTERVIEWER: In your own works, you go beyond reality into the unreal and make it real. As readers of your novels, we accept everything. We can identify with representations of reality. But the unreal becomes so real that we identify with it just as well. So, at certain points we cannot say what is real and what is unreal. That is the magic of your work.

DONOSO: Yes, but that is also the magic of Juan Rulfo, Vargas Llosa and Carlos Fuentes. It is the magic of writing, to make out of the fabrication of reality, which is parallel to the reality we know, another reality which the author has caused to exist.

INTERVIEWER: Is the interplay of fantasy and reality typical of Latin American writing?

DONOSO: I don't know. What about *A Midsummer Night's Dream,* for instance, where you have reality, irreality and sub-reality? It is in the nature of writing.

INTERVIEWER: How would you respond to what Alfred MacAdam has said of you: "Donoso depicts in his satire the literary work of art in action, a grotesque work in progress that fights to stay alive as it seeks to destroy itself"?

DONOSO: Certainly there is the question of writing itself. I don't accept the idea of writing as exposition. I question the idea of what writing is. In *The Obscene Bird of Night* there is continual questioning of the use of writing, what it means, how it works and what it is. In that sense, I end up with a negative answer.

INTERVIEWER: Your work creates an atmosphere of enclosure. Almost every character is fighting to breathe or to escape boundaries.

DONOSO: Yes, I think most of my novels take place within an enclosed space, or within a set of enclosed spaces like Chinese boxes, one inside another. One must get away from them, destroy those layers, get outside and breathe. But the inverse is also true. There is the delight of being within the womb. There is progression and regression.

INTERVIEWER: Is there no difference between being a baby and being very old?

DONOSO: There is the terror of having to take a position, having to assert, being committed. I think no one wants to do that.

INTERVIEWER: When you are writing, do your characters lead you or do you lead them?

DONOSO: On the whole they lead me, I think, quite a bit.

INTERVIEWER: So they become almost independent of you?

DONOSO: Sometimes it is characters, sometimes it is space, sometimes it is time, sometimes it is working with a word or a phrase that leads me on to something else. I work with models, with plans which I continually tend to betray. I begin by having a very set plan and then I go on betraying it, but if I did not have that first plan to betray I would not be able to write.

INTERVIEWER: Do you revise your work?

DONOSO: Oh my God, yes.

INTERVIEWER: So you may write many versions of the same page?

DONOSO: Ten, twenty, thirty, fifty.

INTERVIEWER: How do you decide which is the right one?

DONOSO: I do not decide, the page decides.

INTERVIEWER: And is it not too painful to throw away something that you have written when you have decided that it is not the best version?

DONOSO: No, it's a wonderful feeling. Everything is so clear. When you finally discard something and it is so right to discard it, then you say, "Damn it, it's right, I was right."

INTERVIEWER: How would you describe writing as a profession?

DONOSO: Lonely. I remember talking to Luis Buñuel, the film director. He used to come to visit me when I lived in Calaceite, a small town in central Spain, and he would say, "I envy you because you are responsible for what you do, alone, and there is nobody who interferes in your creation." Then I said to Buñuel, "I envy the fact that you do not work alone. My only companion is my typewriter and my piece of paper."

INTERVIEWER: To write, is it to die or to live?

DONOSO: Or to sleep. No, it is to live, very definitely. I have no other way of keeping alive. It is my way, not of teaching anything, but certainly of trying to understand, of putting things in some kind of shape, in some order. The whole idea of writing, as in any kind of artistic endeavor, is not to find the meaning but to find the shape, and the shape itself is the meaning.

INTERVIEWER: And yet your novel represents a chaotic world.

DONOSO: But it has a shape because it has a style, it has a limit because I set my own restrictions when writing a novel.

INTERVIEWER: What do you try to do in your novels?

DONOSO: I try to demystify, to take this enormous feeling of mystery and of awe that there is in literature and laugh and say, "Okay, I can do something that is just for kicks." We Latin American writers tend to be terribly self-important. But everything is intrinsic to my novels, the images I conjure up in them, the world that some people will believe is there, but I have no pretension to any kind of truth. I know no truth.

Part 2

INTERVIEWER: What is the role of the mask or disguise in your recent works?

DONOSO: But, don't you think that you, as a professor, should know that rather than I? No, I am putting you on. I really do feel that I know something about what the role of the mask is, or the sequences of masks and disguises that a person, a novel, a language, a space can take on. Let me think back for a moment. I won't start at the beginning because that would be much too long. I'd say up to 1970, I wrote novels which were 100 percent Chilean. I had no doubts about the Chilean idiom, I had no doubts about Chilean settings, the Chilean space, I had no doubts about my Chilean identity. There was no choosing anything, there was no trying to be anything but Chilean. But then I had lived something like seven years out of Chile, and Chile was sort of receding into the background. It was easier to grasp, to get hold of the Chilean language, while living in the States than while living in Spain. What Spain did was to superimpose a Spanish mask on my Chilean mask, a mask of the Spanish language onto my mask of Chilean Spanish. And I had to choose. Up to *The Obscene Bird of Night* everything was Chilean. Then I lived in Spain and began to say *bañador* (swimsuit) instead of *traje de baño* (swimming trunks), and my daughter laughed at me when I said *quiero salir* (I want to go out) instead of *quiero dar un paseo* (I want to go for a walk). I had to make a choice between the Spanish mask and the Chilean mask continually. And that became more and more difficult as time went by. Then somehow I felt that I gave my all with Chile in *The Obscene Bird of Night.* Above all, I think that a novel is an exercise in lucidity, which means using everything, not only one's capacity to think, but also lucidity inasmuch as it means imagination, emotion, knowledge and everything else. So that particular exercise was very extreme. After that I retreated and didn't want to be bothered with language anymore. I wanted to write in just blank language or any language that came to me easily. So I wrote *A Personal History of the Boom,* which is just expository, and there was no real challenge insofar as the language went. Then I wrote *Sacred Families: Three Novellas.* In that particular work, I didn't go back to a Chilean setting but rather to a Spanish one. I was unable, however, to assume the Spanish language. I could only recreate the setting as a mask but not the language as a mask. Then I began writing *A House in the Country,* which was another extreme exercise in lucidity, reaching out with my all. And something strange happened. I could use neither the language of Chile nor the language of Spain, neither the Chilean setting (because of obvious political problems posed in that novel) nor the Spanish one. So I chose both a masked language and a masked literary space. I wrote a novel which takes place neither in Chile nor in Spain but in a land of pure fantasy. I chose a language which is yet another mask, that of a very stiff nineteenth-century language that is not in use in either Chile or Spain today. *La misteriosa desaparición de la marquesita de Loria* is a mask without a soul, and it's really an exercise in furbelows, I suppose. *El jardín de al lado* is a very realistic novel; it is a psychological study and there are few masks, though I imagine scholars will find them.

INTERVIEWER: Can you expand on *El jardín de al lado?*

DONOSO: When I moved to Madrid I decided I wanted to

write a novel about the world of political exiles, the world of people who live outside their own countries, who can't or won't go back, and then I wrote *El jardín de al lado*. That's the background for it. It is the terrible rootlessness, the whole idea of the political exiles in Europe not being able to grasp their own identities anymore. Time had gone by and had begun to erode them and there was a senselessness about it all which was very tragic. *El jardín de al lado* takes place in Madrid, a little bit in Chile as far as memory is concerned, a little bit in Siches, which is a small watering place near Barcelona, and also in Tangier. It is bitter, very bitter, I would say, very angry.

INTERVIEWER: You lived away from Chile for about eighteen years. Why did you return to your native land? Was it to reconquer your own language?

DONOSO: I wouldn't give an awful lot of very intelligent excuses. The truth is I was beginning to feel old, and I had been away for so many years. The Chilean situation is not what one would desire in any way, but the time had come to complete the cycle. I left Chile because I was unable to write there, and then I left Spain when I began to feel that the language there was constricting my writing. In a way I am glad I went back to Chile; in a way I am not. I didn't expect things to be exactly as they are.

INTERVIEWER: Is there any similarity between what you are writing now and the novels you wrote previously?

DONOSO: What I am writing now is a different matter, but we can talk about it later. In the meantime, I have done something rather unorthodox by my standards. I have written a book of poetry called *Poemas de un novelista,* and a very small Chilean publishing house printed it. I very much have the feeling that when I write a novel I set out to do something very concrete; it has a size, a shape, a plan, I feel the tone of it singing in me as I start out doing it. I may not have every detail clear in my mind, but things begin to happen, seeds begin to sprout.

INTERVIEWER: How did you feel when you were writing those poems?

DONOSO: I did not write them just like that. I have always written a little bit of poetry, very little. But during my time in Calaceite, where I lived for four years while I was writing *A House in the Country,* I had the feeling that I was writing it very consciously as a metaphor. But in the meantime I had a private life, a life of my own, and somehow this private life got into poetry, became poetry, some of it very weak probably. It's not supposed to be great poetry. I was rather disappointed when my editor in Chile said, "This is going to be a great publishing event, but it may not be a great literary event." During that period I wrote a diary, "Diario de un invierno en Calaceite" (Diary of a Winter at Calaceite), which is one of the chapters of the book of poetry.

INTERVIEWER: How would you compare writing poetry with writing prose?

DONOSO: Somehow the poetry happened to me. Novels don't happen to me. They are. One lives inside them, it's an atmosphere, a space one creates where things are possible, where one feels them, where one lives within other rules than those of the outside world. They are my own rules, which I create for myself and for my characters. In poetry I don't create any rules; I know very little about metrics, for instance. But there is a feeling of breadth, of space, there's a terrific commitment in writing poetry. One is responsible for absolutely every single line one writes, every semicolon one puts in or leaves out. This was one phase. Then I wrote another batch of poems when I was in Siches, and these were mostly concerned with portraits, I'm very interested in portraits of every kind. When I was a young man at Princeton, for instance, I wrote a paper about the difference between the portraits of the High Renaissance and the portraits of the mannerist painters. In this batch I have a portrait of *Madame Rivière* by Ingres; a portrait of my mother, taken in 1922 by a Chilean photographer called Soré; and one of my father—a doctor and professor of medicine—who looks like a tiny spot in the amphitheater where young men and women listened to him. There is another poem to the Roman portraits in the Capitolino Museum in Rome, a portrait of Seneca, and all those wonderful marble busts. And then there is yet another batch of poems which I wrote later in Madrid, which are freer. I never really intended to publish them at all, it was just a private thing. I put them away in a drawer, and when I just didn't feel like writing prose I took them out, and corrected an adjective, changed a line, added a stanza and so on, until I finally went to Chile. I wanted very much to have another book of mine published in Chile because I hadn't published anything there for twenty-five years. Ganymedes, a young poet and publisher, came to me and asked, "Do you have anything I could publish?" and I replied, "No. There are these poems, but they're no good." He said, "Let me look at them," and after he glanced at them he concluded, "They're not so bad." So there we go.

INTERVIEWER: According to what you've mentioned, you've written mostly in Spain. Have you done any writing in Chile since your return?

DONOSO: Yes, I've been writing articles once a month for the news agency EFE. And I've started on a new volume of short stories. I hadn't written short stories for thirty years. The first story is called "Una recepción en casa de Madame Verdurin" (A Reception at the House of Madame Verdurin), which takes place in Chile, but everybody uses Proustian names. In a dingy bar in Chile somebody is called Guermantes and somebody is Charlus and so on. It's all in the Proustian language, but takes place more or less in the bas-fonds of Santiago, with a group of young Proustian writers looking at things with Proustian eyes. Then there's another short story. When Rimbaud lived in Abyssinia, he knew a Dutch merchant who worked for King Menelik and I make this Dutch merchant into a more intimate friend of Rimbaud than what we know is true. I discover a batch of this man's letters addressed to a friend of his in Europe, telling him about the wonderful poetry that Rimbaud is now writing, poetry which has completely disappeared. There is absolutely no trace that he ever wrote any poetry at all while he was there, but I pretended that he did.

INTERVIEWER: Which genre do you prefer?

DONOSO: The novel. There is absolutely no question about it. Walking into a novel is like walking into my house. I feel at ease there, it's enough that I have a handle, a first sentence, a jumping board. I feel I have more range in a novel. I survey a vast part of my experience with a novel, while in poetry I have to keep the focus straight all the time so I can't change my tone and I love to change tones. I like to play tricks, to be ambiguous and to be contradictory, and in poetry that's rather difficult, at least for me.

INTERVIEWER: I believe this is your way of achieving freedom, by playing these games, because you destroy in order to create.

DONOSO: A writer never thinks of himself as creating, somehow. He thinks of himself as something completely different. It's like taking a chunk of wet clay. You have the stick that holds the clay up, and then you more or less plan a form, you adjust the clay here and there, formless yet, and then you begin dabbing here, and cutting there, and thus you achieve a balance. It's always a play of balances and surfaces which have meaning, continuity, unity. But you play, you can add or take away as much clay as you want. All writing includes playing games, although they are minor aspects of the craft.

INTERVIEWER: Is your obsession with space also present in your poetry?

DONOSO: I would say not, probably not. That's an interesting point to make.

INTERVIEWER: What about the role of dogs?

DONOSO: I don't think I have a dog in my poetry. I must put one in at once. But I think my poetry is rather flat, prosy, and intellectual.

INTERVIEWER: And yet your novels are poetic.

DONOSO: That's right, that's just what I was trying to explain. For instance, this may be an interesting parallel: in *A House in the Country*—which I think is as poetic, allegorical and metaphorical as my writing gets—one theme is the ritual killing of pigs. In the village where I lived in Spain, every family during winter killed a pig, just before Christmas, in the street. They brought out an old table they kept for just that purpose. It was a family ritual, very savage and very brutal. And that pig killing, which I wrote about allegorically and poetically in my novel, is very realistically described in my poetry.

INTERVIEWER: You hate generalizations, you hate anything that limits you.

DONOSO: I hate simplification. Somehow, when a novelist tries to speak about his work, he simplifies. And the gist of a novel, the gist of a work of art is the non-simplification, the big canvas where everything happens. In every work of art there is an actuality, there is a permanently restated truth which is itself, which is the absolute, which is the flesh of the art piece. To simplify on my part would be redundant.

INTERVIEWER: Last year you said, "I think a novelist is a man who does not want to teach, or say something, but wants to know something."

DONOSO: A novelist is more than an answerer of questions. He is an asker of questions, I think, about the world at large, and about himself. One writes a novel not so much because one wants to say something but because one wants to know what one is, what one wants to say, what the world is like.

INTERVIEWER: So when you write a novel, you actually discover yourself, or a part of yourself.

DONOSO: Yes, absolutely.

INTERVIEWER: If I ask this question I know you are going to jump at me, but I'll ask anyway: who is José Donoso?

DONOSO: I was somebody last year, I am somebody this year, I will probably be somebody else next year. The truth of me is in my novels.

INTERVIEWER: So this is the mutation that appears in your characters?

DONOSO: Of course.

INTERVIEWER: In which environment do you write best?

DONOSO: If I knew, I would be there, but I don't know. I'm a rather sane person, and I tend to follow my impulses. And when my impulse was to leave Chile, I think I was right. And I've changed homes and places very often, and I think I've been right all the way, up to now. I may be wrong now, having gone back to Chile. I don't know, I hope not.

INTERVIEWER: Is writing a lonely profession?

DONOSO: Yes, it is, very much so. There is the great ego trip of suddenly taking a bus and watching the person who is sitting next to you, and that person is reading your novel, and then you are not alone. But you can't say, "Look here, I'm the author."

INTERVIEWER: Would you recommend writing as a profession to other people?

DONOSO: By all means. It's one of the great professions.

INTERVIEWER: Are there any young writers in Chile now?

DONOSO: I've just arrived, I don't quite know. Then again "young" is such a relative age. For a person as old as I am, young could be forty or forty-five, and when you say young I suppose you mean twenty-five. I now have two literary workshops in Santiago, and I've come into contact with a few young writers. I haven't had time to be able to assess what they're doing or where they're going. I have a feeling that one of the characteristics of contemporary Chile is that it's become terribly remote; there are very few books, very few movies. So these young writers can't compare themselves with what is happening in the rest of the world. I have terrible feelings of loneliness and isolation in Chile at this point, and something must be done about it.

INTERVIEWER: But isn't this the same type of isolation you were speaking about just before the Boom, when no one knew what was being done?

DONOSO: Sure, but that was a different kind. Then it was a small world, and for us a benign world, where friends traveled with books in their pockets and so on. Now there is a terrible world of competition, of throat-slashing.

INTERVIEWER: Do you still feel the same closeness with such writers as Carlos Fuentes and Guillermo Cabrera Infante, all the writers who belonged to the Boom?

DONOSO: The Boom was a very circumstantial thing. It was an event that happened during a very short period, in a given place and at a given time. It was in Barcelona at the end of the 1960s and the beginning of the 1970s. Most of us lived there and people traveled there and it was a center of operations. But then people began to leave Barcelona and there was also a political question that became diversified and people didn't have the same ideas. As in everything, look at what happened to Spanish lyrical poetry; did it last even ten or fifteen years? The Generation of 1927 belongs to a time, a period. What about Mexican mural painting? It's very much of a period and of a time. It's a form which suddenly becomes, for a period, the language of a culture.

INTERVIEWER: If a young writer were to ask for advice, what would be the first thing you'd tell him?

DONOSO: To write, write, write, all the time.

Part 3

INTERVIEWER: Pepe, I last saw you in 1981 at Winthrop College, when I interviewed you at a symposium held in your honor. Do you explain your reversion to realism by the fact that you have gone back to your roots, to Chile?

DONOSO: I don't think these literary turning backs have any explanation, I think they just happen. One can't reduce a literary phenomenon to its causes, it's not a question of cause and effect. But I imagine it could be said, or you could think of it that way.

I wonder how much Chile is my roots; everything is so up in the air that I can't be sure about that.

INTERVIEWER: Now that you have returned to Chile after more than eighteen years of absence, you no longer need to recreate it through nostalgia and memory. Do you feel your style has changed as a result?

DONOSO: Those are things that I said because I had to define them and I had to give them a shape. It could be easier said that way, yes.

INTERVIEWER: When speaking of the Boom, you said, "We all were writing the same novel." Do you feel that all your novels are versions of the same novel?

DONOSO: My daughter says they are. She says they are a terrible bore because to her all my novels are alike, which I hope they are not. But yes, one is a limited person, and one's experience is limited.

INTERVIEWER: Why did you say that when you finish writing a book, you actually feel physically sick? Is it the drama of parting with the text? Is it that you are very possessive of your own works? I notice that you do say "my book," and that you insist on the *my*.

DONOSO: Yes, but I don't know, it is something that happens. When I am writing a book, I live on an island, which is myself and the book. I am completely self-sufficient. And then when I finish the book and the island is taken from me, I do not have anything to feed on anymore.

INTERVIEWER: Do you go through the same suffering during the process of writing?

DONOSO: No, the process of writing has been lately, I would say in my last four books, one of extreme happiness. I have written very happily, with extreme joy in the act of writing. I am most myself when I write.

INTERVIEWER: So if I ask you why you write, is it to experience that happiness?

DONOSO: I can't answer that. I don't know why I write. I

write because I want to know why I write.

INTERVIEWER: Do you think that in the last three novels you have felt this happiness because you were in Chile?

DONOSO: No, because I am an older man, more mature, I know my craft, I know what to expect.

INTERVIEWER: When do you know it is time for you to pick up your pen and start writing?

DONOSO: It happens. I need to when I need breathing space. I need a breath of fresh air, which is literature. When I create, the fresh air is not real life, the fresh air is the air of the imagination.

INTERVIEWER: When do you know it is going to be a poem, or a short story, or a novel, or for that matter, a play?

DONOSO: It is never anything but a novel or a short story. It has only been very accidentally a play, or very accidentally an essay, or very accidentally poems. I am a prose writer.

INTERVIEWER: Yet you have moments which are very poetic in your prose.

DONOSO: Oh sure, there can't be any literature without poetry.

INTERVIEWER: *Sueños de mala muerte* (Nasty Nightmares), a novel within the novel *Cuatro para Delfina,* is to me one of your best works because of its tremendous realism. How did you come to write this story?

DONOSO: I wish I knew. I don't know how I get to write stories. They are bits of experience, things I have seen. Just as you like to put together a collage, I construct from fragments of memories, things I have seen or felt. I summon feelings and, at one point, they seem to acquire cohesion and identity. They stick together and become one entity. And then from that seed, the line of the short story or the novel is born.

INTERVIEWER: "Los habitantes de una ruina inconclusa" (Dwellers of an Unfinished Ruin) is a breathtaking work. What made you write such a story?

DONOSO: What makes someone write anything? Deep feeling, vision.

INTERVIEWER: In the sense that Chile is all around?

DONOSO: I assume, I don't know, it probably is. But I don't write because Chile is all around, I write because there is a very small field of experience, which means probably all of Chile, but what I am writing is not about all of Chile, what I am writing about is what is very closely around.

INTERVIEWER: And who is that man who comes to the old couple in "Los habitantes"? What does he represent?

DONOSO: That's for you to say.

INTERVIEWER: What does the scarf represent in that particular story? It seems as if the woman by putting it on becomes all the poor people of Chile and can feel their pain.

DONOSO: That's for you to say. Of course, critics always see more in books than writers. But I don't write things that represent anything. I write about things that are. Literature doesn't represent anything; literature *is*.

INTERVIEWER: In "Los habitantes de una ruina inconclusa," the structure is rebuilt after many years with the original stones, which are out of date. All of a sudden, it is as if there were some trace of hope.

DONOSO: There is some repetition, not hope.

INTERVIEWER: Do you consider *Cuatro para Delfina* realistic and symbolic?

DONOSO: That's for you to say.

INTERVIEWER: Who is Delfina Guzmán, the dedicatee?

DONOSO: Delfina Guzmán is one of my best friends and she is a very great Chilean actress. It was with her that I had the idea of turning *Sueños de mala muerte* into a play. I adapted it for the theater with the help of the people on stage. It was a team effort.

INTERVIEWER: Why do your characters feel the need to hide behind layers of masks in your works?

DONOSO: Perhaps because I do.

INTERVIEWER: And can you explain that?

DONOSO: No.

INTERVIEWER: So you are wearing a mask?

DONOSO: Of course. I'm a private person and my characters are private people.

INTERVIEWER: Do you think that you will ever change your perspective on space, and that from a stifling, dark enclosure where your characters gasp for air, you will ever set them free in a wide-open, sunny area?

DONOSO: I can't see that sunny, open area very much, frankly. I assume it exists.

INTERVIEWER: If, for instance, everything around you were to breathe freedom and peace, would you then have to change the perspective?

DONOSO: I hope to be intelligent enough to do it.

INTERVIEWER: What is Chile to you, now that you have recovered its reality?

DONOSO: I don't know whether I have recovered its reality. I live there, I am one of the people who is undergoing the process of its history. Before, I was outside its history, I was living my own history.

INTERVIEWER: And now you are part of it.

DONOSO: I am part of its destiny, yes.

INTERVIEWER: And you find it easier as a writer and as a man to be there?

DONOSO: No, it is not easier, it is very hard.

INTERVIEWER: But still you chose to be there?

DONOSO: Yes, it is the same situation as with your family. Sometimes, your family is not something which you particularly like. But it is your family. I wish my father had been different, I wish my brothers had been different, I wish lots of things like that. But I want them, I feel closer to them than to anybody else. Many times, I don't have anything to say to them, many times I think they are idiots, but still I feel very, very close to them.

INTERVIEWER: What is reality to you?

DONOSO: Oh, don't ask that terrible question. I wish I knew, there are so many things I don't know. It's not a question I can answer.

INTERVIEWER: Your works are rather pessimistic.

DONOSO: I am a very pessimistic person. I am an atheist. Can an atheist be anything but pessimistic?

INTERVIEWER: So you are not at all religious.

DONOSO: No, absolutely not. I am not religious. If I had said agnostic, it would mean that there would be a possibility of being religious. I don't believe in the life hereafter, I don't believe in God, I don't believe in survival of consciousness. I have nothing to do with God, nothing whatsoever. I don't even like Him.

INTERVIEWER: But if you don't like Him, it means that you accept his existence.

DONOSO: No, that sounds very Jesuitical. I don't like the way He is represented. He is just something that doesn't exist in my life.

INTERVIEWER: So, how do you look for something higher than ourselves?

DONOSO: I write history, the love of what I have around me. What else? But certainly not more than that.

INTERVIEWER: Is writing for you a reflection of yourself?

DONOSO: No, writing is my road to knowledge, it is my way of getting to know my thoughts, and my knowledge of the world.

INTERVIEWER: What is language for you?

DONOSO: Language is the instrument with which I work, it is the material I use. It is being able to do things with it, being its master, rather than letting it be yours.

INTERVIEWER: Seven years ago, you said that your characters enjoyed some degree of free will. Would you agree with this statement today?

DONOSO: No, they don't have free will, I invent them.

INTERVIEWER: You invent them and you lead them?

DONOSO: Sure, it's ridiculous for them to believe anything on their own.

INTERVIEWER: So your characters never become people for you?

DONOSO: I would be a very bad writer if they did. I wouldn't be a writer, I'd be something else, like a doctor or a scientist.

INTERVIEWER: Are you fond of your characters?

DONOSO: As characters, yes. I am fond of writing, I love writing.

INTERVIEWER: Why do you usually lead them to their deaths? Why do you destroy them?

DONOSO: I've told you, because I think that life is destruction. I don't believe in the hereafter or the survival of personal consciousness. What I have done mostly is create novels which end in destruction.

INTERVIEWER: Are you very fond of your novels?

DONOSO: I'm fond of my novels, I'm fond of my writing, I'm fond of words, I'm fond of creating, of molding a scene, of seeing how the characters react when they get together—this I'm very fond of.

INTERVIEWER: Would you say that Cervantes has influenced you?

DONOSO: No, not at all, not at all.

INTERVIEWER: Do you believe in fairylands?

DONOSO: I believe that the imagination can do things. Fairies are created by man, as was God. God was invented by man.

Rosario Ferré

Rosario Ferré

Rosario Ferré was born in Ponce, Puerto Rico, in 1942, into a politically oriented family. Luis Ferré, her father, is the former governor of Puerto Rico.

She graduated from Manhattanville College, New York, as an English and French major, later obtaining her Master's degree in Spanish and Latin American literature from the University of Puerto Rico. She received her doctoral degree from the University of Maryland in 1987, with a thesis on Julio Cortázar that will soon be published as *Cortázar el romántico en su observatorio* (Cortázar the Romantic in His Observatory).

Rosario Ferré began writing in 1970, when her short story "La muñeca menor," translated as "The Youngest Doll" in 1980, was published in the first issue of *Zona de carga y descarga.* That literary magazine, which she founded and on which she served as coeditor, lasted from 1970 to 1972. It brought recognition to many of the then young and unknown Puerto Rican writers. From 1980 to 1982 she published a column on literary criticism called "Carga y Descarga" in *El Mundo,* one of Puerto Rico's main newspapers. Her column was similar in content to her former magazine and therefore bore the same title.

Her first book, *Papeles de Pandora* (1976), contains fourteen short stories and six poems, in which she has revived the ancient Greek myth of Pandora. An English translation (omitting the poems) will be published in 1990 as *The Youngest Doll and Other Stories.* She likes to play with myths and write about them from a feminist point of view. This first work brought her international fame and recognition. Many critics have called her a writer in the tradition of the "Boom," but she does not particularly care to be included in that category. She prefers to be thought of as a chronicler of her island.

She is the author of works of poetry, short stories (both for children and for adults), and a novel composed of intertwined stories and essays. As she explained in the following interview, she enjoys short-story writing the most: "I do feel I have a special affinity for short stories." Among her works are the following: *El medio pollito* (The Half-Chick), 1976; *Sitio a Eros* (Eros Besieged), 1980, a book of feminist essays; *Los cuentos de Juan Bobo* (The Stories of Juan Bobo), 1981; *Fábulas de la garza desangrada* (Fables of the Bled Heron), 1982; *El acomodador Felisberto Hernández y la literatura fantástica* (The Usher Felisberto Hernández and Fantastic Literature), 1986; *Maldito amor,* 1986, translated by the author as *Sweet Diamond Dust,* 1989; and *El árbol y sus sombras* (The Tree and Its Shadows), 1989, literary essays. She is working on a book of poems and short stories, *Las dos Venecias* (Venice and Its Image). Rosario Ferré's work has also appeared in many anthologies of women writers and in the most important literary magazines of both her island and Latin America.

In 1986, she became Writer-in-Residence at the Center for Inter-American Relations, New York, and she was also appointed Referee for Caribbean Projects at the Wilson Center, Washington, D.C. She has lectured extensively across the United States as a literary critic and has taught at Berkeley and Rutgers.

INTERVIEWER: Rosario, in your works you give life to your characters and then you take it away. Why do almost all your stories end dramatically with a violent death?

FERRÉ: That feeling of violence is an expression of the current situation in Puerto Rico, which has one of the highest crime rates anywhere in the world. This is due to the deep conflicts created by the clash between the two cultures of modern consumerism, with its materialistic approach to life, and a much older way of living and of being. This is probably why there are many deaths in my work, as you pointed out.

INTERVIEWER: In your last book, *Sweet Diamond Dust,* you say of death, "Like her twin sister love, she is the mother of all, irrespective of caste or class." Does death appeal to you as an element of justice, or does it frighten you?

FERRÉ: Of course I'm afraid of it, like everyone else. But I do believe that beyond this feeling, there is a concept of social justice to death: in a culture where there are great economic and social disparities, death is the great equalizer, it is as real for the rich as for the poor.

INTERVIEWER: Adriana, the character in "Isolda," exclaims, "English, English, always English everywhere!" Your work is like an ode to the Spanish language. Do you see English as a threat to your identity?

FERRÉ: No, absolutely not. Adriana is a character speaking from a particular perspective: she was educated in military bases and had no real contact with her own culture. That is not I speaking, because I don't have that problem. I feel that English is a very important and essential language nowadays. I have even translated my novel into English myself.

INTERVIEWER: But you have never written a novel in English.

FERRÉ: No, I cannot write in English, it's an impossible task. I can translate, but I cannot write directly in it.

INTERVIEWER: Do you think Latin Americans speak a borrowed language because they express themselves with the tongue of the motherland rather than the indigenous languages?

FERRÉ: I'd rather like to think that the motherland, Spain, lent us her language, but we appropriated it. It is no longer Castilian Spanish that we speak, no longer Spanish from Spain. The indigenous languages, furthermore, coexist with the national language.

INTERVIEWER: What does language mean for you?

FERRÉ: The word is extremely important. As a writer, it is

my means for self-definition, the tool to express my idio-
syncracies, my personality. It is also like a painter's brush
which I use to depict the reality of my people.

INTERVIEWER: You write stories for children and adults, as
well as poetry. In which genre do you feel most comfortable?

FERRÉ: Curiously, with the tale, be it a story for children or
for adults. Even my book of poems, *Fábulas en la garza
desangrada,* is really a series of tales in prose. The book *Sitio
a Eros* is a series of essays also narrated in the form of short
stories, and *Sweet Diamond Dust* is really four short novels
strung together into one. So I do feel I have a special affinity for
short stories.

INTERVIEWER: Have you ever considered writing a long
novel?

FERRÉ: I wrote *Sweet Diamond Dust* in the way that I did
because I think I have a talent for short stories. When I attempt
to write a long text, I usually get bored by the time I reach the
hundredth page, and this is why I like to vary my prose and skip
from subject to subject. I encapsulate one story and then move
to another, in such a way that I juggle many balls, each with its
own integrity.

INTERVIEWER: Do you think female writers express themselves differently from their male counterparts, and that all
persons are limited by their worlds, or do you consider it possible
to break through these barriers?

FERRÉ: That's a very important question. I think men can
never really know the female universe, and vice versa. The point
of perspective is always very different. But this does not mean
that one cannot break through the barriers and try to understand
the other a little better, attempt to fill the other's shoes. This
type of understanding is essential.

INTERVIEWER: Almost all of your characters are women.
Do you consider yourself a feminist writer?

FERRÉ: I consider myself a feminist in certain respects. But
I am not a feminist writer exclusively, because I am concerned

with a wide array of subjects, and I think my work reflects that diversity. I also believe that literature has no gender because both sexes use the word as their basic building block. I strongly disagree, therefore, with the theory that there is a type of female writing separate and distinct from male writing.

INTERVIEWER: Do you control your characters or do they control you, and do they feel a struggle for domination among themselves?

FERRÉ: I don't think they struggle to dominate, although many of them are at odds with each other, due to a series of conflicts engendered by social and economic reasons.

INTERVIEWER: But they don't fight with you, or you with them?

FERRÉ: I wouldn't know how to answer that question. Characters have a life of their own—it is not that they fight against me, but rather that they do what they want. On many occasions I have had an outline for a story which I was eventually unable to bring to fruition because the characters changed. I very much believe in the influence of magic and the subconscious on the literary process.

INTERVIEWER: You have just taken the words out of my mouth. Why does magic play such an important role in your work?

FERRÉ: I think that magic has to do with the subconscious, much as the ancient sorcerers believed. The identification of man with his material surroundings and his active participation in that world are detailed in the books of Carlos Castañeda, for example, as well as, on a different level, with the books of sociologists like Lévy-Bruhl and Ernest Cassirer, or Lévi-Strauss. The magical identification has a lot to do with literature, this alternate way of viewing the world.

INTERVIEWER: What about masks?

FERRÉ: They are also relevant to the creative process, of course. In the same way that objects have a life of their own, people are really an amalgam of several persons, not just one.

My characters are almost always a combination of the characteristics of three or four people that I bring together in a sort of collage.

INTERVIEWER: What led you to writing?

FERRÉ: I have always wanted to understand certain things about myself and my life, but in order to know what I think, I have to write it down first. Right now, for instance, as I am speaking to you, I am frightened because I don't know what I am going to say next since I didn't get to see your questions. In my specific case, there is a very direct relationship between the written word and the evolution of my thinking.

INTERVIEWER: So if I asked you why you write, you would say . . .

FERRÉ: Because I want to know how I think.

INTERVIEWER: Do you play with words, the blank page and the reader?

FERRÉ: The blank page is generally the place where I establish a dialogue with myself. Of course, it is important to be aware that writing is directed to a third person, but the empty page and I have a very special relationship. Unlike other writers, I do not have this great fear of the "blank page." In fact, it is completely the opposite for me: I am very frightened of the page which, even before I start writing, overflows with words. I have to control them in order to avoid their invasion of the page.

INTERVIEWER: Do you think about a particular reader or the reader in general when you write?

FERRÉ: Generally speaking, I write for my friends, for people who are close to me.

INTERVIEWER: Do you like to polish your work?

FERRÉ: Yes, I usually revise a short story at least eighteen times.

INTERVIEWER: So how do you know when you reach your goal?

FERRÉ: It is a clear intuition, but it is at the same time mysterious. It is as though the finished work had existed previously but had somehow disappeared from the earth, and all I did was rediscover it. Marguerite Yourcenar compared that flash of discovery to the mysterious moment when the baker knows it is time to stop kneading the dough.

INTERVIEWER: What is your reaction when you have finished a work?

FERRÉ: I almost always like it immediately after finishing it. I continue to think that I wrote something quite good for a period of maybe six months or a year. But after a year and a half I begin to see some flaws in it, after two years it begins to look pretty bad, after three years it is horrendous, and by the fourth year I want to burn the book.

INTERVIEWER: How do you come up with the titles for your books?

FERRÉ: *Maldito amor* occurred to me through music, because it is a Puerto Rican dance, by Juan Morel Campos, which is closely identified with a specific social class: the Puerto Rican sugarcane plantation owners from the end of the nineteenth century and the beginning of the twentieth. But I have come up with titles through different paths. *Las fábulas de la garza desangrada* comes from the Chinese novel *The Dream of the Red Chamber* which I had been reading at the time. I chose *Papeles de Pandora* because of the phonetic sound of the double "P"; it seemed like a title that would be easy to remember. So the reasons vary; I have no set guidelines.

INTERVIEWER: What is the relationship that exists between the Puerto Rican reality that surrounds you and the reality that you create through your use of fantasy, which is very important in your works?

FERRÉ: Puerto Rico, like all the countries of the Caribbean, is a nation where fantastic reality, the world of magic, is ever present. There are various sects of white magic, such as *Santería*. It is a reality that is very palpable in our environment, and this is why there are no great differences between fantasy and reality. This is also true in the work of writers like García

Márquez, whom I consider a Caribbean writer because Aracataca, which is the setting for the imaginary Macondo, is in the Caribbean. All Caribbean writers have this in common.

INTERVIEWER: Your work is like García Márquez's in that respect because you give that feeling of reality to fantasy and vice versa.

FERRÉ: Yes, there is an interchange of reality and fantasy that is quite apparent. *The Kingdom of This World* and *Explosion in a Cathedral,* both by Alejo Carpentier, also use this technique, which he named *realismo mágico* (magic realism).

INTERVIEWER: Do you know where fantasy begins and reality ends?

FERRÉ: No, I feel that the two are inseparable.

INTERVIEWER: Do you think of yourself as an heir to the Spanish American Boom precisely because of this constant interplay between fantasy and reality?

FERRÉ: I think the Boom was a very limited phenomenon in itself which initiated a period of great literary activity in Spanish America. But women were never a part of the Boom. I don't think I am part of it and I don't think I would want to be. I'd like to be thought of as an independent writer.

INTERVIEWER: You are that, in every way. Since you wrote your doctoral thesis on Cortázar, do you see some resemblance between his work and yours?

FERRÉ: In the sense of the interplay between the magic of the universe and palpable reality, I think there is a similarity. Cortázar's short stories imbue reality with magic, and magic is an expression of the subconscious. Objects acquire a life of their own, as in "Casa tomada" (The Haunted House). In this story, two brothers live in a house, and all of a sudden they begin hearing voices. The house begins to speak at night, and the brothers have to close off every room because the voices or spirits are taking over. Finally, the brothers are driven from their home by the voices, which can be interpreted simultaneously as supernatural beings and as the voices of *Peronismo,* the political movement in power at the time in Argentina. This short story could have been written in the Caribbean, and that is why I like Cortázar so much.

INTERVIEWER: A moment ago you said that after a period of three years you no longer care for your work. Nevertheless, do you have a favorite book from among those you have written?

FERRÉ: My novel *Sweet Diamond Dust,* which I suppose I will not like three years from now.

INTERVIEWER: You speak as if you were not the "mother" of your books.

FERRÉ: Books grow and become something else, so in a way I still love them but I respect the fact that they are something different.

INTERVIEWER: If you had five children then, you would only like the last one!

FERRÉ: No, they grow up and become separate from me, so I have to respect their little defects, their idiosyncrasies and their independence. I continue to like them, but I don't want to dominate them, or say that they are mine exclusively. But mothers, in their heart of hearts, would always like their children to be perfect.

INTERVIEWER: What attracts you more: the past with all its glories or the progress of modern life?

FERRÉ: I wouldn't know how to answer that. The past holds little appeal for me, and the future is not any more appealing. I'll stick with the present.

INTERVIEWER: I have the feeling that your work is like a personal biography of your people. Would I be wrong in calling you a chronicler of your beloved Puerto Rico?

FERRÉ: No, you would not. That is a very nice title.

INTERVIEWER: Why do you turn to mythology in your book *Fábulas de la garza desangrada?*

FERRÉ: I tried to reinterpret various female myths, like Desdemona's story, for instance, who was strangled by Othello. I changed the endings of many stories in classical and traditional

European mythology which dealt with women. For example, Ariadne, who was abandoned by Theseus in the original myth, abandons him in my story. She is the one who had the string leading to the exit of the labyrinth, and instead of giving it to Theseus, who then abandons her, I turned the tables and made Ariadne the one able to extricate herself from it. It's not that I want to victimize men, but I think that women have been the victims throughout the centuries, a fact which has been incorporated into mythology and which I thought it was high time to change.

INTERVIEWER: Could you explain the following verse from that book: "I am a tree with bleeding branches. Through my tumultuous veins the rebels who sleep in my shade come to life every night"?

FERRÉ: That's a line of Antigone, who is the very paradigm of the rebellious woman. She stood up to her uncle Creon and caused his political downfall through her act of defiance, her determination to bury her brother Polyneices. The latter had been condemned not to be buried outside the walls of Thebes, which was a kind of edict against love and, to a certain extent, against liberty in the political sense. But she was determined to bury her brother, so Creon had her killed, which proved to be his downfall. The idea is that through her veins love, which is compared to the blossoms of the *flamboyán* (flame tree), is reborn every day. She is the symbol of rebellion against tyranny through the power of love.

INTERVIEWER: The last poem in that book is identical to the first one, but it is written backwards, and one has to use a mirror to read it. Why?

FERRÉ: Precisely because reading in front of a mirror is one of the themes of the book.

INTERVIEWER: So writing is a reflection of life.

FERRÉ: It is a parable of life, and also its paradox, that one needs to read it forward and backward, from left to right, and right to left.

INTERVIEWER: What is poetry for you?

FERRÉ: Unlike Gustavo Bécquer, I do not think that "Poetry is you"! Do you remember that poem which he wrote to his beloved? I do not think along those lines. I could never say to my love, "Poetry is you." I wouldn't have the presumption to glorify a man as "my muse" simply because I wrote a poem and he inspired it. In a way, what Bécquer did in that poem is what most male authors have done through the centuries. He was asserting his creative power and relegating woman to the passive role of "the muse"! That's very convenient but I'm not sure it's very fair. Writing poetry is a profession like any other, which can be done by men or women.

INTERVIEWER: So you don't believe in inspiration?

FERRÉ: Yes, I do believe in inspiration, but more so in dedication.

INTERVIEWER: Do you see some literary development in your work in the ten years separating the publications of *Papeles de Pandora* and *Sweet Diamond Dust?*

FERRÉ: There is a very great difference between both books. I think I have greater control, objectivity, and distance in the second one.

INTERVIEWER: Are you working on a new book?

FERRÉ: Right now I am working on a book of poems and short stories that will be called *Las dos Venecias.*

INTERVIEWER: Why do you say you like to translate but would be unable to write something original in English?

FERRÉ: Because it is a very different process. Translating is interpreting, whereas writing an original text has a lot to do with forces that are oftentimes beyond our control. One has to have a very intimate relationship with the language, have spoken it since birth, to make it the handmaid of imagination. Otherwise it is impossible.

INTERVIEWER: Since we are nearing the five-hundredth anniversary of the discovery of America, I wonder if you would like to comment on it?

FERRÉ: There is a very good book on a related subject,

Eduardo Galiano's *Genesis,* a three-volume work. He recounts a series of anecdotes which are really the roots of the Spanish American experience. It is a very poetic work because he has gathered the most moving moments of the chronicles. It is only now that we are beginning to understand many things about the conquest of America, and this book is a part of that process of reevaluation. I certainly don't think that the discovery and colonization of America by Spain is anything that should be glorified. The first Indians who came into contact with the Spaniards were the *Taínos,* the native Puerto Rican Indians, who were a very peaceful people. The relationship which developed at first was very interesting because the Indians had no idea what the Spaniards would eventually do, and they trusted them and befriended them. The Indian leader Agüeybana even offered his daughter in marriage to Juan Ponce de León. But then they realized that what the Spaniards were doing was taking them as slaves, and this is when they began to rebel, without any success. When one thinks of what happened, it is truly an extermination of a people, comparable only to what happened with the Jews in World War II.

Carlos Fuentes

Carlos Fuentes

Mexican novelist Carlos Fuentes is also known for his short stories, essays and plays. He is the winner of the 1967 Biblioteca Breve Prize of Spain, the 1977 Rómulo Gallegos Prize of Venezuela, the 1979 Alfonso Reyes International Prize, and the 1987 Cervantes Prize, the Spanish award considered to be equivalent to the Nobel Prize in the Hispanic world.

A central figure of the "Boom," he has been the most influential in bringing international recognition to Latin American fiction, both through his own works and through his comments on the works of others. Some of his reflections on the Boom are included in his book *La nueva novela hispanoamericana* (The New Latin American Novel), 1969.

Born in 1928, the son of a career diplomat, he received both a Mexican and an international upbringing. He spent his formative years in the United States, Latin America and Europe. As a result, he acquired a global perspective and a need to explain his country to others and to immerse himself in it.

Fuentes also entered the diplomatic world. From 1974 to 1977, he served as Mexican Ambassador to France. Since then, he has found teaching to be more compatible with writing and has become a popular figure on American campuses. He has been Distinguished Visiting Professor at some of the most important universities in the United States, and has also taught at the Colegio National in Mexico and at St. Catherine's College, Cambridge.

Fuentes is a very articulate and persuasive writer and a well-known figure on American television. I recall that after we had finished taping our three interviews at CBS studios, the whole crew applauded and told him that, should he decide to run for president, they would vote for him.

Carlos Fuentes is the author of countless books, translated into many languages. Among his major works are: *La región más transparente,* 1958 (*Where the Air Is Clear,* 1960); *La muerte de Artemio*

Cruz, 1962 (*The Death of Artemio Cruz,* 1964); *Aura,* 1962 (*Aura,* 1965); *Cambio de piel,* 1967 (*A Change of Skin,* 1968); *Terra Nostra,* 1975 (English translation, 1976); *Una familia lejana,* 1980 (*Distant Relations,* 1982); *Agua quemada,* 1981 (English translation published first, *Burnt Water,* 1980); *Orquídeas a la luz de la luna,* 1982 (*Orchids in the Moonlight,* a play which premiered at Harvard University in 1982); *La cabeza de la hidra,* 1978 (*The Hydra Head,* 1978); *Gringo viejo,* 1985 (*The Old Gringo,* 1985). *Cristóbal nonato,* 1987 (*Christopher Unborn,* 1989), his latest and most controversial novel, is a harsh analysis of the five hundred years that have elapsed since Columbus discovered America. The story is told by Cristóbal Palomares, the first child to be born on October 12, 1992, as he views the world from his mother's womb.

INTERVIEWER: As the son of a Mexican diplomat and a diplomat yourself, you have lived in many countries. You went to school in Washington, Santiago de Chile and Geneva. Since then you have lived abroad, yet your novels are essentially Mexican. Has living outside your country given you a greater awareness of what Mexico is?

FUENTES: Most certainly, I think I have a perspective on Mexico that I would not have had without these exiles, which were all dictated either by family necessity, because of my father's profession, or because of my own life and the demands placed upon me. I grew up in Washington, D.C., in the 1930s. My father was a counselor at the Mexican Embassy and he was very, very keen on having me understand that I was a Mexican, and he taught me the history and geography of Mexico. I thought it was a country he had invented in order to entertain me, in order to feed my imagination. The country came alive for me one day, one precise day, on March 18, 1938, when President Lázaro Cárdenas nationalized the oil holdings that had been in the hands of foreign companies. Until that day I had been a very well-liked boy at my public school in Washington. I acted in plays, I was part of the baseball team—a rather bad baseball player, but liked nevertheless. I was popular, but suddenly I ceased to be popular because there were all these headlines in the American press screaming against the action taken by Mexico, the action taken by the "communist" government of Mexico, the "Red President" Cárdenas, talking about invasions, sanctions against Mexico. I became very unpopular and so found out that I was part of that imaginary country. It was a peculiar experience which deeply influenced my work.

INTERVIEWER: Do you think you can actually write about Mexico and be outside of it?

FUENTES: Well, I go to Mexico constantly. I have my Mexican bath every five or six months. I have never lost touch with the country and I have lived there many long periods of my life.

INTERVIEWER: Doesn't it create a problem of language? How can one keep up with the everyday spoken language?

FUENTES: No, on the contrary, it is very difficult for me to write when I am in Mexico because I am surrounded by the language and it becomes the means of everyday expression for me. It is what language is for most of us—a collective means of communication, a debased coin of communication. When I sit down to write, I have to transform this debased currency into gold again. And I find that, if I am using it and reading it in newspapers or elsewhere, I don't have the same critical distance toward it and the same challenge to make copper into gold that I have when I am outside and can see the country and its language from a distance.

INTERVIEWER: You have said that you speak a borrowed language inherited since the time of the conquest. For that reason, you feel that the contemporary Spanish American novelist must make the Spanish language his own by playing with it, pulling it apart and then giving it a rebirth. Could you speak a little about your own ways of torturing the language in order to revitalize it?

FUENTES: That is the challenge we all had in Spanish America since the time of the conquest—especially if you belong to a country, such as mine, which has very deep Indian roots and the sense of an historical past, that there was something before the Europeans came. I am a *mestizo.* I am of both Spanish and Indian ancestry. I don't feel, as the Mexican Indian, the Mexican peasant, does, that the Spanish language is an imposed language. The Indian in Mexico speaks the language with suspicion, with a special intonation, with a singsong quality which he retains from the old Indian languages, and also with a sense of vengeance and resentment. Still, the Spanish language is a great language, which permits us to be, in some minimal way, a cultural unity.

INTERVIEWER: I notice that you even go so far as writing backwards. For instance, in *Terra Nostra,* you say, "Oigas, oigas. Sagio, sagio" (Listen, listen. Netsil, netsil.). You do that to revitalize the language.

FUENTES: Yes, I want to go back to the powerful roots of the language, because Spanish Americans have a sense of dispossession toward it. Suddenly this circular attitude toward the Spanish language has become that of Spain also. I think that owing to the failure, the defeat, the subversion of democracy in Spain in the 1930s and the forty-year-long Franco dictatorship, the Spaniards also felt they had been deprived of their language by the slogans and the rhetoric of the dictatorship. And so, they became Spanish Americans in a way. They had to face the same challenge. It is therefore no coincidence that there was this flowering, this rebirth of the Spanish American novel and, at the same time, of the Spanish novel.

INTERVIEWER: André Breton has said that Mexico is a land of surrealism. Do you agree with this?

FUENTES: Yes. He really called it the land of black humor. The commentators made it the elected country of surrealism. Mexico is above all a baroque country; it is also a surrealist country because of the whole problem of desire and reality. After all, what surrealism purports to be is an instantaneous bridge between your hopes and realities. It is a way of bridging that enormous gulf between what we desire and what we can have. The avenues offered by Breton are dreams, free associations, sex, etc. Well, Mexico is a country where there is always such a gap between your dreams, your desires and reality, that perforce it had to become a surrealist country in the sense Breton was talking about.

INTERVIEWER: In many of your novels you deal with modern society in Mexico but within it you show the weight of the past, the conquest by Cortés, the impact of the Mexican revolution, the ever-present concept of sacrifice of the Aztecs superimposed on modern Mexico. Why are most of your novels built on this double structure of the old gods and the new?

FUENTES: I am very wary of the whole enlightenment tradition in Latin America, which bids us to forget the past. It cuts us off from the past, which was deemed barbaric by the philosophers of the eighteenth century. In order to forget our Indian and Spanish background, we decided to become men of the European Enlightenment. I think you cannot have a living present with a dead past. The past is present and if we don't realize it we run into deep historical, political and social troubles. Take, for example, the agrarian reform in Mexico after the revolution. It was decided it would have a sort of general application without due consideration to the particularities of the regions, the traditions of the people and even of the tribes. Therefore, it failed in great measure, owing to the fact that it became a cultural abstraction which did not take the past into consideration.

INTERVIEWER: You once said, "Cárdenas made me realize that a blow of the present could make us recover the past for the future; that our dignity, our identity, depended in great measure on recovering this past." Am I right in saying that this is exactly what you are achieving through your novels—the recovery of the past in order to situate Mexico in the modern world?

FUENTES: We had no past for three hundred years. The Spanish colony created a cultural world in which it was very difficult to express oneself. People were silenced. Take, for example, the case of the famous Dominican Friar Bartolomé de Las Casas. His great book in defense of the Indians, where he outlined the brutal treatment inflicted on them by the system of the conquest, was written in the 1530s and was not published until the 1890s or 1900s. It is incredible! Similarly, El Inca, Garcilaso de la Vega, exalted in his works both the Indian past of the colony and the Spanish Viceroy in Peru, but his works were not published. Sor Juana Inés de la Cruz was practically silenced, stifled. So we had a silent past and I think we have to recapture that past and make it alive in some way, give it relevance to our lives today. You cannot have three hundred years of silence behind you.

INTERVIEWER: One of your characters in *A Change of Skin* uses the metaphor of the pyramid to explain present-day Mexico: "Everything in Mexico forms a pyramid: politics, economics, love, culture." And then he goes on to say, "We are all disguising one face when we look down, another when we look up." Is this your own personal feeling or is it your character speaking?

FUENTES: It is my character speaking but it is also my personal feeling. It is in evidence in Mexico. Octavio Paz has written a lot about the pyramid also. The Belgian writer 't Serstevens wrote a book called *Mexique à trois étages* (Mexico on Three Levels), which also shows that the country is built like a pyramid. If you travel from the coast, in Acapulco on the Pacific and Veracruz on the Gulf, you ascend through terraces to a summit, to a sacred summit, which is the City of Mexico, from which no one dares emigrate if he wants to hold power in my country. When the Spanish conquerors found that beautiful place, they named it Cuernavaca, the place of eternal, spring-like climate. They said to Cortés, "Let's go there, it's so much nicer than this harsh plateau of Mexico City." And, of course, Cortés said, "No, we have to build the Spanish cathedral on top of the Indian temple and we have to build the palace of the Viceroy of New Spain on top of the palace of Montezuma, on top of the ruins." And Mexico City has always had this sacred quality of being at the summit of the pyramid where, by the way, only one person can stand.

INTERVIEWER: You have also said, "Mexico is a country with a tiger sleeping on its belly and we are all afraid that at any moment it may awake." What did you mean by this?

FUENTES: I meant many things. Mexico is different from other countries in Spanish America in the sense that the revolution of independence from Spain in 1810 was originally a popular revolution, the revolution of the peasantry of Mexico, of the Indians of Mexico, who really rose against colonial power with sticks and stones. It was not a coup d'état by the Spanish Creole officers against the monarchy in Spain. The Mexican revolution of independence ended up by being that, but originally it was not. Since then, Mexico has been a country where no aristocracy, no elite has been able to establish itself for a long time. There's always a convulsion eventually, which breaks up the formation of the elite, or upper crust, and opens up a new dimension, a new perspective to the country. I think that Mexico has been the Latin American country of Indian extraction with the greatest social porosity, thanks to what I just mentioned and to the fact that oligarchies don't stay there too long. Eventually, the tiger roars and devours them and the country opens up its greater porosity. Mexico is a very great meritocracy; it is not an oligarchy or anything of the sort, as many countries contend to be.

INTERVIEWER: In *Where the Air Is Clear,* one of your characters says something that reminds me of Don Quixote and which I like very much: "Don't deny the one title I want to leave

my children . . . [that of] a good Mexican." Do you identify
with this character?

FUENTES: Yes, in a way, but I also wish a good Mexican to
be a good Latin American and a good citizen of the world, and
not a strictly chauvinistic, flag-waving Mexican.

INTERVIEWER: In the same novel you also say, "One does
not explain Mexico, one believes in Mexico with fury, with
passion." What is Mexico for you?

FUENTES: Mexico is that—it's fury, it's passion, you have to
believe in it and you have to carry it in your guts. It presents so
many alternatives and so many contradictions between love
and hate, between hope and the loss of hope, that you really
have to come to it through a sort of act of faith. Tertullian, the
father of the Church, used to propose a test for the good Christian by saying, "It is true because it is unbelievable," which is
the only way to show faith in God. God is totally unbelievable.
The act of faith consists of believing in the unbelievable. Mexico
resembles this. You have to come to it through a certain act of
faith. That's why I write novels, by the way, because I believe
in the unbelievable!

INTERVIEWER: I would like to talk about the importance of
the mirror in practically all of your novels. The characters
either have a double or are looking at themselves through a
mirror. Why does this concept of the doppelgänger, the double
or twin, prevail in your work?

FUENTES: It's more than the concept of the double or the
twin, because I am very concerned with the problem of identity,
which comes from the fact that I am a Latin American and a
Mexican and a man of the Third World, and identity is at the
center of our preoccupations. We don't have a set identity we
can easily climb into the way a Frenchman or Englishman or
even a citizen of the United States can—although a U.S. citizen
has a less definite identity than a European, I would say. We
are trying to fashion our identity to discover it and this sometimes leads to deep schizophrenia and to impulses of doubling

and seeing ourselves in a world of mirrors. It also comes, I think, from a double tradition, the tradition of the Indian cosmology and civilization, and the great tradition of Spanish literature with its idea of asking if life is a dream, or if the dream is life, which is so strong in Calderón de la Barca, for example. The old Aztec god Quetzalcoatl always thought of himself as a god until the moment a demon came with a mirror and showed him he had a face. And he said, "Then I am not a god! I have a face like men," and went out and left Mexico and promised he would return. The exile of Quetzalcoatl is a myth which mirrors the history of Mexico because the god discovered that he was a human being, that he had a face. And most of our history springs from this discovery, from this troubling discovery.

INTERVIEWER: The idea of disguise, mask, distortion or change of identity seems very important to you. Is it your way of achieving a new dimension?

FUENTES: A very good Mexican writer, Salvador Elisondo, has said that you can never disguise yourself as something worse than your own self. Probably, what I am trying to find is that real self, which is after all nothing but another disguise. But I am also indicating the dimension of the masquerade, which is very important in the baroque culture of Spain and Latin America—the fact that you have to participate in great masquerades and put on masks and disguise yourself in order to exist. This is done even at the level of poor peasants in Mexico. All the earnings of the small agricultural community, of the family farm, are spent on masks and firecrackers for All Saints' Day, and then on that day alone, out of 365 days, you exist because you are masked!

INTERVIEWER: In your works you use minute details and even give weight and shape to objects, so that you finally trick the reader into believing that what you are describing is reality, when in fact it is not. Could you speak about your use of what can be referred to as unreal realism?

FUENTES: Well, that is the old Platonic trick of taking the

reader into the cavern and making believe the shadows are real. That is part of the trick of the novel. When I was writing *Terra Nostra,* I showed the first chapters to my old friend Luis Buñuel, the Spanish film director, who said, "It is very nice, but you can't keep a long novel going if it is on a purely fantastical level. You have to give it some weight." And I saw that he was absolutely right and that the way to make the fantasy work was to give a great presence to objects, furniture, eating utensils, dogs, birds, cages and beds and everything.

INTERVIEWER: When you write, do you have the reader in mind?

FUENTES: I have a few readers in mind, about ten or twenty of them.

INTERVIEWER: Do you think of the reader as an intruder or do you consider him another character?

FUENTES: The reader is present in the sense that I am not going to say everything I have to say. I am going to leave a door open, so that the reader can complete and collaborate with me in the creation of the novel.

INTERVIEWER: So, you actually give a very active role to the reader?

FUENTES: Yes, but I don't think of the reader in the same way that some best-selling authors think of the reader, namely, "This is what the reader will like. This will make him drowsy and happy and contented and this is my recipe for writing the best-seller." No, it is not that, of course.

INTERVIEWER: Could I then deduce from this that you enjoy playing hide and seek with your reader? You make him struggle as if he were one of your characters, without ever leading him by the hand, and you let him find his own way through the narrow labyrinth of the real and the unreal.

FUENTES: I hope so. That's the only way he can be a co-creator of the novel.

INTERVIEWER: How do you see yourself in relation to your characters?

FUENTES: I don't see myself as either the manipulator I am sometimes accused of being or as the man who fools himself by thinking the characters can be psychologically free. I am not interested in the security of psychology as practiced by the nineteenth-century novelists. Flaubert could say, "I am Madame Bovary," because he truly believed that Madame Bovary had a certain psychological weight in reality. I don't believe we live in a world where we can have that security any longer. The characters in the measure that they are characters are being destroyed. They are in fusion and confusion. They are becoming something else. There is an encounter, a mixture of the individual character, of the individual psychology and the culture and the civilization. To a degree, I would say that in a novel such as *Terra Nostra* the civilization takes over and becomes the protagonist of the novel. This disconcerts many people, that it should be a whole civilization which becomes a character and not an individual.

INTERVIEWER: What would you say is the relationship of the narrators to the other characters and, in turn, what is your own relationship to the narrators?

FUENTES: The narrator is, in a way, creating the other characters and situations, but they are creating the narrator as well. It is a battle between the points of view in the novel, the way you perceive the novel from within, the conflict of the novel with itself, with its own verbality, its structures, with its characters. They are in a duel, but it is not a duel in which the narrator always wins. I can come out deeply wounded from the battle with the narrator and with the characters—characters which, I insist, I do not like to see under a strictly psychological light as resembling a novel of the nineteenth century. I prefer to see them much more as bearers of civilizations, of a cultural situation, of a cultural nexus of some sort.

INTERVIEWER: Do you lead your characters or do they lead you?

FUENTES: Since they are not characters in the psychological

fashion, the problem becomes irrelevant. It is not a question of being led, it is a question of existing, of being. I hope they are as much as I am, and sometimes they are more than I am, sometimes less.

INTERVIEWER: Could you describe some of the techniques you use in writing? For instance, the way that you use recurring versions of the same episodes throughout the novel?

FUENTES: I am very convinced that in art and also in real life there are many things that are born at a given moment and don't really reappear in your life until many years later. And suddenly you realize they've formed a thread in your life of which you are totally unconscious and which really has been the vein of your life, as though there were a mine or a lode of silver or gold running under the surface. It is there, and something crops up, something disappears again. It is like many characters in Kafka who appear and disappear. They have been forgotten, and we say, "Where is he?" and "Was he ever here?" But this happens a lot, it happens in the poetic reality, that is in the inner reality of your life—consider memory, consider people you have loved, consider names, consider songs and places.

INTERVIEWER: How do you achieve structural unity?

FUENTES: I don't know that I achieve structural unity. In a sense, a novelist is an architect or an engineer who builds bridges. I always know very clearly how to build the bridge on this or that bank of the river. The problem is constructing the center, the middle, as it is for an engineer. I know where I begin and where I am going to end, more or less. Probably I create an invisible structure, a sort of cathedral made out of thin air, and then I give it verbality, which is what writing is about. Writers give verbal reality to this structure which exists only in their imagination.

INTERVIEWER: You are a master at building up climax. We as readers are left breathless at the end of your novels. Can you say something about the rhythm of your language?

FUENTES: I am much more interested in rhythm than in

practically any other thing when I am writing, much more so
than in style. I disregard style a great deal so that I can get into
the actual rhythm of the prose, which I think is going to carry
the reality of the novel, going to be its carnality, identical to its
verbality, identical to its rhythm. Whatever will be found in the
novel in the way of plot or paradox or poetical intuition or even
characterization has to be born out of the density, the rhythm
and the flow of the prose. So for me it is an all-important aspect.
It suggests the problem of letting go like a waterfall and control-
ling the waterfall, to get some energy out of it. It is something
that I am constantly struggling with when I am writing a novel,
especially since it is a long, protracted period of writing. It takes
a long time to get these engines moving and to get the energy
from the waterfall, without ever letting it become a little trickle.

INTERVIEWER: Could you explain how in your novels you
make all times—past, present and future—simultaneous?

FUENTES: Do I really do that? You make me very happy
because I try to achieve that. Whether I do so is a question open
to doubt.

INTERVIEWER: You definitely do that!

FUENTES: I am very happy. You have made my day! I think
every writer, and certainly every modern writer, is trying, consciously or unconsciously, to defeat the fatality of the successive
order of writing. It is not as instantaneous or simultaneous as
painting, architecture or sculpture. We are trying always to
defeat this in order to reach a simultaneous order of time. Why?
I think there is a profound cultural criticism in it. It is a rejection
of the linear time of the West, this linear progression of time
toward a happy future which is at the very core of the thinking of
the modern West. But it sacrifices the other times of the world,
including the circular time of the aboriginal peoples, the Aztecs,
the Africans, the Incas and many others. There is a rejection of
this implicit in the great works that have revolutionized the
literature of the twentieth century. Consider Proust, Joyce,
Virginia Woolf and Faulkner. So, we are in rebellion against

this purely linear succession of language. Is it possible to make language simultaneous? Within a book, it is possible to operate this revolution of time, which, in a way, is a cultural revolution.

INTERVIEWER: In *The Death of Artemio Cruz* you use the past, present and future to convey the three voices of Artemio Cruz: "I" for the present, "he" for the past, and "you" for the future. Why do you do that?

FUENTES: Simply because I want to get as many facets of the reality of Artemio Cruz and his world as I can. In my novels, I am very interested in presenting crossroads where personal and historical destinies meet. For me, that is the clash that counts: the individual and history and what happens to them when they come together. In order to give all the facets of that clash, I must understand that Artemio Cruz—and the history in which he lives, and which surrounds him, and which will outlive him—has a past, a present and a future. So does any man who has an "I," a "you" and a "he" wrestling inside him, or speaking to him from the outside. It's very important that Artemio Cruz very easily could have been a villain, a nasty character, a man who betrayed the revolution. I don't want him to be that. I want to show all his qualities, as well as his tremendous defects. He is the man who is representative of modern Mexico, of the process of modern Mexico, which, as in the bullring, involves a contrast of lights and shadows, neither totally black nor totally white. I believe very much in the gray areas, and I thought this literary technique I employed in *Artemio Cruz,* three tenses and three persons, would give a much richer and a more diversified picture of the man and his country than a purely linear succession.

INTERVIEWER: How do you arrive at a title? Do you come upon it in the course of writing or do you think about it before you start writing?

FUENTES: Only afterward, at the end.

INTERVIEWER: What does the title *A Change of Skin* mean to you?

FUENTES: It means many things. Here are characters who are interchanging their skins, sexually of course, because it is a sort of *ménage à quatre*—they are all having sexual relations with one another. There is the whole problem of their identities being changed. And then there is the symbolic aspect of four characters who are traveling from Mexico City to Veracruz in a broken Volkswagen and finally are trapped forever in the pyramid of Cholula. The Great God of the Flayed Skin, the God of Spring who flayed himself in order to change his skin every year, was the God of Chipetote, a very important divinity in the Aztec pantheon, a symbol of both sacrifice and renewal, which is the theme of the novel.

INTERVIEWER: In *A Change of Skin* the narrator, who also describes himself as a taxi driver and is therefore another character, says, "I am a rebel without a cause" and "an angry young man still angry enough but no longer so young." Do you identify with him in any way?

FUENTES: At that moment I did. That was written in 1967. I was something of an *enfant terrible,* a terrible young man. But I decided not to be a terrible old man, so I've ceased to be a rebel without a cause in the sense that my character speaks of.

INTERVIEWER: Besides playing with changes of identities, you also play tricks with history, that is with historical figures as well as literary ones. Can you explain the reasons for taking liberties with history, for transforming it into a fiction and converting the fiction into reality?

FUENTES: In *Terra Nostra* there is a history of a dynasty, which is the Hapsburg dynasty in Spain. I take a great many liberties with it. Solemn critics in Spain and Latin America say: "Mr. Fuentes does not know history, he ignores the dates, he doesn't know that Charles V was the father of Philip II and the son of Philip the Fair. He just makes them go away so that Philip the Fair becomes the father of Philip II and Charles V disappears." They never ask themselves why Charles V disappears, why there is this crucial need in the novel to devour the father at the same time that you devour history. It is a sort of cannibalism toward history and toward the father, which eliminates both the sexual and the historical aspects of the novel. History is as it is imagined by us. True history is not a succession of dates on the calendar. True history is something which happens inside us. We live it, we imagine it, we preclude certain events, we admit others, we give full relevance to some things, we forget others, we block them because we don't want to remember our father or our mother, for instance. I am following very deep obsessions which are mine but which also reflect the obsessions of the culture.

INTERVIEWER: Can this world, which in *Terra Nostra* you call the Next World and which is neither real nor unreal, exist outside of poetic creation?

FUENTES: Of course not, it exists only in *Terra Nostra,* that is the whole point. If it existed around the corner, at the delicatessen, I wouldn't write about it. Fiction is a new creation, there is no reflection of the world. Fiction is something added to the world. At least that is the prideful pretense of the novelist.

INTERVIEWER: How would you define *Terra Nostra?* Is it a modern bible or chronicle?

FUENTES: A bible, of all things! Well, in the sense that the Bible is a very cruel book, full of genocide and desperation and crime, *Terra Nostra* would be biblical. But that's not what you mean, of course, so I would not say it was a bible, no.

INTERVIEWER: A chronicle?

FUENTES: I would not say it was a chronicle, because a chronicle purports to be faithful and this is a profoundly unfaithful book. No, it would be a heretics' chant, a *canto* by heretics, yes, that would be it.

INTERVIEWER: What made you write *Terra Nostra,* which takes in the entire spectrum of human experience?

FUENTES: Everything about me, everything in my life. You know, this is like the imaginary museum of the Hispanic world. It is all the things that make us tick, as descendants of Spain in the New World. All our obsessions about sex, honor, pride, history, freedom, art, family—everything is there.

INTERVIEWER: In *Terra Nostra,* you give us two apparently contradictory messages, that of the destruction of the world and that of a future prolific creation. Is this one more game you are playing with reality and the unreal? What is your message?

FUENTES: I don't have a message. Messages are sent by Western Union. I don't do that. But at the end there is a sort of apocalypse, which is not apocalyptic because it is a condition for a reunion. There is a man in bed with a woman who in the act of love become one, become the original hermaphrodite. I don't think Adam and Eve were separate in the beginning—I think there was a man-woman, woman-man capable of loving him-herself and of having a child through him-herself.

INTERVIEWER: Is *Terra Nostra* a pessimistic work?

FUENTES: I wouldn't think of pessimism and optimism because those are Pollyanna attitudes toward life. We are trying to avoid that.

INTERVIEWER: Do you see yourself in this novel as a prophet announcing doom or do you see yourself as a redeemer?

FUENTES: No, that is very pretentious. I am talking about my obsessions, I am trying to articulate them into a vision of the cultural ambience. There is the whole problem of dispersion and unity. The dispersion of the novel—political and cultural —comes from this taillight of Tiberius on the Isle of Capri, condemning his descendants to proliferation. He says: "I am the Caesar, and in order to be one I must be the last. And after me you can only have two; and after two, four; and after four, eight; and after eight, sixteen; and after sixteen, thirty-two, so that the world is divided and lost, and I am remembered as the only Caesar, the only Emperor." This is taken up by Philip II, who then denies the existence of the outside world and even the discovery of the New World of America, in order to be unique. But that is a perversion of the unique. What I offer is the fecundity of the unique in the recovery of the sexual self, the man and the woman who become one at the end of the novel.

INTERVIEWER: In *Terra Nostra,* various characters take on the role of the narrator. How would you describe this shifting of narrative perspective?

FUENTES: *Terra Nostra* implies taking the whole universe, which is all my past. My cultural past tries to become a present in this novel. It is the past I value, or fear, or possess, or wish to possess because I feel I have been dispossessed. It is a very personal novel in that sense, very pertinent, at times very idiosyncratic. I am trying to capture that cultural past, that richness of the civilization through a multitude of voices, a multitude of eyes that can help me do this. Sometimes it is a witch girl, Celestina, who does it, sometimes it is Cervantes who has come to life again and does me the favor of narrating the novel. Sometimes it is an obscure monk who is painting a medieval fresco in secrecy, in silence, so as not to be condemned as a heretic. They form a chorus, which is the narrative voice of the novel. I have always been a great admirer of Thomas Mann. And there is a beautiful novel by Mann called *The Holy Sinner.* It is a novel about a man who becomes a pope. Mann starts the novel by saying that he is the spirit of narration descending on a little beach, where he finds this man who is going to be the protagonist of the novel, and he follows him with great narrative freedom. Probably it is the spirit of narration that wants to be the narrator of *Terra Nostra,* although there are several narrators.

INTERVIEWER: In *Terra Nostra* you go beyond the idea of a single mirror to take us into a hall of mirrors when Brother Julian, the painter-priest, says, "I paint so that I may see, I see so that I may paint, I gaze at what I paint and what I paint, when painted, gazes at me and finally gazes at you who gaze at me when you gaze upon my painting." This is a breathtaking journey into reflections!

FUENTES: Leonardo da Vinci said that painting was a mental thing. And this is an illustration of a bit of that thought, because here you have a painting which appears in the novel and suddenly takes over as a Renaissance painting. It takes over from the medieval paintings which do not see or do not follow this immensely complicated process of mirroring the spectator who mirrors the painting, and so on. The Byzantine icon and the medieval painting purport to be every place at the same time with one figure which is that of God, the pan-creator. The Renaissance world introduces a variety, a baroque roundness of possibilities of looking at the object, or the painting. This is what this painting hopes to be. There is more than that. *Terra Nostra* is a novel driven by an obsession with the Don Juan character. And in the novel the Don Juan character is a man who would like to be his mother but who is condemned to be a reflection of women. He ends up in a prison of mirrors, in perpetual lovemaking with a nun, who gnaws his masculinity off, while condemning him to look at himself for all eternity in nothing but mirrors.

INTERVIEWER: Your works have been translated into many languages. Do you take an active part in the actual translating process of your books?

FUENTES: If I don't know the language, no. Since I don't know Serbo-Croatian, I wouldn't participate in that. But in English and French and Italian I do. I will cooperate with the translators as much as I can.

INTERVIEWER: Is there a particular language that best lends itself to your style?

FUENTES: Let me tell you briefly the story of the translation of *Terra Nostra* into French and into English. *Terra Nostra* is built on the premise of the recovery of the roots of the Spanish language, of the vast richness of the Spanish language in the Middle Ages and in the Renaissance, which we have forgotten. We have impoverished our language. For Margaret Peden, my excellent English-language translator, there was no problem because English has always been so rich that she could go to many medieval and Elizabethan sources and find the equivalents. With French, it was a different matter. Céline Zins, who is a magnificent translator and a great poet in her own right, said to me, "There is no equivalent for your language in French." So we decided that she had to do a very spectacular, acrobatic thing, which was to go to Rabelais's *Gargantua and Pantagruel,* books that used an incredibly rich, baroque, forceful language, and then follow that language before it became the strict classical language ordered by Boileau in the precepts of his *Art poétique.* In order to translate my novel, we had to capture language as it had been at the moment when France ceased to be a jungle and became the Garden of Versailles. Let me say that I think the translation into French is far better than the original Spanish; it is such a creation that I promote it in French much more than in Spanish.

INTERVIEWER: One of the characters in *Terra Nostra* says, "I write when I feel like it and I write when I don't." When do you write?

FUENTES: I have learned to write in my head. I used to be a chain-smoker and thought that I depended on that for writing. I decided to prove to myself that I didn't, so I had to go cold turkey and continue writing. But then I discovered that, in order to avoid the tension of facing the white page every morning, what I had to do was to take long walks thinking of what I was going to write and only write it in my head. I found that for twenty-five years I had been suffering in anguish because I did not know exactly what I was going to write before I sat down in front of the blank page. Now I take long walks, for instance in the woods in Princeton, near the houses where Thomas Mann and Albert Einstein lived. They inspire me and I write everything in my mind. I write five or six pages in my head, then I go to the typewriter and it's there and the anguish is gone away.

INTERVIEWER: Do you polish your works? Do you go over them?

FUENTES: Yes, I have a system of working. I start off by writing longhand in notebooks, and correcting the notebooks a second time. I always leave a white page in front—the little techniques of writing, the secrets of the kitchen—and then I type it, which means a third correction, and I type the correction and finally I get five or six drafts before I think it is all right.

INTERVIEWER: When did you first realize that you wanted to be a novelist?

FUENTES: I knew I was going to be a writer from the very first moment. When I was seven years old, I was writing magazines for myself with news stories and all sorts of things.

INTERVIEWER: Do you consider your novels to be a criticism of society, or a third and new dimension of the world, or an intellectual challenge?

FUENTES: The main thing is that my novels are very much linked to the social and historical reality of Mexico and of Latin America, and perhaps of the world. Quite simply, there is the question of the relation of the writer to society. I do not regard it in the Sartrean sense of the writer's *engagement,* the obligation of the writer to serve society, to make it better, to be a philanthropist toward society. On the contrary, I think that society has a responsibility toward the writer. The novels, the plays, the poems of great literature are all the products of society, they arise from historical reality, but they become autonomous in a way. They go beyond society, they outlive the historical circumstances which bred them. *Don Quixote* is more than a novel of the seventeenth century, and there is not a Guelf or a Ghibelline alive today but Dante Alighieri keeps marching on. The work has gone beyond the immediate historical and social imperatives.

INTERVIEWER: You have written quite a few movie scripts. Would you say that the cinema has influenced your work?

FUENTES: I have written movie scripts because in the 1960s García Márquez and I formed a syndicate of sorts in Mexico, a syndicate of two, to earn some money from the cinema in order to be able to write books. But our philosophy was to take the money and run. The cinema has been a great influence on me, and yet I write novels that are not cinematographical. *Aura,* the only one of my books made into a movie, was a disaster. The director and screenwriter never understood what it was about. My novels were not written to be seen as films, but I have been influenced by the works of Buñuel, Orson Welles and Erich von Stroheim. I've always felt a great link between their visual world and what I am trying to say, my obsessions. I have the work of these directors present in my imagination when I write.

INTERVIEWER: Who are the writers who have influenced you?

FUENTES: In the 1940s two young brilliant Mexican writers came to the fore, Juan Rulfo and Juan José Arriola. The lazy critics, who abound in every country, started looking for influences. Is he influenced by this, or that? And they asked Alfonso Reyes, the great Mexican polymath, "What are the principal influences on these two young writers?" and he replied, "Two thousand years of literature." We are influenced by two thousand years of literature. There is a book I read religiously every year, and I do say religiously because I read it during Holy Week and Easter. Every year, I spend a few days reading *Don Quixote.* This is probably the book that has influenced me the most. But I feel very close to Balzac and to Laurence Sterne in *Tristram Shandy.* Among modern, twentieth-century writers, Faulkner has probably influenced me and other Latin American writers the most.

INTERVIEWER: Do you see your own influence on other writers?

FUENTES: No, fortunately I don't. I have not had any descendants, in that sense.

INTERVIEWER: Even though you say your art is more verbal than visual, I see the definite imprint of Goya upon your work. Is that right?

FUENTES: Yes, in *Terra Nostra,* Goya, Bosch and other painters become actual participants. In that novel, there is a painting by Luca Signorelli which becomes a painting by Hieronymous Bosch, which becomes a painting by El Greco, which becomes a painting by Goya. Throughout the novel, it's the same painting undergoing a series of metamorphoses.

INTERVIEWER: Two vital components of your art are humor and lyricism. How do you make them compatible?

FUENTES: Octavio Paz once said that reading me was like being present at an Aztec sacrifice in Times Square. There is an element in modern humor which comes from that outrageous idea Lautréamont had in the *Songs of Maldoror,* saying that true poetry is the unexpected encounter of an umbrella and a sewing machine on an operating table in a hospital. There is this juxtaposition of elements which clash, which can produce at the same time fear and tenderness, very contradictory sentiments of humor and fear. I think that out of them is born a sort of lyricism, a lyricism of the absurd, of recognition, of shock, of encounter, of admission of guilts and fears—which is also in a way a psychiatric procedure through literature.

INTERVIEWER: Would I be right in saying that poetry has played an important part in the contemporary novel and has a special place in your work?

FUENTES: I think poetry is very important for any novelist, since the genre of the novel has broken down so much, and what was considered to be the genre, let's say in 1890, is no longer so. It has broken down because the novel has been invaded by the media, by movies and television, which have taken away so many things. It's the same with plots and situations. You don't have to describe flowers in the novel if you can see them on TV in color. What for? You come down to the fact that the novel has to find its common literary roots, its reality, its essence in the poetic facts of literature. The common ground of all litera-ture is poetry, so if you think of the great novels of the twentieth century—*Ulysses, Mrs. Dalloway, Remembrance of Things Past,* and *Absalom, Absalom!*—you come upon novels that have a profound poetical structure and linkage to the language of poetry. Of course, poetry is very important. I never go to bed without reading three or four poems.

INTERVIEWER: Since the 1960s the novel has taken over the role that used to belong to poetry as an expression of the Latin American continent. Can you account for this change of expression?

FUENTES: I think that the challenge of creating a language of our own, a language for our culture, our Hispanic American culture of the New World, was originally a challenge placed on the chronicle, the great epics of discovery: the diaries of Columbus, Amerigo Vespucci, the chronicle of the conquest of Mexico by Bernal Díaz del Castillo, the great epic chant of the conquest of Chile, *La Araucana* by Alonso de Ercilla. With the onset of independence throughout Latin America, it became a challenge the poets felt very strongly. Basically, our literature has been a literature of poets, especially since Rubén Darío and *Modernismo* (the modernist movement) at the end of the nineteenth century. I think poets developed the language, which then permitted novelists to continue this evolution. Without poets such as Pablo Neruda, César Vallejo, Gabriela Mistral, Vicente Huidobro, Octavio Paz, we would not have written anything. We would not have felt we had instruments with which to challenge the language of everyday life that we write about in our novels.

INTERVIEWER: Can you explain the so-called Boom, the literary phenomenon that produced a renaissance of the novel throughout Latin America in the 1960s?

FUENTES: What has been called the Boom is, I think, simply a new stage in our literary development. It is a stage in which this great tradition of ours comes to a further blossoming in the realm of the narrative. We must not forget that Spanish America has a very old literature, it has a great tradition I will just outline briefly. It starts in the Spanish language with the writings of Columbus and Amerigo Vespucci about the New World. But in the countries of Indian ancestry, such as Mexico and Central America, there was already a great deal of literature. So what we have is the full flowering of a tradition which doesn't culminate with the so-called Boom. It is not the writing of one generation; it includes writers as old as Borges, who died in his late eighties, or as young as Vargas Llosa, who is hardly in his fifties. So, it is not a generation but more a movement in which many strands of our tradition come together and transform the quality and the nature of narrative fiction in Latin America.

INTERVIEWER: José Donoso has spoken of your definite influence on the Boom, the literary stimulus of your first novels, your generosity in helping other writers. In fact, he has called you "one of the precipitating agents of the Boom." What is your reaction to this?

FUENTES: I don't know. I know that when I wrote my first novel, *Where the Air Is Clear,* I was simply responding to the reality of the Mexican experience, both social and literary: the postrevolutionary society, the creation of a Mexican bourgeoisie after the revolution, its contradictions, the whole process. Mexico City is a gigantic city, growing larger all the time. It is going to become the biggest city in the world, with twenty-five million people by the end of the century. This was not reflected in any way in our literature, so I wrote this novel out of a sense of urgency, to give expression to a reality which was surrounding me. I was well aware, as Tom Stoppard put it so well, that art does not change society, it is merely changed by society. I did not change my society but I was changed by it, and my first novel arose out of these circumstances. I did not know at the time that in Chile there was a man called Donoso who was doing the same thing, and in Cuba another man called Cabrera Infante, and in Paris an exiled Argentine called Cortázar. We suddenly came together in a sort of constellation.

INTERVIEWER: What has been the role of Spain in the promotion of the Boom?

FUENTES: I think the Spanish public and the Spanish writers were caught off-guard by a sudden rush, a sudden invasion of good Latin American writing. They should not have been, because at the end of the nineteenth century the great Nicaraguan poet

Rubén Darío revolutionized the poetry of Spain. In the twentieth century, Neruda fused with the great generation of García Lorca, Alberti, and Cernuda. During the dictatorship in Spain, and afterward, the Latin American novelists arrived and awakened their Spanish colleagues. The caravels of Columbus keep going back and forth across the Atlantic Ocean all the time. Sometimes they come from Spain to America, sometimes we send them back from America to Spain.

INTERVIEWER: Why do you believe that the work of Juan Goytisolo stands like a bridge between the contemporary Spanish and Latin American novels?

FUENTES: Of all the Spanish novelists, Goytisolo, who wrote *Count Julian, Juan the Landless* and *Marks of Identity,* is the one who has best understood that we are in the same boat or in the same caravel. Spaniards and Latin Americans suffer the same alienation, the same sense of dispossession toward the language. Spaniards have had to suffer a rhetoric similar to the one we have endured in our newspapers in Mexico, Argentina, Bolivia, Central America. We are being bombarded by the same influences. We are aware that language is one of the elements of power, that it is not gratuitous, that power employs language. Politicians, heads of state, and political parties abuse language, and the writer has to say in response to that misuse, "Yes, but there is another language, there is another possibility of saying things, of naming things and emotions that is not that of *you,* Mr. Politician, that of *you,* Mr. Candidate for Office, that of *you,* Mr. Union Leader."

INTERVIEWER: Do you think Goytisolo stands alone or are there other writers who have the same modern outlook on the novel?

FUENTES: I think that you can cut no one off from his tradition, that behind Goytisolo there is Francisco Ayala and novelists of the immediate postwar period in Spain, such as Sánchez Ferlosio, the author of *El jarama,* a great novel; Luis Martín-Santos, the author of *Time of Silence,* one of the most beautiful novels written in Spain; and the other Goytisolo brother, Luis, an excellent novelist too. No, he is not alone.

INTERVIEWER: What are some of the basic characteristics that the writers of the Boom have in common?

FUENTES: First of all, the critical attitude toward language —that language has to be criticized in order to be effective, in order to be creative, in order to really communicate. We all feel we are the heirs to a magnificent language, the language of Cervantes, Calderón, Góngora and Quevedo, which went dead on us. From the middle of the seventeenth century until approximately the end of the nineteenth century, there were no great books written in Spain. That is a long, long period. So we said, "No, we don't want this great language to go to sleep on us." It had become like Sleeping Beauty. We came upon her in the woods and said, "What are you doing sleeping? Get up!" We started smacking her in the face, shaking her. To a great extent this is what we have done with the Spanish language.

INTERVIEWER: Donoso mentions a spectacular party given at your home in Mexico in 1965 to celebrate the starting point of the Boom, and he also speaks of a party in Barcelona given at the home of Juan Goytisolo to mark the coming to an end of that glorious era. Is this another myth about the Boom? In what year would you say the Boom came to a close?

FUENTES: I think it has not come to an end. I think it began with Christopher Columbus, and will probably end October 12, 1992, when we will all be five centuries old.

INTERVIEWER: Who are the writers of your generation to whom you feel closest?

FUENTES: We are all very different. Fortunately, I have good friends. I am quite close to Mario Vargas Llosa, Gabriel García Márquez, Guillermo Cabrera Infante, and I was a friend of the late Julio Cortázar. Of course, I must also mention the great Cuban novelist Alejo Carpentier, to whom we owe so much.

INTERVIEWER: What influence did Borges have on the writers of the Boom?

FUENTES: Borges was a unique writer. You won't find a second Borges, there is no such thing. If people tried to imitate Borges, they would fall flat on their faces. He is inimitable. People have tried to imitate García Márquez. *One Hundred Years of Solitude* has had one hundred imitations, which have been one hundred flops. It is impossible. I find that Borges had a greater influence abroad. You can see his influence on American writers such as Donald Barthelme and John Hawkes. Borges did something to the Spanish language. He proved it was good for something more than making florid speeches. He took a horrible old tree and pounded it and made it a nice shrub, but you can't do that again. He has done it once and for all.

INTERVIEWER: In the last twenty years, the Latin American novel has crossed the boundaries of its continent to join the foreground of Western fiction. Why do you think the Latin American novel has achieved this international recognition?

FUENTES: I think it is a novel born of a sense of urgency. A French writer may feel that he has nothing new to say because everything has been said in the past, and forms are exhausted. If there are other things that have to be said, it is up to the newspapers or television or movies or sociology to say them. But because of all the omissions in our society, we Latin American writers have to say things that nobody else has said. I also think it is comparable only to the literature of Eastern Europe in terms of quality, quantity and urgency. In a sense, adversity breeds good writing.

INTERVIEWER: Do you believe that the experience of exile has played a role in the development of the novel?

FUENTES: Certainly. I think that the sense of perspective is very important for a writer. I say this very humbly because as a writer I am always in voluntary exile. There are other writers from Latin America who are not in voluntary exile. If they returned to their countries, they would not get past the airport, or they would land in jail, or be killed by terrorists. So, when we talk of exile, it is best to be humble.

INTERVIEWER: What is there about the Latin American novel that makes it so appealing to readers from other continents?

FUENTES: *Terra Nostra,* a novel which is not easy, has had its greatest success in France and Germany. When I was in Germany, I wondered why the principal newspaper, the *Frankfurter Allgemeiner Zeitung,* would publish it as a serial in fifteen chapters. I found that, for the first time in many years, the Europeans had doubts about their identity. Therefore, they recognized themselves in our works, which are basically quests for identity and creations of identity through language and imagination. Also, I think some of the novels have a genuinely universal appeal based on their poetic truth, which makes them readable anywhere. García Márquez's *One Hundred Years of Solitude* has been an equally great success in Italy, Israel, the Soviet Union and Japan. As a matter of fact, it is the only novel I know that has been read by my mother and my cook, and they both understand it perfectly well.

INTERVIEWER: The United States, and for that matter all other non-Hispanic countries, look at the Latin American novel as a single entity. Do you think of the novel as being Mexican, Cuban, Peruvian, or simply Latin American?

FUENTES: I accept all the differences, the richness of diversity, and thank God for it. Let's not sacrifice the vast differences which exist between Argentina and Mexico. We all write in the Spanish language, that is the great unity we have. We impoverish ourselves if we subdivide too much between Spanish, Mexican, Peruvian, Argentine and Cuban literatures.

INTERVIEWER: How did the drastic break with the traditional concept of realism manifest itself in contemporary Hispanic fiction?

FUENTES: I think it came about through the whole process of self-identification that we have been speaking about. The Mexican revolution produced a very powerful kind of novel, which is a realistic chronicle of the recognition of Mexico by

Mexicans, such as *The Underdogs* by Mariano Azuela, or *The Eagle and the Serpent* by Martín Luis Guzmán. But then you have a second wave, such as *Pedro Páramo* by Juan Rulfo and *The Edge of the Storm* by Agustín Yáñez, in which there is a deeper reality of imagination, almost of witchcraft, that which Alejo Carpentier called "magic realism." Reality is not exhausted in the realistic surface, but also includes all that you have not yet dreamt.

INTERVIEWER: It is as if Cervantes suddenly had awakened after centuries of sleep to conquer Latin America with his interplay of reality and fantasy.

FUENTES: Yes, but who woke him up? The Latin Americans, do not forget that.

INTERVIEWER: Why is this interplay of reality and fantasy such a vital part of the Latin American novel?

FUENTES: What is reality? I don't know if we are in New York City, somewhere between 6:30 and 7:00 in the morning doing a television program, or whether we are dreaming we are doing this program, or whether we are being dreamt by the wonderful gentleman in the control room. There is an Italian movie by the Taviani brothers which has a very effective sequence. Suddenly at the end, there is a moment of enormous power and fright which encapsulates the whole film retrospectively. The actress says, "Great God, wake me up, get me out of this dream." Dreams are a dimension of reality. We have hardly plumbed our subconscious, we have hardly plumbed the world of our dreams, which is at least eight hours of our reality every day. A writer tries to give some sort of expression to that.

INTERVIEWER: Is that why, perhaps, in so many of the novels written today, the invisible world of the dead is described with the same dynamics as the world of the living, or even made more vital than the world of the living?

FUENTES: Coleridge asked this question in a poem. To paraphrase, he said: "Imagine you're dreaming that you are in Paradise and that somebody puts a rose in your hand. But then you wake up and a rose is in your hand. What then?"

INTERVIEWER: In *Terra Nostra,* you give your characters more than one life so that they die several deaths, first as they go from the Old World to the New, and once again when they travel to create the Next World. Why is this so?

FUENTES: I believe that life and death are purely conventional matters. We are not sure that we die, we are not even sure we have been born, so I underline this in novels such as *Terra Nostra.* We come back to the problem of the lack of historical fidelity. Only in this way can I have one queen of Spain representing all the queens of Spain and crying, lamenting, moaning over the corpse of her son, who is all the kings of Spain. I am interested in the dynasty, in the concept of the sequence of time, of the cosmogony behind it.

INTERVIEWER: Juan Rulfo's *Pedro Páramo* is a perfect example of a novel in which the world of the dead takes on the vitality of the world of the living and creates a third dimension. What can you say about the work of this great Mexican novelist?

FUENTES: Juan Rulfo was the greatest Mexican novelist. He has written something no one can surpass. There is such a wedding there of fiction and truth, of life and death, of shadows and light, that you cannot separate one from the other. This is the great success of *Pedro Páramo.* It is a novel which, you finally realize, takes place among the dead, among people who are buried and are talking to each other from grave to grave. You realize this little by little, so while the novel takes place among the dead, only the dead could give life to this novel.

INTERVIEWER: Another master at erasing the boundaries between the dead and the living is, of course, García Márquez. *One Hundred Years of Solitude* and *Terra Nostra* tell us about the creation and the destruction of the world. If you related the two works to each other as family, would you see them as close or distant relatives?

FUENTES: We are very different writers. I wish I had many of the powers of García Márquez. He is a man who has a tremendous imagination of detail in action, which is wonderful and for which I envy him very, very much.

INTERVIEWER: *Terra Nostra,* for me, is a book that attracts as if it were a magnet. How can you explain its magic?

FUENTES: Well, there are many people who do not like it, you know, who feel it is a repulsive book, primarily because of its weight and its length. They say, "It is only good as a door stopper" or "You would need a sabbatical to read it," things like that. And there are many people who enjoy it and go into it. I am convinced that it is the sort of book that doesn't lose readers—it gains them little by little.

INTERVIEWER: Do you consider it a novel?

FUENTES: It is a metanovel, in a way. It is a novel of novels.

INTERVIEWER: In your opinion, what makes up a novel?

FUENTES: A novel is made up of the astonishment we feel when, like Don Quixote, we leave our houses and go on the road and see that the world does not resemble what we thought and what we read. What makes up a novel is this awareness that the world is vaster than we are.

INTERVIEWER: What do you think of the future of the Latin American novel? Do you think that it will be able to have the same dynamics, the same creativity as it did in the 1960s?

FUENTES: Yes, I think this has been amply proven. We have come out of the Boom and we are now going into what I would call the "Bio Boom." Something very extraordinary is happening in Latin American writing. For the first time, we are greatly concerned with autobiography, with the chronicle, with telling the truths about our lives, our societies, our times, as they really were and are. We don't have a great tradition of memoirs and biographies, contrary to the Anglo-Saxons or the French. We have been very sparse about this, mostly because it has been very dangerous to tell the truth about what actually happened in life and in politics. Then all of a sudden, there was a great novel by Vargas Llosa called *Aunt Julia and the Scriptwriter,* which is the novel of the life of Vargas Llosa as it is reflected in soap operas. It is his life in one chapter and a soap opera in the next. And then there are the writings of Cabrera Infante about his life in Cuba as a young man, and the cultural life of Cuba. He has incredible candor, he tells the truth about everything and everybody, which is absolutely unusual in Latin America. I think this will be a phenomenon of the near future. Donoso started it a bit with his *The Boom in Spanish American Literature: A Personal History.*

INTERVIEWER: Do you think it is possible to make new experiments with the novel, or has everything been tried?

FUENTES: I think you can now make all the experiments you want, because there is no avant-garde. The idea of progress on which the avant-garde was postulated has died, and therefore you can write any way you want, which is the most experimental way of writing. You can try to write like Dostoevsky or Cervantes. You won't succeed, of course, but that will be the experiment. Remember the short story by Borges, "Pierre Menard, Author of the *Quixote,*" in which Pierre Menard sits down and writes *Don Quixote* and shows it to his friends, who say, "But this is not another novel, it is *Don Quixote* typed by you," to which he replies, "Oh yes, it is the same novel, only with a different intention."

INTERVIEWER: Are you especially close to one particular novel or do you feel like a father to all of your novels?

FUENTES: When you're writing the novel, you're very close to it. Then you cease writing it. It's like a child. You cut off the umbilical cord and it goes off into the world. But I feel that I have written only *a* novel, like Balzac. All my novels are part of a mural with different colors, tensions and figures. So I won't say I have finished any of my books yet.

INTERVIEWER: How do you see yourself as a writer?

FUENTES: That is the one answer I don't have. After answering, I believe, ninety questions from you, now at the end I don't have an answer.

Isaac Goldemberg

Isaac Goldemberg

Isaac Goldemberg was born on November 15, 1945, in Chepén, a small town in the north of Peru, of a Jewish father and a Peruvian mother. As a child, he learned how to read by picking up words here and there in a missal, as well as from the subtitles of Hollywood movies.

In 1953, he moved to Lima to stay with his father, and there began his Jewish awareness and a constant search for identity: "I began to ask myself 'Who am I? What am I?' I had to stop being in order to become." In 1954, he attended the Jewish school León Pinelo where he learned Hebrew. In 1959, he went to the celebrated Peruvian Military School Leoncio Prado, where he was the only Jewish boy. That same year marked an important event in his life: his bar mitzvah.

Isaac Goldemberg is a well-known novelist and poet who began writing in 1958. His first book, *La vida a plazos de Don Jacobo Lerner,* came out in 1978, a year after the English translation, *The Fragmented Life of Don Jacobo Lerner.* The novel, part autobiography, is based on his Judeo-Christian experiences. His next work, *Hombre de paso / Just Passing Through,* 1981, is a long autobiographical poem presented in a bilingual edition. His second novel, *Tiempo al tiempo,* 1984 (*Play by Play,* 1985), is also representative of his search for identity and his attempt to reconcile his two cultures by joining the Cross and the Star of David. His most recent book is *La vida al contado* (Life Paid in Cash), a collection of poems to be published in Peru in 1989. He is working on a new novel, *En la puerta del horno* (At the Oven's Door).

Isaac Goldemberg has traveled widely in search of his roots. In 1962, he went to Israel to study agronomy and live in a kibbutz. At the end of 1963, he went to Barcelona to study medicine. Since 1964 he has been living in New York, where he taught Latin American literature at New York University until recently. He is now coordinator of the New York Latin American Book Fair and co-director of the Latin American Writers Institute at City College.

Isaac Goldemberg has created many writing workshops throughout the Hispanic communities of Greater New York. He was a writer-in-residence at the Center for Inter-American Relations and Ollantay Center for the Arts.

The following interviews were held in 1981 and 1987. In the interim, Goldemberg returned to his Peruvian origins, a radical change which is dramatically reflected in his remarks.

Part 1

INTERVIEWER: Isaac, you were born in Peru of a Spanish and Indian mother and a Jewish father. Your first novel, *The Fragmented Life of Don Jacobo Lerner,* is at the same time a great Peruvian novel and a great Jewish novel. In it, you tell the story of Jacobo, a Jewish immigrant who is incapable of adjusting to the small Jewish Peruvian community or to Peruvian society. How were you able to bring together these two contradictory worlds, and from them create a work of art?

GOLDEMBERG: I would say that the elements of the novel are autobiographical and, to some extent, biographical. The figure of Don Jacobo Lerner, the main character of the novel, is loosely modeled after my father. And the other important character of the novel, the child Efraím, is modeled after my own life. But the novel is really a work of fiction; I would not call it an autobiography. When you think of an autobiography, you know that it also contains elements of fiction. When you start reading it, one of the first questions that you ask yourself is "who is telling the story?" Immediately, you have to establish a difference between the person who is narrating the story, even if it is autobiographical, and the person whose name appears in the book as the author of that book.

INTERVIEWER: Why was this novel, although written in

Spanish, first published in English?

GOLDEMBERG: The reason is very simple. I didn't have any contacts in the Latin American publishing world—I had been living in New York for a long time. I didn't know anybody in my own country who would publish the book. And friends of mine, professors, read the book, and they thought that it should be published. They recommended it to several publishing houses, and one of them decided to publish it.

INTERVIEWER: The *New York Times* has said of it: "It is a nightmare world of frustrated hopes, of narrowness and claustrophobia, where no one can afford to be generous, and where people become insane and destructive." Isn't this pessimistic trend typical of many contemporary Latin American writers?

GOLDEMBERG: Yes, I would agree with that. If you think of works like *One Hundred Years of Solitude* by García Márquez or *Pedro Páramo* by Juan Rulfo, you discover that those novels usually portray chaos and destruction. In particular, the family line, so significant in Latin America, is destroyed.

INTERVIEWER: How was the novel received in Peru?

GOLDEMBERG: It was received well, by and large, by Peruvian critics in newspapers and magazines. But I was attacked by certain members of the Jewish community because they felt that some of the aspects of Jewish life that I portrayed in the book were anti-Semitic. I, of course, completely disagree with that.

INTERVIEWER: Your characters are torn between the new world, which represents assimilation, and the old world, which symbolizes cultural retention. Your novel shows almost no solace in the life of a provincial town of northern Peru, where you were actually born, nor in the Jewish community of Lima. Why are these two worlds so tragic?

GOLDEMBERG: I would say that life, as it is depicted in the book, is representative of both worlds, which are remarkably similar. In both communities, daily existence is ruled by almost the same present.

INTERVIEWER: But why is it so tragic? So pessimistic?

GOLDEMBERG: I don't know if it is pessimistic. I would like to say that it is more realistic than pessimistic, considering the atmosphere in which the child has been placed.

INTERVIEWER: Why do utter solitude and the search for one's identity play such an important part in your novel?

GOLDEMBERG: For personal reasons, and because I think that the theme of solitude and exile is an integral part of the Latin American condition. I believe that to be a Latin American, even in one's own country, is to be an exile. The writer himself lives in exile; his work is published in exile. When Adam and Eve were expelled from the Garden of Eden, it meant that they had to begin to make things. So work is a part of exile. And of course, I cannot forget I am Jewish.

INTERVIEWER: The picture of Efraím, Jacobo's illegitimate son, is a haunting one. The reader cannot forget how the child struggles to piece together an image of the absent Jewish father he does not know, and whom he confuses with Christ. In the last paragraph of the novel, young Efraím, while talking to a spider, says: "That's why I'm going to cut your little legs off, and I squeeze your head with my fingers, and I tear it off slowly, and I crunch your body, so that you can't feel anything when I chew you." What made you write this striking scene of total loneliness and despair?

GOLDEMBERG: The spider is building its web, and Efraím is watching this. The structure of the web is the thing that fascinates Efraím because it offers some sort of security that he doesn't have. Because of his lack of security, he becomes a destructive character, and he has to destroy the spider in order to identify with it. And I think the spider also symbolizes, in a way, the figure of his father.

INTERVIEWER: Like your compatriot Mario Vargas Llosa, you have developed the skills of fragmentation, which is reflected even in the title of the English version, *The Fragmented Life of Don Jacobo Lerner.* You present five different first-person narrators: Efraím, Samuel Edelman, Miriam Abramovich, Sara Lerner, Juan Paredes, and a third-person narrator. Is fragmentation for you a way of bringing out the spiritual and physical disintegration of your characters?

GOLDEMBERG: I guess in the last analysis it is. But I discovered this a posteriori; I did not set out to write the novel in this way. I think that the novel is akin to a living organism; it acquires a life of its own as it develops and becomes independent from the writer. When I started writing it, I did not plan to fragment the chapters or the sections in such a way.

INTERVIEWER: So, after a while, the characters were leading you?

GOLDEMBERG: Exactly. The structure of the novel began to take shape.

INTERVIEWER: How do you combine humor with suffering and do you consider your sense of humor a Jewish one?

GOLDEMBERG: I would say so, yes. I think that the sense of humor that appears in my novels, which many Peruvian critics have mentioned, is something alien to Peruvian literature. I would have to agree with that because it is not very prevalent in most of the novels written by Peruvians, although they have their own brand of humor.

INTERVIEWER: You left Peru at the age of sixteen. You lived for two years in Israel, in a kibbutz. In 1964, you moved to New York, which you now consider your home.

GOLDEMBERG: It is my home, but I think for most New Yorkers it is a kind of a temporary home. I don't think that anyone who lives in New York, especially if he is a foreigner, can make New York into a permanent home. I have lived for over twenty years in this city, and in that sense it is my home, but at the same time I feel that it is only temporary. I think that almost everyone here is just passing through. My real home is actually an ideal place that I have left behind. I would say that it is perhaps my hometown, where I was born.

INTERVIEWER: Your characters are transplanted, displaced,

and go through a constant inner and outer exile. Do you also live in a self-imposed exile?

GOLDEMBERG: Yes, it is self-imposed. I would like to go back to Peru, but I feel that I would be completely alienated in my own country. Perhaps the only way that I could go back to Peru and live happily there would be to go back to that small town just outside of Lima.

INTERVIEWER: Could you say something about your second novel, *Play by Play?*

GOLDEMBERG: It is a sequel to the first one. In my first novel, the child is left in the town and goes mad. And then I thought of the possibility, again following autobiographical lines, of taking the child out of that environment and bringing him to Lima, within the Jewish community, to see what would happen to him in that new atmosphere.

INTERVIEWER: But in your second novel the child has a different name.

GOLDEMBERG: Yes, he has a different name because he is a different character, based on a friend of mine. When I went back to Peru four years ago, I learned that a friend of mine with a history very similar to mine—he was also the offspring of a Catholic mother and a Jewish father—had emigrated to Israel, gone to a kibbutz and committed suicide there. This is more or less what I did, except that I didn't kill myself. So, that sort of destiny made me think about the possibilities of writing a novel based on his life and, at the same time, on my own.

INTERVIEWER: You have lived in New York for almost half of your life, and yet your novels are based on memories of your childhood and your youth in Peru. Why is your past such a vital part of your present?

GOLDEMBERG: Yes, I have the feeling that in at least three or four more novels I'm going to write about Peru and about the things that I have experienced. Perhaps it weighs so heavily on me because I feel I am in the very peculiar position of being capable of writing about the two realities I know best: the

Catholic and the Jewish. I feel privileged to have lived in both realities, and perhaps I am the only one right now who can deal with them.

INTERVIEWER: How much of your work is autobiographical?

GOLDEMBERG: A lot of it is, although I think that most works of fiction are.

INTERVIEWER: In your novels, you have created very skillfully an interplay of reality with fantasy. Can you explain the use you make of imagined chronicles and of *Alma Hebrea,* a fictitious Jewish magazine which you keep on quoting in *The Fragmented Life of Don Jacobo Lerner?*

GOLDEMBERG: When I started writing the novel, I realized that, in order for the reader to understand what was going on in the life of the character, I had to present a background of Peruvian and Jewish histories. And when I say history, I'm talking about the psychology of Peruvians, the psychology of Jews, their philosophy. But I didn't want to write a 500-page book. I realized that I wasn't ready for it. So I remembered that, when I was growing up in Peru, there was a small magazine that circulated in the Jewish community. I tried to recreate that magazine and it turned out to work well.

INTERVIEWER: So it is not completely fictitious. It is based on something real.

GOLDEMBERG: Right. There are many magazines like that in every Jewish community. Here in New York, there are hundreds.

INTERVIEWER: Am I mistaken if I see in your work the influence of the nineteenth-century Peruvian writer Ricardo Palma, precisely because of the way he plays with history and fantasy?

GOLDEMBERG: Yes, as a child I read Palma quite a bit, and I'm sure there is some unconscious influence. I hadn't thought about it, but I'm sure there is. My books have a very colonial element to them.

INTERVIEWER: The *New York Times* has called your first novel "a moving exploration of the human condition." In it, you have touched upon every human emotion, from sanity to madness. What made you write the powerful scene in which Don Jacobo is possessed by his friend's *Dibuk,* a spirit? And the only cure left for him is that of exorcism.

GOLDEMBERG: All the things that I'm telling you about the book are things that I thought about when I finished it and I read it. Jacobo feels that he has committed the worst possible sin by having a child with a woman who was not Jewish. He pays for this by being possessed by the wandering soul of his friend, who is also a sinner. The only way to get rid of the sin and to get rid of the guilt is by going through his exorcism, which is sort of comical in the book. It is not really serious.

INTERVIEWER: Do you consider your first novel experimental?

GOLDEMBERG: No, I don't experiment really. I think it is a very traditional novel. It has different techniques, but it is very traditional. I think that it is easy to read and I wouldn't call it experimental.

INTERVIEWER: In your novel, nevertheless, you do what Cervantes did long ago: you call on many different styles. You use poetic prose, journalistic prose, with imaginary reprints of magazines and official documents, and you even imitate the Spanish language as spoken by a Jewish immigrant. How did you achieve that mastery of the language?

GOLDEMBERG: I tried to remember how my father spoke, because I couldn't remember my father's voice, which is very interesting. But I remembered the voice of his friends and tried to recreate that.

INTERVIEWER: You worked on the bilingual edition of your poetry, *Hombres de paso / Just Passing Through.* Have you ever tried writing in English?

GOLDEMBERG: No, I haven't and I don't plan to.

INTERVIEWER: There is a definite bond between your poetry

and your prose as far as themes are concerned. You always seem to go back to your roots, being Jewish and Peruvian.

GOLDEMBERG: I am very preoccupied with history and myth. I'm also concerned with integrating myself as an individual. In order to do that, I can only go back to my roots. I feel that by investigating my family, my ancestors, their different beliefs and cultures, I can come to a better understanding of myself. Of course, that has to transcend my experience and become art. And I hope that I am achieving this.

INTERVIEWER: What is poetry for you?

GOLDEMBERG: Poetry is something very elusive. I don't like to talk in terms of poetry. For many people, poetry is something that is floating around, and the poet has to catch it and grab it as if it were a butterfly. I am more concerned with the poem as a form, which has really nothing to do with what poetry is.

INTERVIEWER: What is a novel for you, then?

GOLDEMBERG: It is almost the same thing. The novel is the form or the concrete thing that one can see and touch and read, and fiction is just an abstraction.

INTERVIEWER: As I read your poetry, I was struck by its similarity to your novels—the ideals, the thoughts are the same, to such a degree that I even wondered whether your poetry was a companion to the novel, or the novel a companion to your poetry. Do your novels precede the poems, or is it the other way around?

GOLDEMBERG: With the first novel I wrote, the poems were preceding the novel. I was writing a certain kind of poetry that showed me at a certain moment that I was ready to write that novel.

INTERVIEWER: Do you consider yourself more a novelist or a poet?

GOLDEMBERG: When I am working on a novel, I am a novelist. When I am working with poetry, I am a poet.

INTERVIEWER: When did you first begin writing?

GOLDEMBERG: It was a long time ago, I was twelve years old.

INTERVIEWER: And it was prose?

GOLDEMBERG: It was prose. I had read a book by Steinbeck, *The Grapes of Wrath.* I was very impressed by it and thought that I could write a novel myself. I started writing the novel, but I discovered that the landscape that I was describing, and the characters, resembled characters in the Midwest, in the United States. I was not dealing with the people that I was supposed to be dealing with. I finally wrote it twenty years later.

INTERVIEWER: Is writing a profession?

GOLDEMBERG: It is a profession because I think that you have to be disciplined. It is not a profession in the sense that it makes money for you. I don't think that most writers who are "serious" about their writing work with the idea that they are going to make money with their books. I don't think that's the main concern that a writer has. But it is a profession in the sense that you have to be committed to your work and possess self-discipline.

INTERVIEWER: Do you write to express a message or do you do it because you need to?

GOLDEMBERG: It is something I need to do. There is no message involved, because I think that can be very tricky and very dangerous. I have a story to tell and I would like to tell it in the best way I can. If there is any message, it is a matter for other people to decide.

INTERVIEWER: Is writing a lonely profession?

GOLDEMBERG: Very lonely. It is the loneliest profession that I can think of. Because you are working with words, and they are very abstract.

INTERVIEWER: What is the language for you?

GOLDEMBERG: First of all it is sound, someone saying something to somebody else. If you use a typewriter, it is also a typographical image, so the two things are really combined.

INTERVIEWER: Is music very important for you?

GOLDEMBERG: Yes, it is important.

INTERVIEWER: Do you sing?

GOLDEMBERG: Yes, I like to sing and I'm learning to play the guitar.

INTERVIEWER: Have you ever thought of singing some of your poetry?

GOLDEMBERG: Yes, I have taped music to some of my poems. Because I don't know how to write music, I had to use a tape recorder to remember the melody that I composed.

INTERVIEWER: Who is Isaac Goldemberg?

GOLDEMBERG: Isaac Goldemberg is someone who is still in search of a home. I see myself as someone who is just beginning his profession, and I have many, many things to learn. Perhaps in twenty years I will be able to write something that I'll really be proud of.

Part 2

INTERVIEWER: Since I last interviewed you, would you say that you have found yourself and that you are no longer in search of an identity?

GOLDEMBERG: What I found out is that my identity was there all the time; I was only looking for ways to get to the point where I could recognize myself. I think that I have achieved this not only through my writing but also because of my frequent travels back to my country in the last five years. I have been able to go back to my family on my mother's side. Some of them were people I had not seen in thirty years. Through the stories that they told me while sitting around the table, I discovered that they remembered me in very affectionate terms—it was as if I had never left them. I feel that now I am fully integrated, culturally and also on a personal basis. My mother still lives in Chepén, in the house of my grandfather, which she inherited at his death. Like her, I was born and raised there, and it was quite an experience to visit her because even though the house is falling apart, it is a strong symbol of my childhood.

INTERVIEWER: It was quite a long time since you last saw your mother?

GOLDEMBERG: Yes, in 1985, it was about ten years since I had seen her.

INTERVIEWER: And when you saw her, it was as if you had never left?

GOLDEMBERG: That's the feeling I always get when I see her. Being with her again has helped me clear up many unresolved doubts about my childhood, particularly my trip to Lima, when she sent me to live with my father. I had been mistaken about many of her reasons for doing this. The truth of the matter is that my mother sent me away out of love, thinking that my father, who was a man of relative means, would be able to give me a better life and a better education.

INTERVIEWER: How did you manage to reconcile your Peruvian and Jewish identities?

GOLDEMBERG: It was through very close contacts with my mother's family. When I was sent to Lima as a child, I felt that I had to erase my past in Chepén in order to become fully Jewish. I also thought I would never be able to return to my hometown; it was as if that part of my culture had been obliterated forever. Now I realize that I was wrong, and that I could go back to my Peruvian roots and reclaim them.

INTERVIEWER: How do you view your relationships with both Israel and Peru?

GOLDEMBERG: I don't see Israel as my fatherland. For me, Israel is a place that offers every Jew in the world a choice: to settle there, if he so wishes. My relationship with Israel is more ideological than emotional. My relationship to Peru, by contrast, is an ancestral one, to which I am tied as if by an umbilical cord. That is truly my land.

INTERVIEWER: You now identify much more with your mother than you did before?

GOLDEMBERG: Very, very much so, to the point that I have discovered certain traits in myself that I cannot see coming from my father. My mother is a woman with a great imagination, a great storyteller, and so are all my aunts, her sisters. Even though they are not intellectuals and they don't read very much (they hardly read at all), they know that I am a writer and they take great satisfaction in telling me stories about Chepén. They feel very proud of my writing about my hometown and they would like me to continue. Through their stories, I have begun to remember conversations that I overheard when I was six. My mother, her sisters, and my grandmother used to go into the kitchen every afternoon and prepare dinner. I would always join them and help with the preparation of the food, and they would hold long conversations about everything that was going on in the town. As I am beginning to remember their voices, I am thinking of writing a novel which would consist only of their stories.

INTERVIEWER: It could be called "Six Voices from Chepén."

GOLDEMBERG: Yes, but the tentative title that I have for this book, if I ever write it, is "En la puerta del horno" (At the Oven's Gate).

INTERVIEWER: So I see there is a big difference in you since we last spoke, because you were mostly concerned with your father then. Six years have passed since that interview. Now you seem to have moved back to your origins on your mother's side.

GOLDEMBERG: I don't think it is so much that. They were always there, but I refused to see them, but now they have become vital and concrete again.

INTERVIEWER: Have you started working on your new novel?

GOLDEMBERG: It's all in my mind, which, for me, is already writing. I think writing begins with the conception of ideas and images. The first step is to see the novel in terms of images and voices. The second step, the actual writing, takes place when the images and the voices are already distinct, almost forceful.

INTERVIEWER: And when do you think this will happen?

GOLDEMBERG: I plan to go back to Chepén to stay at my

mother's house for three or four weeks. I am going to spend every afternoon in the kitchen, reliving the experiences that I had as a child. I will talk with my mother, my aunts and my grandmother, and when I come back, I think I will be ready to write that book.

INTERVIEWER: Must writing be autobiographical for you?

GOLDEMBERG: It would seem so. I have many notebooks with ideas for stories, novels, and poems that someday I would like to write, but they have remained there only as ideas. Although they touch upon things that I feel deeply about, I don't think they are really connected to my being. They are like ingenious, intellectual, imaginative, playful exercises, but nothing more. I take great delight, even in conversations, in being witty, in creating stories out of the blue, but I don't feel strongly enough to actually construct a novel around them. But anything that is connected to my own autobiographical experience, however, finds a way into the writing itself. I am not really afraid of people saying, "Goldemberg can only write about himself or his own experiences." My experiences have enriched me, and I feel it is my duty to keep on writing about them. I think I am making a contribution to understanding what it is to be a Peruvian, a Jew, or a Peruvian Jew.

INTERVIEWER: So you believe that the writer has a duty and a mission?

GOLDEMBERG: I wouldn't say mission, because the word has religious overtones. Perhaps because of my two cultures, I see it as a duty to record the history of a particular people.

INTERVIEWER: What is writing to you?

GOLDEMBERG: It is a full-time occupation that the writer performs most of the day, not only when he or she is sitting down in front of the typewriter. Although this sounds almost like an oxymoron or an antithesis, I think that writers, to a large extent, have the unfortunate fortune of seeing reality in terms of writing itself or the possibility for writing. Many times, this turns us into outsiders. Sometimes I have the feeling that only for very brief moments do we participate fully with what's going on around us. Most of the time, a writer's position with respect to reality is that of an outsider, somebody who is looking in and recording what he sees.

INTERVIEWER: What are words to you?

GOLDEMBERG: Instruments, utensils that the writer uses in order to build something that is very concrete. Many writers feel that words are elusive, hard to catch, but I think if they say this they are not really locked in with the material that they are trying to write. For me, words are utensils in the same way that a hammer or a saw are tools for a carpenter.

INTERVIEWER: So what is your reaction to the famous "blank page"?

GOLDEMBERG: In the past, it used to be one of fear. As Nicanor Parra says in one of his antipoems, and I am paraphrasing, what the poet has to do in front of a blank page is not to ruin it, let alone try to improve it. This is the fear that we writers have when we sit in front of the blank page. I think that I have managed to lose some of this fear by viewing the blank page merely as the repository of the voice. It is the social tool that the writer uses.

INTERVIEWER: Why do you write?

GOLDEMBERG: Because I think that certain things can only be told by using words, through the telling of stories. In many periods of my life, and I am sure that this has happened to many writers, I have said to myself that I would never write again, that it was too lonely an activity. It would be nicer to work with other people in order to fight the solitude, for instance on a movie. Even a painter can hang his works on the wall and nobody will say anything. Hanging a poem on the wall, on the other hand, has a very strange connotation, it almost seems too arrogant. So writing, to that extent, is a much more private activity, on all levels.

INTERVIEWER: And how do you feel in front of the finished work?

GOLDEMBERG: It's an accomplishment. I have a very strong respect for the book itself as a form. When I started writing as a young boy, my main ambition was to have a book published and see it displayed on a bookshelf. I like to reread what I write— many writers say that when their book is published, they never go back to it, they want nothing more to do with it. For me, it is the opposite: it is precisely because I feel that the book is no longer mine that I love to read it many times. Even though I feel alien to it, I am also very close to it. And because I feel very familiar with the world that is contained in the book, I am able to discover many things that I did not see when I was working on it. There is a great satisfaction in this; it is like living with someone for many years and discovering new things about that person every day.

INTERVIEWER: Do you think of yourself as a poet or as a novelist?

GOLDEMBERG: I think I answered that in the interview we held six years ago. What I said then is still true today: when I write poetry there is a narrative quality to it, and in my narrative there is a poetic quality. I really don't like to establish a very definite distinction between the two genres.

INTERVIEWER: That's because your prose has a poetic sensibility.

GOLDEMBERG: You could say the same thing of Rulfo, for instance. He was a fiction writer, a narrator, but his prose reads like poetry. I remember that once José Emilio Pacheco, the Mexican poet and novelist, took out certain lines from Rulfo's stories, perhaps even from *Pedro Páramo,* and arranged them as if they were a long poem, and you couldn't tell the difference. They really read like poetry.

INTERVIEWER: How do you view 1992, the celebration of the discovery of America, and the recognition of Israel by Spain?

GOLDEMBERG: The second part of your question, the recognition of Israel by Spain, is undoubtedly a move on

Spain's part to begin to recognize the debt that it owes to the Jewish and Islamic cultures. This is coincidental with the celebration of the 500 years of what they call the discovery of America. It was precisely in 1492 that both the Jews and the Arabs were expelled from Spain. As far as the celebration is concerned, it is obvious that the event has to be remembered. In the last year, we have been bombarded in newspapers, magazines, and television by the enormous propaganda and publicity apparatus that Spain has constructed to convince us that the Spanish presence in Latin America is strong, as if we didn't know. Anytime you watch a program on television that relates to that presence, what they usually show are either the colonial buildings in the cities and the small towns, or, invariably, at least ten churches. It seems that they are trying to tell Latin Americans that we should be thankful for the two things that Spain has given us, language and religion. Sometimes I get the feeling that the Spaniards still haven't realized that the language is ours, it's not as if they had given it to us on consignment. Even religion in Latin America has been changed forever, through the mixing with the native religious beliefs and those of immigrants. Were I to speak from the point of view of a Catholic, I would have to say that the religion is no longer the same. I think that the so-called "discovery" should not be a celebration but a critical remembrance of what really happened, what it really meant for America, for Spain and for the world in general. And I hope that our countries and our governments will not fall into the deplorable position of yet again celebrating the conquerors.

INTERVIEWER: Do you identify with the Spaniards in any way?

GOLDEMBERG: I have Spanish blood on my grandfather's side, from the north of Spain, and my grandmother's ancestors were from Andalusia. But I think that ideologically the Hispanic culture in Latin America has done a lot of harm. Sometimes, even the most progressive and the most well-intentioned leaders in Latin America cannot get rid of this Hispanic attitude toward their own people. Your question reminds me of something that I experienced in Peru two years ago when I went back after seven years of absence: I went to the Plaza de Armas in Lima, where, interestingly enough, you can see the Cathedral, the Palacio de Gobierno [Government Palace], and a gigantic statue of Francisco Pizarro, the Spanish conqueror of Peru. When I say a gigantic statue, I am not exaggerating; what impressed me was not only its size but the ferocity of this man; he looked like a centaur. His helmet had two long horns, as if he were really a devil, and he was holding his sword up in the air menacingly. As I looked around and I saw the many Indians who had come down from the Andes to live in the capital, I began to wonder what it meant for them to have such a big statue of a conqueror who came to annihilate their race. As I was reflecting on this, a woman, who looked half mad, went by. She saw me staring at the statue and said the exact words I was thinking—it was unbelievable! She said, "This piece of crap should be sent back to Spain as a present from the Peruvian people. We don't want it here because it has nothing to do with us." And that is the way I feel. When the so-called celebration of the 500 years comes, we Peruvians should send that statue to Spain because it belongs to them, not to us.

INTERVIEWER: And what statue would you place there?

GOLDEMBERG: Ironically enough, the statue of Manco Capac, who is the founder of the Inca Empire, is located in La Victoria neighborhood, which is populated mostly by workers, a lot of black people, and now by a lot of Indians also. As I told you, Pizarro is looking up at the sky menacingly, very sure of himself, and the statue of Manco Capac, smaller in size, shows the founder of the Inca Empire looking at the ground. Maybe we don't need statues, maybe all statues should be brought down. But if we are going to have one, I would place a new statue of Manco Capac, a new monument, where Pizarro's is now.

INTERVIEWER: What about El Inca, Garcilaso de la Vega?

GOLDEMBERG: I don't know if writers should be glorified in such a way, perhaps no one should. But he is a figure who interests me a great deal for many reasons. A large and wide avenue in Lima bears his name, in opposition to Vallejo, who is perhaps the second major figure in Peru as far as writing is concerned, but who has only been given a very small street.

INTERVIEWER: And Ricardo Palma?

GOLDEMBERG: Ricardo Palma also has a street, but it is not very impressive either.

INTERVIEWER: Are you a friend of Vargas Llosa?

GOLDEMBERG: No, although we have met twice and he's helped me a great deal. I know that he was instrumental in getting my first novel published in Spanish in Peru. He recommended it to the owner of the publishing house that brought it out. When I was working on my second novel, he had the opportunity to read the first two chapters, and he liked them very much and urged me to keep on writing and to finish the novel. He has always spoken very kindly about my work.

INTERVIEWER: What is your reaction to the statement made by Grace Paley about your novel *Play by Play,* when she says: "This is a wonderful, lively book. It somersaults out of the Andes, leaps from home Spanish into Yiddish exile, out of Peruvian exile into family Yiddish. It is like a poem wildly plotted among the contradictions of the life of a boy who is an Indian, a Peruvian and a Jew"?

GOLDEMBERG: When I first saw the blurb that Grace very kindly agreed to write for the cover of my book, my first impression was that she was an excellent reader. She had captured in a very profound way everything that the book contained: the technique, the poetry that runs throughout it, and also the rhythm. When she spoke about a book that leaps out of the Andes into another world, I saw that she had seen exactly what I had intended to do: to write a story that takes place in Peru and relates very closely to Peruvian culture, but at the same time is able to transcend it. And perhaps that was accomplished primarily because of the Jewish elements in the story. Grace Paley was able to identify intuitively, not only because she is Jewish but also because she is a writer and she is very politically committed to Latin American history and reality. She saw in a very clear way all the conflicts that our Latin American reality contains.

INTERVIEWER: What does the word *exile* mean to you?

GOLDEMBERG: The first word that comes to my mind is *dispersion,* not in a negative way, but rather in the positive sense. It enables the exiled person to mentally, intellectually, and even poetically occupy many spaces. When I was growing up in Peru and I found out that I was Jewish, I was told about the two thousand years of exile that the Jewish people had suffered. All of a sudden, my world became larger, it expanded automatically, because I knew that my ancestors had been in many lands, and to some extent I was part of those lands. At the same time, as a Jew, I felt that in my own country I lived in exile. I also felt that the Indians lived in exile themselves, but in a very strange sort of exile, because they were occupying their own territory but it was not theirs. As Jews, our eyes were always placed on the possibility of going to Israel and recovering our territory, whereas the Indians, even though they were already occupying their land, lived in cultural exile.

INTERVIEWER: You chose exile.

GOLDEMBERG: I was really young, I left Peru when I was sixteen and my ambition was to travel, to see all those places, but always with the intention of returning. It never crossed my mind that I would not settle there again. I did make an attempt in 1964. I went back to Peru, I wanted to study in Lima, thinking that I was going to stay there, but because of economic reasons, I had to leave.

INTERVIEWER: And now?

GOLDEMBERG: Now I entertain the idea of going back to Peru to settle there, but I have responsibilities in New York: my children are here and it is my home. There are many things that tie me to the city, so perhaps the ideal situation would be to live in Peru part of the time and live in New York the rest of the time.

INTERVIEWER: Six years ago, when I asked you "Who is Isaac Goldemberg?", you replied, "Someone who is still in search of a home." What would you say today if I asked you that same question?

GOLDEMBERG: I would answer something very similar, but with the clarification that my search of a home is not a physical one. I am searching for a spiritual home, which can be built anywhere. Maybe my home is my writing.

INTERVIEWER: A moment ago, when we stopped the interview briefly, you said, "Speaking in English is somewhat artificial because I cannot express myself fully." Let us continue this interview in Spanish, which later I will translate. Is speaking in your mother tongue any different than speaking in English?

GOLDEMBERG: It is different in the sense that every interview necessarily entails a mask: the interviewer has a mask and the interviewee has a mask. If we had done this interview entirely in Spanish, my mask would have been different; it wouldn't have been the same as the one I used to respond to questions in English.

INTERVIEWER: But it would be a mask anyway?

GOLDEMBERG: Yes. Regardless of how sincere an image the interviewee wants to present, what is ultimately going to be revealed is a mask. The voice speaks from behind the mask always. The thing is that I am more accustomed to wearing my Spanish mask than my English one, because I use the latter very infrequently. If we had continued our conversation in English for hours, however, perhaps there would have come a time when I would be accustomed to speaking through the English mask. By using English, nevertheless, many things remain unsaid; we are left with quite a few empty spaces that would have been filled more thoroughly had we used our Spanish masks all along. The image would have been more complete.

INTERVIEWER: And what would you add to what we have been saying, now that you have the use of your Spanish mask?

GOLDEMBERG: The main addition is that I am speaking with a little more feeling. I think my English mask works on a more intellectual level. I have been speaking more with my brain than with my heart. The beauty of an interview, or any human enterprise, is to achieve a union between the two: to be able to think with feeling and to feel with intelligence.

INTERVIEWER: In other words, had we carried out this interview in Spanish, we might have seen that poetic fluidity which is apparent in your prose?

GOLDEMBERG: I believe it would have been more natural because, for me, one word suggests another in Spanish, whereas in English words do not suggest alternatives. This is particularly true when I have spent some time without speaking English.

INTERVIEWER: So if we wanted to express that poetic fluidity, what would you now say about your mother, or yourself, or history?

GOLDEMBERG: As I was telling you during our brief pause, when I was speaking about my mother and my hometown, I found myself in a strange situation because I was translating something that I had lived in my own tongue, I was translating simultaneously. And the effort required to do this left me no time for imagination and poetry, because I was more concerned with communicating the idea than the feeling underlying it. These experiences that we have been discussing took place in Spanish and talking about them in English places a wall between their essential "reality" and what I was trying to say.

INTERVIEWER: Do you think that in an interview one can never speak without masks interfering?

GOLDEMBERG: Not only in an interview but in any social interaction. I think we move through society with our masks on at all times.

INTERVIEWER: Do you never take off your masks?

GOLDEMBERG: We can't even take them off when we are alone. From the moment we wake to the moment we go to sleep, we are completely masked. Perhaps when we sleep is the only time when we can really remove our masks.

INTERVIEWER: Then dreaming is very important for you?

GOLDEMBERG: Very important. It is the only time when our true selves are revealed. Understanding this when one awakes is another matter altogether because we then try to comprehend our true selves through the mask which we put on as soon as we rise. I think, therefore, that we will never be able to unmask ourselves during our waking hours.

INTERVIEWER: So even with your own children or your wife, you cannot remove your mask?

GOLDEMBERG: It's impossible. It's a mask that has been acquired over a long, long period. I have no idea what I would be like without my mask.

INTERVIEWER: Not even with your own mother?

GOLDEMBERG: Not even with her. I think every intelligent individual tries to reveal himself as much as possible through the thinnest mask possible. But I don't believe we will ever be able to remove it completely.

INTERVIEWER: So if I were to ask you once again who Isaac Goldemberg is, what would you answer, now that you have on the thinnest mask possible?

GOLDEMBERG: I would tell you that in the last two years Isaac Goldemberg has been a person who has changed masks constantly to discover which one is the most appropriate.

INTERVIEWER: What is this new mask like in comparison to the one you wore six years ago when I first interviewed you?

GOLDEMBERG: It is a mask with more defined physical traits, it is more assured than the image I present, and it has no desire of being strictly bound but is willing to accept changes. It is a mask willing to acknowledge that experience is like a sculptor who carves the changes day by day and that the color of my mask could vary tomorrow without being fake. Basically, it is growing and evolving.

INTERVIEWER: Do you see growth and evolution in the six-year interim?

GOLDEMBERG: Absolutely. I am more at peace with myself, more willing to acknowledge my limitations, although I was always aware of them. I want to turn them to my advantage, make them a means for freedom. Without being grandiose, I think that all writers strive to be great writers, that is our greatest dream, because if the opposite were true, it would not be worth the effort. When we finally realize, however, that we will never be a great writer, then we have to shape our thinking to the notions that writing is never going to abandon us or we it. The most we can do is attempt to write as well as possible.

Juan Carlos Onetti

Juan Carlos Onetti

Juan Carlos Onetti, novelist and short-story writer and one of the most enigmatic literary figures from Latin America, was born in Montevideo, Uruguay, on July 1, 1909. His great-grandfather was private secretary to General Rivera, who took part in the Wars of Independence and fought against the dictator Rosas.

Little is known of Onetti's early years. He seems to have drawn a veil over his childhood to preserve it as a private and sacred refuge. He does admit, however, that at the age of thirteen he went through a Knut Hamsun period and read all of his books. He would hide in a cupboard with a cat and a book. He also tells of his leaving school as a youth because he could not pass a course in drawing.

Onetti published his first short story at the age of twenty-three. In 1939, he became an editor for the newly founded weekly *Marcha,* for which he worked until 1941. He had a column which he signed "Periquito el Aguador" and also wrote humorous articles under the pen name "Grucho Marx," without the "o." His short story "Convalecencia" (Convalescence), written under the name of his cousin H. C. Ramos, won the first prize at a literary contest sponsored by *Marcha.* During those years in Montevideo, Onetti took part in intellectual gatherings at the well-known Café Metro.

From 1941 to 1954, Onetti worked for the Reuters News Agency, first in Montevideo, and later in Buenos Aires. He feels a sense of endearment to both cities and they form the backbone of his novels, although they do not always appear under these names. Like Faulkner, he has created his own city, the fictitious world of Santa María, an enclosed space where characters come and go within the cycle of his saga. And to him that world is as real as reality itself.

In 1955, Onetti interrupted his voluntary exile and went back to Montevideo. In 1957, he was appointed Director of the Public Libraries and became a member of the board of directors of the Comedia Nacional. In 1962, he was awarded the Uruguayan National Literary Prize for his works published in 1959 and 1960, and in 1980 received the Cervantes Prize.

Juan Carlos Onetti is the author of numerous novels and short stories, among them: *El pozo* (The Pit), 1939; *Tiempo de abrazar* (A Time to Embrace), which came in second in a contest sponsored by Farrar and Rinehart of New York in 1940; *Tierra de nadie* (No Man's Land), awarded the second prize in a contest sponsored by Losada, Buenos Aires, 1941; *Para esta noche* (For Tonight), 1943; *La vida breve,* 1950 (*A Brief Life,* 1976); *Un sueño realizado y otros cuentos* (A Dream Come True and Other Stories), 1941; *Los adioses* (The Goodbyes), 1954; *Para una tumba sin nombre,* 1954 (*For a Nameless Grave,* 1980); *La cara de la desgracia* (The Face of Misfortune), 1960; *El astillero,* 1961 (*The Shipyard,* 1968, winner of the William Faulkner Foundation Certificate of Merit, 1963, and awarded the Italian Prize for Best Foreign Work in Translation, 1975); *Tan triste como ella* (As Sad as She), 1963; *Juntacadáveres* (Junta, the Corpse Collector), 1964, runner-up in the 1967 Rómulo Gallegos Prize); *La novia robada y otros cuentos* (The Jilted Bride and Other Stories), 1968; *Obras completas* (Complete Works), 1970; *La muerte y la niña* (Death and the Girl), 1973; *Requiem por Faulkner y otros artículos* (Requiem for Faulkner and Other Essays), 1976; *Cuentos secretos: Periquito el aguador y otras máscaras* (Hidden Stories: Periquito the Water Carrier and Other Masks), 1986; *Presencia y otros cuentos* (A Presence and Other Stories), 1986; *Cuando entonces* (Back Then), 1987.

Juan Carlos Onetti is a very sincere and private person. He does not like to talk about himself, but when he does it is always with a great sense of humor and humility. He has given few interviews throughout his life and in most of them the answers are strikingly shorter than the questions. However, in spite of the lack of importance he gives his works, his writings had a great impact on the Boom. Many Latin American writers, such as Cortázar, García Márquez and Vargas Llosa, have expressed their indebtedness to Onetti.

Juan Carlos Onetti was married four times. Since 1975, he has been living in Madrid with his fourth wife, Dorotea Muhr, whom he married in 1955. He left Uruguay after being imprisoned by the military authorities from January to May 1974. He has a son and a daughter by previous marriages.

ONETTI: I have been waiting for your call since six o'clock this morning. I hardly slept last night. I am a very shy person.

INTERVIEWER: I too am shy.

ONETTI: Then we'll understand each other.

INTERVIEWER: Is your last name of Irish or Italian origin?

ONETTI: It comes from Genoa. A confusion arose, however, because one of my ancestors, who had lived for a long time in Gibraltar, changed his name to O'Netty.

INTERVIEWER: It has been said that in order to be a poet one has to preserve something of one's childhood.

ONETTI: I am in complete agreement with you. All decent and respectable people remember something of their childhood. Mine was a happy one. My parents loved each other dearly.

INTERVIEWER: What childhood memories would you like to evoke?

ONETTI: I couldn't tell you a specific memory, except perhaps a long friendship I had with a cat. I remember him now as if he were here. What was his name? I cannot recall, he had so many. I would hide in the cupboard with my cat and read a book.

INTERVIEWER: What does language mean for you?

ONETTI: For me it is basically a tool and a challenge. Many times I wake up early in the morning because I realize that an adjective I have used is wrong. So it is a continuous but pleasant struggle. But it is never an end in itself, never the moving force.

INTERVIEWER: How are Montevideo and Buenos Aires represented in your work?

ONETTI: There are a lot of references to Montevideo and Buenos Aires in my work. The most important thing is to be sincere. Those two cities have been very dear to me.

INTERVIEWER: The saga of your mythical city, Santa María, begins in *A Brief Life*. Do you see that city as something real, a space with streets, houses, and monuments that you have elaborated as if you were both an architect and a writer? Could you draw up a map of Santa María with the Plaza Brausen, the Petrus Villa, the old Barrio and the new Plaza, as Juan Benet did with his mythical city Región?

ONETTI: I had a map of Santa María but I lost it. So I manage through invented memories.

INTERVIEWER: Do you feel like a citizen of Santa María?

ONETTI: When I write about Santa María, I am one of its residents.

INTERVIEWER: Do you see the evolution of your novels through the urban and social transformation of that mythical city?

ONETTI: It is the reader who sees that evolution, I don't plan it.

INTERVIEWER: Do you think your work represents the heart of the Uruguayan people or is it more representative of the anxiety of the twentieth century?

ONETTI: I would choose the second interpretation.

INTERVIEWER: What does the word freedom mean for you?

ONETTI: If I don't have food to eat, I am not free. If I have to work in an office, performing tasks I don't enjoy, I am not free. Fortunately, I can now live off my books, so I don't have responsibilities of any kind and I feel that I am free.

INTERVIEWER: You have recounted that Ortega y Gasset used to recall to his students the following phrase by Hegel:

"Have the courage to be wrong." Why is that phrase so important for you?

ONETTI: Because a great number of young people do nothing but copy and repeat what previous generations have said. What I would like is for all these young persons to show themselves as they are. Every individual is different, no two people are exactly alike. So they should reveal themselves as they are, with absolute freedom.

INTERVIEWER: In 1957 you were director of the public libraries of Montevideo. What do you feel about the works of others and your own?

ONETTI: I never reread my books, except when I look for some specific information that I need for the novel I am working on. When I finish a novel, I have nothing more to do with it. But I do go through some of the translations—many years ago they made some mistakes in the French translation of one of my works. What I am very interested in is publishing in the United States.

INTERVIEWER: Do you have a favorite among your books?

ONETTI: My favorite is a very short novel that was treated with much disdain, *Los adioses.* I am not saying that I like this novel because of its intellectual value or because it is better than another one, but I have a special feeling for it, I like it more. As far as characters go, my favorite is Dr. Díaz Grey.

INTERVIEWER: You have said, "I would like to truly write, without thinking of anyone and without any other goal than the book itself." What does this mean in terms of the space that we call a book? What geometric shape would you give to the chaotic world of your novels?

ONETTI: I think that is a surrealistic question. It would have the same shape as a book.

INTERVIEWER: What is more important for you: the book as a whole, the relationship between characters, the plot, the language or the literary techniques?

ONETTI: Those are problems that I have never been concerned with. I don't look at the book from the outside; I see myself within it. Things happen there that I have to write about. Characters or a particular technique may be apparent, but I never plan it on purpose. I believe that it is life that moves everything. Life is like this: if there is tenderness, it comes out; if there is a political angle, it comes out.

INTERVIEWER: What is more important: the interior monologue or the dialogue?

ONETTI: The interior monologue has been used too much. Hemingway was magnificent with dialogue, but I am not interested in copying his style, although he wrote wonderful dialogues. Since I mentioned Hemingway, I would like to say that I think the most important North American writer of this century was William Faulkner. Generally speaking, I think that present-day universal literature is in decay.

INTERVIEWER: During the Second World War, you wrote the following words: "My life is my books, a room to live in, two or three old friends, and running into some former student who endures with his hat in his hands the worn-out words I speak to him." If I asked you the same question today, what would you reply?

ONETTI: Things are pretty much the same today: I usually write in bed, although I get up to eat and sometimes I write in the living room. I have very few friends, because I have told many jokes about Spanish literature and, as a result, people don't like me. I have also received the Cervantes Prize and this has provoked petty jealousies.

INTERVIEWER: In an article about Roberto Arlt you said, "To be born means accepting a monstrous pact and, nevertheless, to be alive is the only marvel possible." Do you see life as something ambiguous?

ONETTI: I have always been very aware of the presence of death, because I feel that we are here for a short time and then we disappear. I discovered at an early age that people die and I have never forgotten it.

INTERVIEWER: Why do you think that until the 1960s reading your work was the privilege of minorities?

ONETTI: I think that it is still for minorities. You have brought me good news, because I do believe that I am an author for minorities.

INTERVIEWER: You consider Cortázar the literary father of García Márquez. Don't you feel also like a literary father to him, since in the 1930s you broke with traditional narrative techniques to give fictional reality a new dimension?

ONETTI: I admire García Márquez a lot and we are very close friends. I have read that I changed literature, especially that written in the region of La Plata, which was a gaucholike literature. I rebelled against all that. I believed that we had to write about themes associated with the cities, because I am very much a man of the city, with little interest in nature. My wife does tend a garden on our terrace, but nature doesn't interest me. In order to write, I need people around.

INTERVIEWER: You have said, "According to his detractors, Emir Rodríguez Monegal invented the notion that there was a boom in Latin American literature." What do you think of the Boom?

ONETTI: That's a very complex question. It seems that a group of Spanish and Latin American publishers was responsible for promoting the Boom. I think it had positive elements but it is now over. Some authors were singled out for special treatment. When the Boom occurred, I had already written extensively and I had nothing to do with it.

INTERVIEWER: What are some of the constants of your work? Is irony one of them?

ONETTI: Yes it is. I try not to show it, but when I write, it comes out. I think everything is ironical and that generations come and go. People who become so happy because they have had one hit or because they got a raise inspire irony and pity.

INTERVIEWER: In your days as a journalist, why did you sign your articles with the pseudonyms Periquito el Aguador and

Grucho Marx, without the "o" of Groucho?

ONETTI: I was a journalist to earn a living. Why did I use those pseudonyms? Carlos Quijano, the director of *Marcha,* the weekly for which I worked, came up with Periquito el Aguador. I invented Grucho as a joke, because I wrote articles as a joke.

INTERVIEWER: You worked for the weekly *Marcha* and the Reuters News Agency. Has your work been influenced by journalism?

ONETTI: When I am reading a book and I begin to feel that the writer is doing journalism, I throw it away. They are two separate worlds. Those who write journalism as literature probably do so because they can do nothing else.

INTERVIEWER: Brausen, the narrator of *A Brief Life,* creates Dr. Díaz Grey and the city of Santa María. In *La novia robada,* he becomes "DiosBrausen" (GodBrausen). Could we then call you "DiosOnetti" (GodOnetti)?

ONETTI: I think so, I give you permission. I am the grandfather. Let us say that Brausen is the father and I am the grandfather.

INTERVIEWER: How does Onetti the creator see his creation, Brausen?

ONETTI: Brausen is a complex character juggling many things at once. He tries to be several characters. His only pretense is to be someone else, not any better, but different. So he creates the world of Santa María and then discovers that writing is like being God. It gives him the power of words, of selecting them and modifying people's destinies. But the character that most resembles Juan Carlos Onetti is Dr. Díaz Grey.

INTERVIEWER: How would God Himself see you, His creation, and do you have anything to say about Him?

ONETTI: We don't know if God exists, we cannot prove it. It is possible that when we die He will appear. I don't know.

INTERVIEWER: Do you agree with the following statement by Octavio Paz: "If the holy presence is absent, the self also disappears"?

ONETTI: I think this is what the French call *boutade* or whim. It goes no further than that. To feel a need for God does not mean that He exists. That's material for a parish priest. I don't seek God.

INTERVIEWER: Do you believe that writers wear a series of masks? Are you wearing one now?

ONETTI: It is possible that each book represents the masks of Onetti, although I am definitely not wearing one now.

INTERVIEWER: Gabriela Mistral believed in divine grace and García Lorca in the magic genie. What about you? Do you believe in inspiration?

ONETTI: I write when I feel compelled to. I don't write with discipline; I have seizures that force me to write when I witness a scene or encounter, or overhear a conversation. Sometimes months pass by and nothing happens. But I know that all of a sudden the whole plot will shape up within me and take hold of me, and then I start writing in a frenzy.

INTERVIEWER: You have said several times that "writing is an act of love." Could you add anything to that beautiful statement?   .

ONETTI: Writing means giving of oneself, and separating completely from reality as you leave the subconscious. It is and has always been an affirmation of love; I would even say physical love.

INTERVIEWER: Does writing always have to be a solitary journey?

ONETTI: Yes, absolutely, at least for me.

INTERVIEWER: Do you see writing as a profession or do you do it for pleasure?

ONETTI: For me it is a pleasure and also an unconscious struggle with words.

INTERVIEWER: What do you feel when you write?

ONETTI: I don't feel anything. I feel the characters and the setting, which is almost always a room. What we call the real world disappears for me, and I am not at all conscious of the fact that I am writing. I create, that's all, I write, nothing more.

INTERVIEWER: You have said, "The thing is to write as well as we possibly can." When do you know that you have reached the point when it is time to let go of a novel and turn it over to the publisher?

ONETTI: That has to do with intuition. The same should be true of love when the moment has come for it to end.

INTERVIEWER: Is art the only way to affirm life?

ONETTI: Yes, we affirm life as long as we are alive. At this very moment as I am speaking to you, I am affirming life. You are doing the same; we are both creating.

INTERVIEWER: Do you see literature as a social weapon?

ONETTI: Of course not! Think of Cortázar, for instance. There is nothing political in his books.

INTERVIEWER: You have said, "We believe that literature is an art and therefore sacred. It is always an end rather than a means." Why do you write and for whom?

ONETTI: When someone asked James Joyce that question, he replied, "When I write I am seated at a table and across from me there is a man named James Joyce to whom I am writing some letters." Writing a book is like writing oneself a letter. It gives intense pleasure. I write because I like to. The would-be reader does not exist for me at that moment of creation.

INTERVIEWER: In *A Brief Life,* Brausen says, "If anything were to happen, I could save myself through writing." In *Junta-cadáveres,* Díaz Grey says that in the act of creation there is "something of salvation." Have you found salvation through your books?

ONETTI: I would like to define the term "salvation" a little. Save myself from what? I cannot save myself from disease, death and misfortune.

INTERVIEWER: If to be an artist means always to strive after the truth, why did you choose the seeming paradox of the brothel to describe Larsen's search for the truth?

ONETTI: It is an example of the artist who has failed to reach his goal or ideal.

INTERVIEWER: You have said, "I burned two novels and a half; I wrote long chapters that I knew wouldn't fit in the novel I was then working on. I knew I would have to discard them, but I liked them nonetheless." Why couldn't you include those chapters in the book? Why did you burn those novels?

ONETTI: Perhaps because they wouldn't have been right for the book. They were not meant to go in the novel; they were my whims, something nice that I did for myself.

INTERVIEWER: *For a Nameless Grave* is a book that explains what a novel is, how a story is made and unmade. It shows how an author can play tricks on the readers by providing them with an ambiguous world with five possible variants without ever revealing the truth. What is fantasy? What is reality to you?

ONETTI: There are no tricks. What is reality? Good heavens, no one can answer that question! Reality is this, the moment we are living right now. Fantasy is very close to what we call reality. Writing is a reality for me.

INTERVIEWER: Is fictitious reality a means to define oneself and impose order on disorder?

ONETTI: Perhaps it is, but when I write I don't have a specific purpose in mind. Writing means tackling the theme that has occurred to me. I will repeat what I have always said: literature is an end in itself, not a means for anything.

INTERVIEWER: Throughout the years, the characters that inhabit Santa María have reappeared in several of your books. Is this also true of the book you are currently writing?

ONETTI: Yes, I am giving an important role to Dr. Díaz Grey in the novel I am writing now. But I won't say anything more, because it is bad luck to talk about it. It's not a question of superstition; if you talk about what you are going to write, you'll never write it!

INTERVIEWER: Are your characters based on real life or on your imagination?

ONETTI: On my imagination, although sometimes they are based on things that I know in reality. The novel *La novia robada,* for instance, is based on the fact that the daughter of a friend of mine went to Europe to buy a trousseau, but when she returned there was no wedding, so . . .

INTERVIEWER: In *Tierra de nadie,* Casal says, "Almost everything is locked up in oneself and there is no communication." In *The Shipyard,* Larsen says, "Communication is impossible and even undesirable." Is the author speaking through his characters? Why is your vision of the world one of disintegration?

ONETTI: In the first place, because everything is going to disintegrate. I must also point out the error of attributing everything the characters say to the author.

INTERVIEWER: Why do you think your characters act within the confines of four walls?

ONETTI: That's the way I am, because the most important things in life take place within four walls.

INTERVIEWER: Why are your characters always lying down?

ONETTI: That may be due to nothing more than laziness.

INTERVIEWER: Many of your characters are forty years old and they attempt to rescue their own childhood and their lost innocence through their relationships with young girls.

ONETTI: I don't know if one is seeking salvation. Quite simply, it is an attraction one feels for youth.

INTERVIEWER: Why are so many of your characters (Díaz Grey, Llarvi, Elena Sala, Julián, Julita, Moncha, Gálvez) tempted to commit suicide?

ONETTI: Because I have also had that urge, everyone has.

INTERVIEWER: Who dominates: the characters or the author?

ONETTI: The characters dominate in an unconscious fashion. I have a vague sense of what is going to happen to each character, but sometimes things change. No one dominates, we walk hand in hand.

INTERVIEWER: Are your narrators active creators or passive witnesses?

ONETTI: There are both, but I am the ultimate narrator.

INTERVIEWER: Why do the titles of your books suggest a sense of defeat?

ONETTI: Perhaps because the author is a pessimist.

INTERVIEWER: Could you explain the title of your novel *Dejemos hablar al viento* (Let the Wind Speak)?

ONETTI: What we are waiting for in the novel is for a favorable wind to fan a fire.

INTERVIEWER: What did you feel upon receiving the Cervantes Literature Prize?

ONETTI: I was criticized a lot by journalists for speaking about the money I received for the prize instead of dwelling on the merits of my work.

INTERVIEWER: You once said: "The most important thing I get from my books is a feeling of sincerity, of having always been true to myself." Are there many Onettis? Who is Juan Carlos Onetti?

ONETTI: I continue to agree with that statement. There may be many Onettis but you have to search for them. I am still interested in writing, even more than in love or prizes.

Nicanor Parra

Nicanor Parra

Nicanor Parra was born on September 5, 1914, in Chillán, Chile, the land that has given birth to some of the most outstanding Latin American poets. In 1937, when he was twenty-three, he graduated in mathematics and physics from the Pedagogical Institute of the University of Chile. That same year, he was awarded Chile's Municipal Prize for his first book of poems, *Cancionero sin nombre* (Nameless Songs). Gabriela Mistral, his illustrious compatriot and winner of the 1945 Nobel Prize, said of him, "We have come face to face with a poet who will reach international fame."

Nicanor Parra belongs to the Generation of 1938, which characterized itself with the following proclamation: "Fight the metaphor, death to imagery, long live concrete reality, and once again let there be clarity."

Parra's second book, *Poemas y antipoemas,* 1954, appeared in English in 1967 as *Poems and Antipoems.* It brought about a new direction in Latin American poetry, as it was a clear break with traditional language. Poetry was no longer for the select few, but belonged to all people. The language was no longer purely poetic, it was also prosaic. His vision of the world had become global. Pablo Neruda, another great Chilean poet and winner of the 1971 Nobel Prize, said of that book, "This poetry is a delicacy of early morning gold or a fruit savored in darkness."

Emir Rodríguez Monegal, the late Uruguayan critic, described the Chilean poet in the following words: "Nicanor Parra has reached poetic originality through the simple, and at the same time difficult, method of being himself. His poetry is anticonventional for it does not pretend to be poetry." In his own "Manifesto," Parra proclaimed that, "The poet is a man like any other / A mason who erects his wall / A builder of doors and windows."

Nicanor Parra has published countless books of poetry, which have been translated into many languages. The English translations of *Sermones y prédicas del Cristo de Elqui* and *Nuevos sermones y prédicas del Cristo de Elqui (Sermons and Homilies of the Christ of Elqui)*, published together in 1984, received the Richard Wilbur Prize for that year.

Among his other books are *La cueca larga* (The Endless Cueca Dance), 1958, which his sister Violeta set to music; *Versos de salón* (Sitting Room Verses), 1962; *Canciones Rusas* (Russian Songs), 1966; *Obra gruesa* (Framework), 1969; *Emergency Poems,* 1972; *Artefactos* (Artifacts), 1972; *Chistes parфa desorientar a la policía/ poesía* (Jokes to Mislead the Police/Poets), 1983; *Poesía política* (Political Poetry), 1984; *Hojas de Parra,* 1985; *Antipoems: Selected and New,* 1985.

Nicanor Parra has traveled throughout Europe, the Soviet Union, the Orient and both Americas, giving readings and lectures on other Latin American poets.

From 1943 to 1945, Parra studied advanced mechanics at Brown University, Rhode Island, and from 1949 to 1951 he studied at Oxford University under the cosmologist Edward Arthur Milne. In 1969, Parra won the Chilean National Prize of Literature. He is also a member of the Chilean Academy of the Language. He has served as Chairman of the Department of Physics at the University of Chile and has taught Latin American poetry at such renowned institutions as Louisiana, Columbia, Yale, Chicago, and New York Universities. At present, he no longer considers himself an antipoet but rather an *eco-poet,* a poet of survival. He writes against the ecological collapse and the nuclear holocaust and states: "For me, a poet is not only the voice of the tribe, it is its conscience."

INTERVIEWER: Do you see the influence of Lorca's *Romancero Gitano* (Gypsy Songbook) on your first work, *Cancionero sin nombre?*

PARRA: Of course, on every level imaginable.

INTERVIEWER: In your poem "Rompecabezas" (Puzzle), you say, "It is better to play the fool / and say one thing for another." Is this interview with you going to turn into an anti-interview?

PARRA: You might well think so, because I constantly alternate between sense and nonsense. I have a built-in prejudice against localizing myself at any particular point of the spectrum. This interview could very well degenerate into a damned interview.

INTERVIEWER: What do you mean by "damned"?

PARRA: It means just what it says—nothing more.

INTERVIEWER: Chile is considered the poetic country by definition: the literary movement *Modernismo* originated there with the book *Azul* by Rubén Darío, and Gabriela Mistral and Pablo Neruda, both Nobel laureates for poetry, were born in Chile. Why is that country so fertile for poetry?

PARRA: We should add also the name of Vicente Huidobro, who ought to have received the Nobel Prize. I have thought about the question you raise more than once. Generally speaking, I think it is merely a coincidence that so many poets are Chilean. Why must we seek to impose laws on everything? But if you insist, I might speculate that Chile's geographic isolation (because of both the Cordillera and the sea) has something to do with it. It must also be noted that many excellent wines are produced in that country—so, maybe the isolation and the wine have something to do with poetic output.

INTERVIEWER: There are four phases of Chilean poetry associated with four poets: Vicente Huidobro, Gabriela Mistral, Pablo Neruda and Nicanor Parra. What does each of them represent for poetry?

PARRA: Gabriela Mistral was probably the most classical

poet of the four (I define classical as the balance between thought and emotion). She was a poet who had very little to do with *Modernismo*—she was perhaps prior to it, in my own opinion. Neruda, on the other hand, represents the culmination of this movement. It is usually said that Vicente Huidobro was the avant-garde poet by definition. The vanguard, in this sense, probably came after surrealism, which never fully convinced Huidobro. As far as I am concerned, I would like to see myself as an effort to regain the balance between reason and emotion —something which was lost in the seventeenth century with the works of Dryden and Milton, according to T.S. Eliot. Eliot thought that the last true classical poets were the metaphysical poets. If we stretch the point a little, we could say that anti-poetry is really an attempt to rediscover classical poetry. In this sense, Mistral is probably closer to antipoetry than the poets who came before her, although every echo is felt in antipoetry. So, we are talking about a new classicism in which both the romantic spirit and the rupturist experience of our times have to be integrated.

INTERVIEWER: Huidobro said that the poet was a little god. In your "Manifesto," you proclaimed that "The poet is a man like any other / A mason who erects his wall / A builder of doors and windows." What sort of poet are you now: an anti-poet, an eco-poet?

PARRA: I have evolved toward a poetry of global commitment, a poetry which could be called "Eco-commitment." It calls for us to pledge ourselves to the totality of our planet, since it suffers from a chronic disease and is on the brink of death and ecological collapse. We are also facing a nuclear holocaust, so that we cannot continue to resolve problems by conventional wisdom or the rhetoric of confrontation. We have to become conscious of our situation. This is why I now prefer to call myself an eco-poet, a poet of survival. From the point of view of my daily work, I would refer to myself as a teacher of ecological literacy. I work at the University of Chile, and I don't teach theoretical physics (as I used to) or literature, except this semester when I lecture on Gabriela Mistral—my efforts are all geared to the subject of survival. Strangely enough, I have achieved a new type of social realism—the difference is that I am not concerned exclusively with the totality of the species but with the totality of the planet.

INTERVIEWER: You like to walk around with a notebook under your arm. Do you see the poet as the chronicler of his time?

PARRA: Yes, it is true that I walk around with a notebook; in fact, I would like to carry a tape recorder, or even a film camera with me, because poetry arises spontaneously out of dialogue and conversation. Many of the poems in my recent book, *Hojas de Parra,* are based on phrases I overheard and tried to reproduce as faithfully as possible. This has to do with the concept of poetry as conversation, and I am getting closer to conversation per se, because before I used to elaborate a lot on what I heard.

INTERVIEWER: What is the function of the poet: to create a world, make it intelligible, destroy it or debunk it?

PARRA: I must hark back to the questions of ecological collapse and survival. In these days, poets, writers and readers should all engage in a campaign for global survival—the old categories and distinctions must give way before these new priorities.

INTERVIEWER: So you think we must save the world?

PARRA: Yes, we must first save the planet. If we ever achieve this (and many people believe it is too late), then we may once again be able to engage in some of our prior pastimes.

INTERVIEWER: You have been called a debunker of myths. Do you agree with this?

PARRA: I am very happy to be the recipient of such a label, because I believe that it is ancient culture, with all its attendant paradigms, which has led the world to its present dead-end situation. I always suspected that these paradigms stank of rotting fish. The nuclear holocaust and the ecological collapse are not the results of fate. They are the fatal consequences of the two social philosophies that rule our world: capitalism, on the one hand, and socialism as it has developed.

INTERVIEWER: Can you explain the following verse: "God created the world in one week, but I destroy it in one moment"?

PARRA: I don't know what that verse means. I am not particularly fond of explaining jokes or poems. The joke has to make you laugh immediately and the poem has to reach the medulla instantly—if it does not, no amount of explaining is going to make any difference.

INTERVIEWER: In your poem "Cambios de nombre" (Change of Name), you say, "Any self-respecting poet must have his own dictionary, and before I forget, even God's name will have to be changed." What words do you have in your dictionary, and what name do you give God?

PARRA: Before I answer I would like to say that one should not confuse the words of a poem with the feelings of the author. I do not identify with any poem without reservations. My work has a lot to do with the use of masks—it has a lot in common with Rimbaud in this respect. One should not think that anti-poetry is a new ideology. Affirmations or negations should stand by themselves in their poetic medium; otherwise, they are completely irrelevant.

INTERVIEWER: What is the language of the antipoet? Does he create a new vocabulary by destroying language so as to recreate it?

PARRA: When I started writing poetry, I surmised that there were two languages: poetical language, used by poets, and ordinary language, used by people on the street. Since I couldn't find an explanation for the tremendous abyss between the two languages, I felt an obligation to destroy this separation. I believed that ordinary language was always closer to daily experience than poetic language, and that the latter often reeked of anachronisms and other deficiencies. So I thought I should attempt a poetry of the spoken language, an intuition, by the way, which was later verified a posteriori, especially upon reading Heidegger. This philosopher used to say that poetry is the essence of language. All I would add to this formula is that poetry is the essence of spoken language. Ultimately, I do not want to pronounce myself against literature because it is also a part of the human experience, and as such can be a useful starting point toward poetry. Therefore, one should not be astounded to find a cliché in the middle of a spoken poem.

INTERVIEWER: What new phrases or words did you bring to poetry?

PARRA: Antipoetry represents an opening to the entire dictionary. No word should be discarded out of hand. Consequently, every word is a likely candidate for a poem.

INTERVIEWER: How did you manage to include clichés in poems and make them seem as if they belonged there?

PARRA: It is like a collage one does based on a particular cliché. The oft-quoted phrase does not retain its individual characteristics in an antipoem, but rather achieves a peculiar effect as a part of it. It is the same as when one throws a ball at a basket—the ball has to be spun in just the right way to score the point; it cannot just be thrown any old way.

INTERVIEWER: Do you have a realistic vision of the world as an antipoet or as an eco-poet?

PARRA: I proceed from the assumption that all sensations, all experiences constitute a totality that has to be integrated into poetry. The task of the poet is to construct a model of the universe.

INTERVIEWER: You have said that "poetry can lead a country to ruin if one is not careful with it." Does the poet have a mission, and does his poetry have to communicate a positive message?

PARRA: I now think so. As they say, the poet must not only be the voice of the tribe, but also the conscience of the tribe, especially if his country is in an ambiguous situation like that of Chile. In my country, a return to democracy is absolutely essential because without democracy nothing can be done. One cannot fight for survival, at the very least, because dictatorships, whether capitalist or socialist, do not have the means to process the facts concerning the ecological collapse or the nuclear holocaust.

INTERVIEWER: In her book *La poesía de Nicanor Parra,* Marlene Gottlieb states that you have "achieved the liberation of poetry." What made you break with the traditional molds of poetic language to achieve antipoetry first, and later eco-poetry?

PARRA: I always thought that traditional poetry did not refer to the experiences of the ordinary man, but rather displaced these events to a special plateau. I always believed that it would be more adequate to examine and write about experiences as they are, without embellishments. If "realism" means the sort of belief I have just described, then antipoetry has more to do with it than with symbolism, for instance.

INTERVIEWER: The rallying cry of the generation of 1938, to which you belong, was "Fight the metaphor, death to imagery, long live concrete reality, and once again let there be clarity." Is this phrase representative of your poetry?

PARRA: I do not work with metaphors or images; my concern is another. I do not go seeking the unknown the way Rimbaud, the symbolists, and the *Modernistas* did. I only want to reflect reality as it is seen by the ordinary man.

INTERVIEWER: Could we then call you a poet of clarity and light?

PARRA: When I was twenty and some odd years, I wrote a book, which I never published, called "La Luz del día" (The Light of Day). It is from this work that the idea of poetry of clarity came. I think you are referring to a very learned essay written long ago by the distinguished Chilean critic and poet Tomás Lago.

INTERVIEWER: If we postulate two types of poetry, poetry of night and poetry of dawn, how would you compare your own poetry to Neruda's?

PARRA: Neruda's poetry is more a poetry of night, as he himself said on more than one occasion. But he eventually ended up writing a poetry of dawn, like "Extravagario" and "Las odas elementales" (The Primary Odes). The situation is reversed in my own case; I started with poetry of day, poetry of dawn, but I don't want to deny the validity of shadows in poetry. A poem like "El hombre imaginario" (The Imaginary Man), for instance, is not ashamed to be both musical and symbolic.

INTERVIEWER: How do you manage to juxtapose puzzles and clarity?

PARRA: I am not really sure of what I do. Probably through my sense of smell, which is basic for me.

INTERVIEWER: Your sense of smell more so than that of sight?

PARRA: No, smell in the metaphorical sense. There is also a visual smell and an auditory smell, or we could also call it the seventh sense.

INTERVIEWER: Your first poems were published in 1937 with the title of *Cancionero sin nombre.* Your second book, *Poemas y antipoemas,* appeared in 1954. Could you clarify the terms "poems" and "antipoems"?

PARRA: I thought I had originated the concept of "antipoem." I was unaware that it already existed. It came to me from reading a book by the French poet Henri Pichette, *Apoèmes,* which I saw in a bookstore display in Oxford in 1949 or thereabouts. I was very taken with that book, and as I have said in many interviews, the word *antipoem* came to mind immediately. I thought that Pichette's book would have better been titled "Antipoem," because that word is strong and produces a more powerful impact. The term floated around my consciousness for a while, until I finally dared to use it as a title for one of my books. But I thought something should be added to "antipoems," so I tagged on "poems." The reason I did this is because antipoetry really has to do with contradiction; it is not satisfied with only half of reality, it must encompass the totality of experience. It is more a synthetic rather than an analytical poetry. In those days, I was a student of physics, so I would not be surprised if Bohr's atomic model had influenced me. Bohr believed that the nucleus of the atom had a positive charge, while its surrounding ring had a negative one, and people thought that the atom was the basic element of the physical world. In the same way, the spiritual world would also have positive and negative charges, thus poem and antipoem.

INTERVIEWER: Do you know beforehand which of your verses will turn into a poem and which will turn into an antipoem?

PARRA: Every verse is both, with a few exceptions. Some people think, for instance, that "El hombre imaginario" is more poem than antipoem, and they say this also about *Canciones Rusas.* In reality, I used the term *antipoem* in an offhand way, and as if by sleight of hand I had to carry the label like a cross all my life.

INTERVIEWER: Now that you write eco-poetry, can anti-poetry still be a part of it?

PARRA: Yes. The basic premise of antipoetry was a categorical rejection of any dogma, except the one I am now enunciating. So, I had to work simultaneously with affirmations and negations. In this sense, antipoetry was always a Taoist poetry. It is not a coincidence that for the past ten years I have been interested in Taoist philosophy. I feel that the Tao Te Ching should be considered like a sort of primer of sight, sound and the other senses, with respect to any inner exploration. I can no longer imagine myself without this type of philosophy.

INTERVIEWER: What would be the definition of an eco-poet?

PARRA: The eco-poet also works with contradiction, he defends nature, but he cannot fall into the trap of a new dogmatism. So there are some eco-poems which are apparently anti-ecological, like the following: "I don't see the need for all this fuss, we all know the world is at its end." It must be kept in mind that any type of dogmatism, including ecological dogmatism, produces a hardening of the soul. To avoid this hardening, this new dictatorship, this new central committee, one has to denounce even ecological dogmatism. Paradoxically, this is also the soul regulating itself. The man who only affirms runs the risk of freezing up inside. Constant movement, vital motion is crucially important for me.

INTERVIEWER: In your "Manifesto," you say, "The poets came down from Olympus." Why did you feel the need to take poetry from the world of the chosen and bring it to the street?

PARRA: I think traditional poetry was very elitist, as were its poets. They all had tremendous egos and a reputation as clairvoyants (remember Rimbaud's "Lettre du clairvoyant"). I felt that this approach was thoroughly undemocratic. I believe in horizontal relations rather than vertical ones.

INTERVIEWER: Upon reading your book *Versos de salón,* the Chilean critic Hernán del Solar commented that one could not talk about your books in a soft voice: "One must scream, gesticulate, as if at the outset of a fight." Why does your work create controversy wherever it is read?

PARRA: I would say because I do not write about beauty in the traditional sense, but rather tackle reality with all its qualities and defects. There is a tendency in the arts to overlook problems, to sidestep ugliness, disagreement, nastiness. Antipoetry, however, presents both the hideousness and the beauty of the world.

INTERVIEWER: Do you think that your current poetry would create the same polemics?

PARRA: I don't know, we would have to consult the specialists, who are the distinguished readers.

INTERVIEWER: When Gabriela Mistral read your first book, she said, "We have come face to face with a poet who will achieve international fame." What do you think about that prophecy?

PARRA: She was a very generous woman. It's all I can say.

INTERVIEWER: If she could be with us this afternoon, what would you tell her?

PARRA: I would invite her to join me in the crusade to save the world. I am sure she would accept unconditionally.

INTERVIEWER: In 1962, Fernando Alegría wrote an article called "Nicanor Parra at the Borders of Realism."

PARRA: My poetry is real but it is also unreal. It does not want to be restricted to any particular point on the spiritual spectrum—it is very ambitious.

INTERVIEWER: Alfonso Calderón wrote an article called "Nicanor Parra, a Breathing Exercise." What is your reaction to that?

PARRA: I once described a book of mine as "breathing exercises." I have been grappling with the idea of poetry as a breathing exercise for a long time. In fact, in some of my anthologies, "Breathing Exercise" is used as the title for a group of poems. So, I am not surprised in the least.

INTERVIEWER: Why "breathing," and why "exercise"?

PARRA: Breathing exercise seems like a very mysterious thing to me. Strangely enough, breathing exercise should now be applied to the planet in order for the earth to survive.

INTERVIEWER: In "Advertencia al lector" (Warning to the Reader), you say, "And I bury my pens in the heads of the illustrious readers!" Do you think of the reader when you write, and who is the reader for you?

PARRA: This question interests me greatly, as I have been very preoccupied by it lately. Poetry and antipoetry are very playful, and the games are not played alone, as this is openly frowned upon. Two people are needed to play. My relationship with the reader was always a bit playful; in fact, to use a Chilean term, it was a type of *hueveo* (fooling around). To fool around with the reader and provoke him out of his complacency—this is central to antipoetry. When I was a child, we used to play a lot, especially when the teachers made us single file before entering the classroom. We used to play a game called *chuletas de lujo* (gratuitous knocks), in which we kicked someone's behind without the teacher noticing. I always thought this game was very funny. I am always playing and provoking the reader.

INTERVIEWER: So you want the reader to participate actively in your work?

PARRA: Exactly, that's the idea.

INTERVIEWER: Something similar to what the writers of the "Boom" did with their prose.

PARRA: I really don't know much about the Boom.

INTERVIEWER: You once said, "This is why I keep knocking myself out, to reach the soul of the reader." What is your relation to the reader? Does it differ in a poem, an antipoem, and an eco-poem?

PARRA: Of course. In an eco-poem the goal is to raise the awareness of the reader so he will join the ecological movement, which is defined as "a socioeconomic movement, based on the idea of harmony between human beings and their environment, which fights for a playful, creative, equalitarian, pluralistic life, free of exploitation and premised on communication and cooperation." This quote is known as the "Slab for Salvation," or the "Proposal of Daimiel." Daimiel is a small village in the south of Spain, and this declaration is the work of Spanish ecologists.

INTERVIEWER: What do you demand of the reader?

PARRA: I push him. The idea is to force him to be attentive and to enjoy himself with the author.

INTERVIEWER: Do you see poetry as an autobiographical vehicle in which you recount some anecdote or story in the first person?

PARRA: It could be that as well, of course; one should not discard any method out of hand. For instance, for a period I worked with the surrealistic method of automatic writing. But I have also worked with the method of prefabricated expressions. In *Los versos de salón,* for example, I chose a topic and wrote

down various verses as they occurred to me, and only later
would I organize them. Antipoetry was a highly experimental
endeavor. I must reiterate that I do not reject or deny any
method out of hand.

INTERVIEWER: In "Advertencia al lector," you said, "My
poetry can perfectly well lead nowhere." Would you say the
same thing this afternoon?

PARRA: Absolutely not. It has to lead somewhere, it has to
lead to the salvation of the planet.

INTERVIEWER: In some of your poems you seem to personify
poetry. For instance, "Poetry has behaved well / I have
behaved horrendously / Poetry was the end of me / Poetry is
done with me."

PARRA: Those verses interest me because of their ambivalence. "Poetry was the end of me / Poetry is done with me" can
be interpreted in many different ways. I like this ambiguity. I
succeed in breaking the strictly linear meaning of the poem.
There is also the playful aspect of making these unnecessarily
categorical assertions in all their uselessness.

INTERVIEWER: In your poem "Es olvido" (It's Oblivion),
you say, "Today is a blue spring day, I think I will die of
poetry." Why?

PARRA: I must once again repeat that either the verse is self-
explanatory or there is no explanation possible. When I say "I
will die of poetry," it seems to me that this produces an immediate effect—poetry as illness, poetry as the possibility of
death. I will die of poetry as other people will die of cancer. I
think that it is an interesting and significant statement.

INTERVIEWER: In one poem, you say, "Free us from poets
and prose writers who seek only personal fame." In another,
you state, "I swear I will never write another verse."

PARRA: Once again, I must repeat that one should not
become attached to the literal meaning of the verses, and that
the author should not be identified with the lyrical speaker.
Perhaps the character no longer wanted to write poetry, but this

might not be the author's view. It could also be that the poet was going through a bleak period, but this does not mean that it has to remain bleak forever.

INTERVIEWER: Why do you write?

PARRA: Because I feel the undeniable need to maintain my spirit in balance, for one thing. I think poetry and art are endeavors to maintain spiritual equilibrium. In fact, I think we will not be able to consider eliminating the arts until we achieve the perfect society.

INTERVIEWER: What roles do irony and parody play in your work?

PARRA: It has always been said that irony was a way to distance oneself from the world. I do not identify with Western society, nor am I one hundred percent against it. I am a sort of clown who is freed through toys such as irony and parody, which are not only the products of civilization but also the results of certain innate existential tendencies. I am referring especially to the passing of time, disease, and death. Schiller was quite right when he said man is here to be free and that man can only be free when he plays as little children do. Of course, the toys which adults play with are different from the ones children use. The toys of adults are the passage of time, love denied, diseases and death.

INTERVIEWER: What are the devices needed to write a poem? How do you begin a poem?

PARRA: I consider myself an experimental poet. I don't stand still on any particular spot. Sometimes I begin a poem from a phrase that I have heard somewhere; other times I begin from a reading or a dream. I am open to all possibilities.

INTERVIEWER: What are you writing now?

PARRA: I am writing a text and I am unsure how it will turn out. But at least I have the title, "Cueca a cámara lenta." Cueca is a dynamic and spontaneous dance, so I am very interested in the effect of having this "dance in slow motion." There is a previous expression, "explosion in slow motion," but I wanted to transform this explosion into something more earthy, thus this Chilean dance in slow motion. Perhaps it is a means to demythify folkloric dancing. But at the moment I am very motivated by the title, although not exclusively. I have just completed another book, *Preguntas y respuestas* (Questions and Answers).

INTERVIEWER: Between whom?

PARRA: The characters are not defined. These are questions and answers which can be justified only within the world of words and concepts. It does not mean, in any way, that the person who answers is identifying himself. They are questions and answers in a vacuum, practically speaking.

INTERVIEWER: In one poem you say, "My tongue sticks to the roof of my mouth / I have an unquenchable desire to express myself / But I cannot construct a phrase." What is the word for you?

PARRA: "In the beginning there was the Word," Saint John says somewhere. It is a way of indicating that words have indisputable importance in the lives of humans. When the word disappears, mankind will probably also vanish.

INTERVIEWER: In another poem you say, "He who wants to get to paradise / From the small bourgeois has to evolve / Through road of art for art's sake / And swallow a lot of saliva." What do you think of *Modernismo* and Rubén Darío's art for art's sake?

PARRA: I enjoy the musicality of Verlaine, I take pleasure in the lightning of Rimbaud and the empty steps of Mallarmé. Everything is justified by its time. But I would like to reiterate that we are not here to play these kinds of games, even though antipoetry is defined as playful. The games with which we must concern ourselves now are games for survival.

INTERVIEWER: Juan Ramón Jiménez once said, "I work on my poetry the way one works on God." Gabriela Mistral wrote, "Every act of creation will leave you humbled, because it was inferior to your dream, and inferior to God's marvelous conception, Nature." What would you say?

PARRA: It gives me the shivers to use the word *God*. I would prefer to use the word *Tao* instead. When someone asked Lao Tzu what the Tao was, he shrugged and said, "I don't know, but the more we talk about it, the farther we distance ourselves from it." There is one thing which is clear, however, the Tao seems to be prior to God. That is all I can say about God—I dare say no more. I prefer to work on the human level. I am a poet of the human more than of the divine, although God does slip in there through the back door, since he is a basic foundation of Western society, and the antipoet wants to include everything. But this does not mean that he identifies with Christianity in any way; it is just one of the tools of the trade.

INTERVIEWER: Do you believe in inspiration?

PARRA: Sometimes we are in the mood to write while other times we are not. If by inspiration you mean being in the mood to write a poem, then yes, I believe in it.

INTERVIEWER: Do you like to polish your work?

PARRA: As I said before, I have worked with all conceivable methods: I wrote the last poem of *Poemas y antipoemas* in fifteen minutes, using the automatic writing method, while I spent eleven years polishing the first poem of that work, which was really an infantile and trifling effort.

INTERVIEWER: Do you feel humble before your work?

PARRA: I don't much understand the concept of humility, but I can say that many of the works I write are far superior to their author.

INTERVIEWER: Do you attach more importance to the body or to the soul?

PARRA: I don't know what the difference between body and soul is; I think they are merely crutches and simplistic distinctions. I refuse to dichotomize.

INTERVIEWER: Then why do you say you want "to get to the soul of the reader"?

PARRA: Those are linguistic expressions that have their own

charges and directions. I don't consider myself a preacher in that type of poetry; I don't even preach in *Sermons and Homilies of the Christ of Elqui.* I wrote that book to demonstrate the futility of preaching. Nowadays, I admit, I do nothing but preach, although in relation to the ecological collapse and the nuclear holocaust.

INTERVIEWER: What inspired you to write *The Christ of Elqui?*

PARRA: Like other writers under Chile's dictatorship, I needed to express certain things that cannot be said openly.

INTERVIEWER: Is it a song to freedom then?

PARRA: Absolutely not. In that book I speak through a mask. This is a device that various other authors have used. Enrique Lihn, for instance, made use of a mask which he called Gérard de Pompier. Christian Hunneus spoke through a mask called Gaspar Ruiz, and Enrique Lafourcarde spoke through a mask called Lafourchette, the Count of Lafourchette.

INTERVIEWER: And in this instance, you speak through . . .

PARRA: I am speaking through the mask of the Christ of Elqui, who was a real person, a sort of liberation theosophist who lived in Chile at the beginning of this century, and who was at the same time an illiterate and a neurotic. His name was Domingo Zárate Vega.

INTERVIEWER: So he is not Christ, but the Christ of Elqui.

PARRA: Yes, he is the Christ of Elqui. He let himself be called that. He was a character who was more comical than dramatic.

INTERVIEWER: And how did you develop the section of questions and answers that takes place between the Christ of Elqui and Nicanor Parra?

PARRA: Perhaps it was a voice . . . perhaps a journalist, perhaps an interviewer like you. I think that poetic content can perfectly well come from an interview.

INTERVIEWER: Where did you write that poem? In Chile or abroad?

PARRA: I wrote both the first and the second volumes in Chile. If you recall, that work deals with abstract topics but also with very specific subjects which have a lot to do with Chile's dictatorship.

INTERVIEWER: You have also said, "The Holy Bible / is the only true book / all the others are pretty but false."

PARRA: It is a way of noting the dogmatism of religions and ideologies.

INTERVIEWER: What does the Bible mean to you?

PARRA: In that passage you quoted, I am merely speaking like a preacher. I am imitating him and making fun of him. But in a surreptitious way (because every mockery contains a grain of truth), there is a little ambivalence there which I find relevant.

INTERVIEWER: When you say the Bible is the only book, you are really saying the opposite?

PARRA: Yes and no.

INTERVIEWER: What is God for you?

PARRA: I don't have the God of the Christians nor any personal gods, although I have inevitably been influenced somewhat by Christianity. It has been pummeled into us so much since childhood that it would not be surprising to find an atheist all of a sudden deciding to accept the Sacrament from a Catholic priest.

INTERVIEWER: Yes, but you are not an atheist.

PARRA: No, I do not define myself as an atheist. I think the best way to refer to this subject is the Taoist method. So if I have to define myself on this topic, I would say I am a Taoist monk, or an apprentice Taoist monk.

INTERVIEWER: Can you add something about your concept of God as Father/Mother? When you speak of God in your poem, you say, "Our Mother who art in Heaven..."

PARRA: Obviously I am making a reference to the feminist movement here. Why should God have to be male? God could perfectly well be female. But I am not interested in this issue as much as with the effect that the image of a female God (to which we are not accustomed) produces on the readers. I want to stimulate and provoke them. I want to place them in unexpected situations and see how they will react.

INTERVIEWER: And what does the mother mean to you?

PARRA: In *Sermons and Homilies of the Christ of Elqui* certain views and feelings of the author become apparent. I think that the mother is such an important phenomenon that even she is not aware of its full magnitude. Before the mother dies, men tend to think of her as an object. But once she is gone, certain very mysterious signs appear—it would seem that a mother is far more than we can ever imagine!

INTERVIEWER: It has been said that all poets carry within themselves the children they once were. What does childhood represent for you?

PARRA: Throughout this conversation, I have referred to children's games. I use the behavior of children extensively in my work, as well as the devices of the Chilean circus, which I saw frequently as a child. I was very struck by the interaction between the mischievous clown and Tony, another character of the Chilean circus, who incarnates innocence. Good and bad are always at odds, and according to the philosophy underlying Chilean popular comedy, innocence and goodness will always prevail.

INTERVIEWER: You have an excellent relationship with your children.

PARRA: Let's say I have a relationship with almost all of them, although I have a great deal of trouble with one of my children, to such an extent that I can hardly talk about it.

INTERVIEWER: How many children do you have?

PARRA: Six.

INTERVIEWER: In *Sermons and Homilies of the Christ of Elqui* you write, "Competition does not resolve anything / Because we are not racehorses / I condemn them with all my heart / In this I am intransigent."

PARRA: I identify with the Christ of Elqui there, with respect to every sort of contest or competition. I remember that in Cuba they used to speak about emulation. But I don't even believe in emulating; on this topic, I am in agreement with a basic tenet of philosophical anarchism: "From each according to his will, and to each according to his whimsy."

INTERVIEWER: What are the subjects which most concern you?

PARRA: At this moment, I am most concerned with the survival of the planet—I have said this in many ways and I don't mind repeating myself in the least. What most matters to me is the health of the planet, and the prevention of an ecological collapse and a nuclear holocaust. I used to be interested in other things before, like the puzzle of passing time, diseases, love denied. But I think these are superfluous luxuries by comparison with the tremendous problems confronting us today.

INTERVIEWER: How did this change in perspective come about?

PARRA: In the past, we weren't aware of the condition of our planet; before the book by Rachel Carson, before the ecological alarm which was rung in the United States in the 1960s by the hippies, none of us were really aware of the condition of the earth. Every revolutionary spoke about the forces of evolution, of production; no one spoke about the forces of destruction. Everyone thought the planet was infinite with infinite resources, and with ample space to dispose of all waste products. But then, all of a sudden, we realized that the planet was finite, and our outlook changed completely. It became apparent that the earth was being transformed into a huge dumpster, and that's when the ecological alarm was rung. I was very involved in this changing awareness, as I was in the United States at the time, very close to the hippies in general and to Allen Ginsberg in particular. I took part in the Earth Day celebrations in 1970. I can remember some of the sayings scrawled on the walls like, "Be kind to me, I am a river, Clear Water Campaign." I became aware then of the state of our world, but of course many things have happened since. It has become clear that to be able to answer the question of what must be done, almost all the paradigms of our Western society must be revised.

INTERVIEWER: In "Hay un día feliz" (There is a Happy Day), you say: "Believe me, I never thought for an instant that I would return to this beloved country. But now that I have returned I cannot understand how I could ever separate myself from it." What does Chile mean for you and how would you describe Chilean reality?

PARRA: Chile's present situation is well known. Due to the polarization that inevitably occurs because of the rhetoric of confrontation, a particular dictatorship arose. A dictatorship would have resulted in any event. That is why I now argue for the refutation of the rhetoric of confrontation, because it inevitably leads to polarization, then to dictatorship, and finally to apocalypse.

INTERVIEWER: Have you lived through the experience of exile?

PARRA: I haven't had that distinction. I chose to remain in Chile, although in my country we also speak of internal exile. Obviously, I have more to do with internal exile than with the world of the Chilean establishment.

INTERVIEWER: You tell of your first encounter with the sea in the beautiful poem "Se canta al mar" (I Sing to the Sea). What does it represent for you?

PARRA: In that poem I am merely reproducing the experience I had when my father took me to the south of Chile and I first saw the sea. I was very taken in by it, and so this poem, quite simply, was the result of that first encounter.

INTERVIEWER: What is the meaning of the poem "Viva la cordillera de los Andes / Muera la cordillera de la Costa!" (Long live the Cordillera of the Andes / Death to the Cordillera of the Coast!)?

PARRA: It has none. There is no meaning there except the gratuitousness of the affirmation and the negation. I would now say that I am laughing at all dogma through those two verses.

INTERVIEWER: In your poem "Solo de piano" (Piano Solo), you say, "Trees are nothing but furniture in motion: they are but chairs and tables in perpetual movement!" What does nature mean to you?

PARRA: At that time I had nothing to do with ecology but, strangely enough, there are ecological intuitions there. From this perspective it could be described as a criticism of the capitalist concept of nature: the woods as a source of income, as the possibility of furniture. I am surprised that one can find the seeds of this idea in works written far before the ecological alarm.

INTERVIEWER: Your sister Violeta defined your work *La cueca larga* (The Endless Cueca Dance) as "urban folklore." Can you speak about the collaboration between the two of you?

PARRA: She herself explained this in "Décimas." Violeta was younger than I and she did not have the good fortune to be able to attend universities as I did, so I evolved far more quickly than she at the outset, on the intellectual level. I therefore put my knowledge at her disposal. Between us a sort of telepathy developed; we were like communicating vessels. In fact, one of my poems ends with the phrase, "We are the same person. Don't take me seriously, but believe me." She also wrote a phrase which has often been repeated: "Without Nicanor, there is no Violeta." I don't know if I could say the same thing about her, because since I was much older I saw the world long before she did. I gave her the first push, and then it turned out she had wings of her own and flew much farther than all of us put together.

INTERVIEWER: Why were you awarded the National Prize of Literature in 1969?

PARRA: I really wonder why.

INTERVIEWER: What was your reaction?

PARRA: I had a very uncivilized reaction: I rejected the diploma and the honors but I accepted the check. I argued that the prize wasn't really a prize at all; it should have really been called the National Literary Tip, because it was such a miserly award. At the time, I also said that this was merely a means by which the government attempted to repair its guilty conscience without resolving any problems. Paradoxically, it is the military dictatorship that solved a problem which Chilean democracy was never able to. Everything is so complex. The National Prize for Literature is now a lifetime pension. One must "render unto Caesar the things which are Caesar's."

INTERVIEWER: Is *Martín Fierro* your favorite book?

PARRA: I have said that on many occasions.

INTERVIEWER: Is it related to *La cueca larga* in any way?

PARRA: I would say that it is not, because one cannot hope to accomplish what Hernández did. He pumped that particular mine dry. *Martín Fierro* was the basis for a new world, a new universe, while *La cueca larga* is much more limited in scope. Quite simply, *La cueca larga* has to do with a local Chilean tradition; it is a series of *seguidillas* (popular verses) which are not even octosyllabic as is *Martín Fierro*. But there is some resemblance between them in the sense that they are both relatively popular forms: *La cueca larga* is a more direct type of poetry than *Martín Fierro,* which is written in sextets.

INTERVIEWER: Do you have a favorite work from among all your writings?

PARRA: It is usually said that my most important book is *Poems and Antipoems.* I also have a weakness for *Versos de salón.* I wrote each of those books for a specific reason. Sometimes I think that the only works that are worthy are certain brief texts like *Artefactos.* But these poems are far removed from me now. What happens with books is the same thing that happens with children: as time goes on they become independent of you, and you no longer identify with any of them.

INTERVIEWER: Which authors do you admire?

PARRA: Practically speaking, there is no author whom I do not admire. I once asked a mathematics teacher whom I respected greatly what was his opinion of certain works. Without having to refer to any of them, he simply said that there was no work which was absolutely worthless.

INTERVIEWER: In "Epitafio," you say, "I was what I was: A mixture / Of vinegar and oil / A combination of angel and beast!" In "Autoretrato" (Self-Portrait), you speak of your "cadaverous white cheeks." Why do you like to create a caricature of yourself, almost as if you wanted to punish yourself?

PARRA: I only have to look in the mirror.

INTERVIEWER: Then you don't know how to look at yourself! You have said, "I am the Individual, capitalized."

PARRA: The capital should be replaced with a lower-case letter. Of course, I am no longer the "Individual" now; I would like to be a member of the community.

INTERVIEWER: Which community?

PARRA: The eco-community.

INTERVIEWER: Who is Nicanor Parra?

PARRA: I would really like to know. Nevertheless, when Manuel Rojas, the famous Chilean novelist, was asked about the Parra family, he said, "I thought Nicanor was the genius of the family until I met his sister Violeta, but nowadays I prefer their brother Roberto"—author of a long poem that was made into a hit play.

Elena Poniatowska

Elena Poniatowska

The Mexican writer Elena Poniatowska is both a journalist and a novelist. Winner of the National Journalism Award in 1978 for best interviewer, she has given the interview a new dimension and turned it into a literary genre. It has been said of her that as an interviewer she applies the techniques of an inquisitor, a confessor, a psychiatrist, a torturer and an adviser to the lovelorn, all in one.

Elena Poniatowska was born on May 19, 1933, in Paris, France. She is the descendant of a prominent family that included Prince Poniatowski, Marshal of France under Napoleon, and Stanislaw August, the last King of Poland. When she was eight, she moved to Mexico with her mother and sister. Since then, she has devoted herself completely to her adopted country and to its people. In fact, one of her reasons for writing has been to defend the marginals, the poor people on the streets whose voice has been silenced.

We may call her a chronicler of her time. She personally witnessed the horrors of the student rebellion of 1968. She put down her recollection of that upheaval in a book titled *La noche de Tlatelolco* (*Massacre in Mexico*), considered by many to be her masterpiece. In 1968, her only brother Jan, who was twenty-one, died and all her books since then have been dedicated to him.

Elena Poniatowska looks up to Juan Rulfo and Octavio Paz as writers who have guided and inspired her. Other authors she read when she was growing up were mostly French Catholic writers, such as Jacques and Raïssa Maritain, Daniel Rops, and Georges Bernanos.

Elena Poniatowska began writing simultaneously as a novelist and journalist. In 1954, she published her first novel, *Lilus Kikus,* in which she disclosed the magic world of childhood. At the same time she started writing for the daily *Excélsior* and then began a long career of journalism, to which she has brought the vitality discovered in "new journalism." It has been said of her, "Her gift as a narrator turns whatever she touches into something personal."

Elena Poniatowska is the author of many books, among them:

Hasta no verte Jesús mío, 1969 (*Until We Meet Again,* 1987),
winner of the Mazatlán Prize, 1970; *La noche de Tlatelolco,* 1971
(*Massacre in Mexico,* 1975), winner of the Villaurrutia Prize in 1970
which she rejected; *Querido Diego, te abraza Quiela,* 1978 (*Dear
Diego,* 1986); *De noche vienes* (You Come by Night), 1979; *Fuerte
es el silencio* (Strong Is the Silence), 1980; *Domingo 7* (Sunday 7),
1982; *¡Ay vida, no me mereces!* (Oh Life! You Don't Deserve Me),
1985; *La "Flor de lis"* (Fleur-de-lis), 1988; *Nada nadie* (Nothing,
No One), 1988; *Tina Modotti,* 1989.

  Elena Poniatowska studied in both France and the United States.
She is the mother of three grown children, Emmanuel, Felipe and
Paula. She is the founder of Editorial Siglo Veinti-uno and the
Cineteca Nacional.

INTERVIEWER: You obtained the National Journalism Award
in 1978 for best interviewer. Now the tables are turned, and I
hope you won't mind answering my questions. When did you
first feel the need to write?

PONIATOWSKA: Unlike many noted authors, I cannot say
that I would have died had I been unable to write. On the contrary, there were many things I wanted to do more so than
writing, like singing for instance. When I was fifteen, I dreamed
of singing in a Parisian cabaret, an almost unreachable goal. I
started writing for the daily *Excélsior* in 1954, because I wanted
to go to France to do interviews. I thought that through my
grandfather, who was a well-known writer, I could meet intellectuals and interview them for the paper. But what actually

happened was that I remained in Mexico for two years working for *Excélsior* before I went to France.

INTERVIEWER: Who was your grandfather?

PONIATOWSKA: My grandfather's name was André Poniatowski. He wrote his memoirs and founded the Pacific Sierra Railways in San Francisco, among the many interesting things he did.

INTERVIEWER: Have you ever written poetry?

PONIATOWSKA: When I was young I wrote poetry. In fact, some of those poems were published in an anthology.

INTERVIEWER: But you first started writing as a journalist?

PONIATOWSKA: Yes, although I had written a short novel called *Lilus Kikus.* It was part of a series of books called "Los Presentes" (Today's Writers) which also included the first works of Carlos Fuentes, Jorge Emilio Pacheco and several other Latin American authors.

INTERVIEWER: How did you come up with the title *Lilus Kikus?*

PONIATOWSKA: It was an invention, it just occurred to me.

INTERVIEWER: Do you think one can be a journalist and a novelist at the same time?

PONIATOWSKA: I think one can try to be, and we can see that many writers and novelists were journalists for long periods of their lives. This is particularly true of all testimonial novels, like Truman Capote's *In Cold Blood,* which are based on reporting and journalism. These are in-depth news features transformed into novels. This is also true of the "new journalism," as practiced by people like Tom Wolfe.

INTERVIEWER: Might one say that you employ journalistic techniques in your novels and that you give journalism a literary form?

PONIATOWSKA: Yes, one could say that, although I believe that the novel always goes far beyond journalism. I think that the value of *In Cold Blood* lies in how well written it is and in the fact that it goes much further than journalism.

INTERVIEWER: The new journalism has had a very big influence on your work.

PONIATOWSKA: My work hasn't been influenced very much by either the new journalism or my own life as a journalist, although I owe much to my profession.

INTERVIEWER: Both your narrative and journalistic work blend the genres of letter writing, the interview, the chronicle, the diary, the picaresque story, and poetry into a highly original collage. How did you find your style?

PONIATOWSKA: My style derives from my daily life. In the first place, I was not born in Mexico but in France, and this accounted for my great interest and curiosity in everything that surrounded me, particularly the language of the people, which was a very new one for me. Before learning Spanish, I spoke French and a little English. I was born into a French family of Polish origin. Among my ancestors was the last King of Poland, Stanislaw August, who ruled in the eighteenth century.

INTERVIEWER: Who was Prince Josef Poniatowski?

PONIATOWSKA: Napoleon appointed him Marshal of France. There is a whole series of books on the Poniatowskis, among them *Les Poniatowski de Florence*.

INTERVIEWER: How did you come to identify so much with the Mexican people?

PONIATOWSKA: My father was a Frenchman of Polish extraction, but my mother came from a family of reactionary Mexican landowners. She speaks much better French than she does Spanish, because she was born in Paris. My great-grandmother, Elena Idaroff, was a Russian who married a Mexican, Felipe Iturbe. My grandmother was known as the "Madonna of the Sleeping" because she used to travel a lot with her family by train and lived in hotels in France, England and Spain, where she brought her own sheets, plates and samovar. So all this rootlessness affected me as a child and I wanted to belong to a country. As things turned out, that country happened to be Mexico, where I arrived at the age of eight, longing to be

Mexican with all my heart.

INTERVIEWER: What is amazing is that you have become the spokeswoman for the Mexican people and all their pain and happiness.

PONIATOWSKA: If you say so... all I can say is that I became particularly interested in working-class people. I must say that no one from my own social class or milieu has enriched me as much as Jesusa Palancares, a woman I found extraordinarily fascinating, because her world was so different from mine. In fact, I based a character in one of my novels on her, which she didn't recognize as herself. When I tried to read her the novel, she said I had made everything up and none of it was true.

INTERVIEWER: Can you pinpoint the moment when you make the move from reality to fiction?

PONIATOWSKA: It happens all the time, because I have written fictional stories, and the book which just came out, *Flor de lis,* is fiction as well. But I think that all fiction is based on reality, even that of Borges and Marcel Schwob. It can be a literary reality, but it is still a reality.

INTERVIEWER: What do you think of the cover of your book *Domingo 7* in which you are depicted as the guardian angel of the Mexican people?

PONIATOWSKA: That cover was due to the great generosity of Rogelio Naranjo, who drew a caricature of me in the likeness of one of Dürer's angels.

INTERVIEWER: What does language mean to you?

PONIATOWSKA: In the first place, words are a miracle, and they also represent the possibility of communicating with others. Humans can communicate in so many ways: Gaby Brimmer, for instance, who had cerebral palsy, used to communicate with her eyes and through touch.

INTERVIEWER: It has been said of you, "Her gift as a narrator makes everything she touches personal." Do you think that is why you have given the genre of the interview a new dimension?

PONIATOWSKA: What happened in Mexico is that in the name of objectivity, they used to do interviews and chronicles which were very impersonal and full of clichés. For instance, they used to say, "Ecstatic crowd received President of the Republic," or, "An enthusiastic crowd gives President standing ovation." When I started going to these events, however, I began to look at what was really happening, and if the President tripped, I would write, "The President almost fell flat on his face at the entrance to the Chamber of Deputies." Although this made my reports sound very disrespectful, it also gave them a sort of validity. I used to say things like "The President's wife wore a horrible hat," without the least awareness of what I was doing and without any idea of who was powerful and who was not. So, this created a style that gave greater freshness, and in some measure greater accuracy, to the interview and the chronicle.

INTERVIEWER: It has been said that as an interviewer you are an inquisitor, a confessor, a psychiatrist, a torturer and an adviser to the lovelorn, all in one. What do you think about that?

PONIATOWSKA: I became very close to some of my interviewees, like Luis Buñuel, for instance. I think I am a shy person deep down, and so was Buñuel. But through an interview and a visit we made to a jail where we both had friends locked up, a long and deep friendship was born. In the case of many other interviewees, friendships also developed with people I would not have known had I not been a journalist or interviewer, so I've been very lucky.

INTERVIEWER: How did you come to write *Domingo 7,* that book in which you converse with the seven presidential candidates in 1982?

PONIATOWSKA: That was a journalistic book and it is the one I like least—I don't even have a copy of it in my library. It was done exceedingly quickly and I could have raised far more incisive questions than I did. But, I am not a political expert.

INTERVIEWER: How is it then that you became involved in the world of politics in defending the missing, the marginals and other undocumented people?

PONIATOWSKA: The only posture that I have maintained through the years is my defense of the weak and oppressed of this earth. I believe that everything is political, and as such it should concern all of us. Authors who claim they don't deal with politics in their work are being naïve, because even that is a political stance.

INTERVIEWER: Out of all your interviewees, which did you like best?

PONIATOWSKA: I suppose it would be Luis Buñuel, as he impressed me throughout his life on each occasion we met. I have also been fascinated by scientists even though they are not particularly good subjects for an interview, because they usually don't express themselves very well. Nonetheless, their thoroughness, modesty, and the exactitude of their world has always attracted me. I think that a good interview always results if people have something to say, particularly if they speak about their ideas rather than about themselves. On the other hand, the people who do not impress me are those who sound like a record and have a set message. This usually happens in the case of actors, who put on a show for interviewers. I can see how theatrical they are, because they almost always repeat the same thing.

INTERVIEWER: Why do you also take notes during your interviews, even when you are using a tape recorder?

PONIATOWSKA: Because many tape recorders don't work and because I have been taking notes all my life.

INTERVIEWER: Is your son Felipe still your assistant?

PONIATOWSKA: Whenever he wants, but my children are all grown up, they are over eighteen, and generally speaking they prefer their own activities to those of their mother. My daughter Paula is going to be a veterinarian. My children hate anything that has to do with journalism.

INTERVIEWER: Why do you play with the letters of your name on the cover of *Domingo 7?*

PONIATOWSKA: I put some of the letters upside down to laugh at myself a little. I have also done that with other books. For instance, in the first edition of *De noche vienes,* my daughter did all the letters on the cover, and since she was a child she did them all wrong, even to the point of initially misspelling the title.

INTERVIEWER: How did you decide to write the book *Fuerte es el silencio,* an impressive collage of interviews and statements?

PONIATOWSKA: *Fuerte es el silencio* doesn't have a single interview; it is a series of chronicles on the Mexican situation: the people who disappeared for political reasons, and the hunger strikes of peasants, among other things. It is really a series of essays. They used to ask me to lecture about the 1968 student movement quite often, so I decided to write a book on the subject, *Massacre in Mexico.* People also used to tell me that I should speak about marginalized people and the slums in which they live, so I wrote *Angeles de la ciudad.* The title refers to the poorest people who walk the streets and whom I call angels. That is also why I wrote *La colonia Rubén Jamarillo,* which is located near Cuernavaca.

INTERVIEWER: Doesn't reporting on torture reflect great courage on your part?

PONIATOWSKA: It would be hard for me to qualify it as courage, wouldn't it? I don't have any awareness of it, and if I did I might not be at all courageous.

INTERVIEWER: In *Fuerte es el silencio* you say: "This chronicle tries to follow the path taken by the student movement of 1968." Would I be right in saying that in this book you tried to articulate the concerns of those who are unable to speak for themselves?

PONIATOWSKA: Yes, in Mexico, as in many other Latin American countries, there is a very high level of illiteracy, so there are a great number of people who cannot read the news-papers or get their voices heard. Giving a voice to those who have none has always been one of my goals as a journalist.

INTERVIEWER: Can you say something about the blood-curdling testimony of repression you describe in *Massacre in Mexico?*

PONIATOWSKA: In 1968 there were student movements all over the world. There was one in Mexico too, possibly linked to those in France or Germany. But no student movement was repressed or annihilated as violently as the Mexican one. So I thought that anyone who wanted to be called a journalist had to write on this event which was fundamental in the lives of so many. Even today, young people ask what happened in 1968; in fact, the book has gone through fifty editions.

INTERVIEWER: You have dedicated many of your books to your brother Jan and you always put the date 1968. Why? Did he die in that year?

PONIATOWSKA: He died on December 8, 1968, at the age of twenty-one. He took part in the student movement but he did not die because of it. As with all young people, he showed a lot of promise, so my dedications are a way to prolong his life and have people like you ask me about him. Otherwise no one would know who he was.

INTERVIEWER: García Lorca believed in elves, while Gabriela Mistral, a very good friend of mine, believed in divine grace. When do you know that you are going to write a book and where do you find your inspiration? What propels you toward writing?

PONIATOWSKA: I generally write all my books on request. They asked me to write a screenplay about Tina Modotti, for instance, so I began to research her life, and when the film was cancelled due to a lack of funds, I decided to use the material and write a book. But it took me a lot of work to identify with that woman because I never knew her.

INTERVIEWER: Does your fiction have autobiographical elements?

PONIATOWSKA: Yes, all literature has autobiographical elements. If you read *Change of Skin* by Carlos Fuentes, for instance, you will notice that the main character is none other than Carlos himself, with his ulcer and stomach problems, things which he tried to exorcise through his writing. As he himself said, writing is a type of psychoanalysis or catharsis.

INTERVIEWER: How did you come up with the character of your first novel, *Lilus Kikus?*

PONIATOWSKA: It is a mixture, it contains autobiographical elements together with the story of a young girl I knew at the time.

INTERVIEWER: When you were a child, did you invent your own toys as Lilus Kikus did?

PONIATOWSKA: I was a very solitary child, although I had a brother. In reality, however, we were like all children: a little less solitary than we thought and inventors of our own reality. When I was sick with scarlet fever, my mother gave me a little farm which was made out of wood and had tiny cows and horses. It was my favorite toy.

INTERVIEWER: Are the questions Lilus Kikus asks her mother, her friends and the man in the room next door similar to those Elena Poniatowska asks her interlocutors?

PONIATOWSKA: Yes, whenever I interview people I always think they are going to give me the solution to the mystery and tell me what needs to be done. I continue to be an absurdly candid person, as I have been all my life. I always believe in others more than I do in myself, so interviews are always a search for solutions.

INTERVIEWER: It has been said that "Lilus Kikus is a strange and natural being touched by the grace of Elena Poniatowska." How did you manage to retain the purity of childhood and describe feelings from the perspective of a small girl?

PONIATOWSKA: I think Rulfo may have made that statement about me. I was very lucky as a young writer because I had Octavio Paz and Juan Rulfo as friends, protectors, and guides.

They were extremely generous in praising my work. But I think it is more a reflection of the goodness of their hearts.

INTERVIEWER: In your book *Dear Diego* you make us feel the physical presence of the great Mexican painter Diego Rivera through the imaginary letters of Angelina Beloff. Where does reality end and fiction begin in that novel and why did you write it?

PONIATOWSKA: Océano publishers asked me to write a prologue to the two novels of Lupe Marín, and that's why I read *The Fabulous Life of Diego Rivera* by Bertram Wolfe and discovered Angelina Beloff. That character fascinated me, and without finishing the book I started writing the letters that I thought Angelina Beloff would have penned to Diego Rivera. And that's how that small novel was born.

INTERVIEWER: In the book, Angelina Beloff says: "He looked like a photographer with a pencil in his hand instead of a camera." How is it that you know so much about painting? Do you paint yourself?

PONIATOWSKA: No, but my first cousin Mariana Poniatowska does, and I have interviewed many painters and been close to them for a long time. I even wrote a book with the painter Alberto Beltrán called *Todo empezó el domingo,* and I watched him draw and paint almost every day for a year.

INTERVIEWER: Beloff also says, "I think that painting is like this: you forget everything and lose the notions of time, other people, obligations and daily life which surround you without your being aware of them." Is writing like this for you, creating in a state of near obsession?

PONIATOWSKA: If one is writing something that one enjoys, then writing can be described as taking place in the context of great happiness and great anxiety.

INTERVIEWER: What do you think of the Boom: do you feel linked to that movement?

PONIATOWSKA: I am very happy with the response that Latin American literature has had, but it also hurts me that

writers as valuable as José Donoso have not been included in
the Boom. I also think that the Boom was a publicity event.

INTERVIEWER: In *¡Ay vida, no me mereces!* you said, "I
have to admit that I am Fuentesized and that I belong to a
generation that does not want to be de-Fuentesized." Do you
think that there are pre-Fuentes and post-Fuentes literatures?

PONIATOWSKA: No, I think that Fuentes opened the door to
a new type of novel, and that later writers—such as José
Agustín and Gustavo Sainz—owe him a great debt.

INTERVIEWER: But couldn't one say the same thing about
the literature before and after Juan Rulfo's *Pedro Páramo?*

PONIATOWSKA: Yes, but although there are Rulfian writers,
Rulfo's world was so original and so closed really, that he was
truly the only master of his own world. Rulfo was an isolated
and solitary man and his literature is too, whereas Fuentes has
been influenced by many figures in literature. For instance, in
Fuentes one can recognize William Faulkner and John Dos
Passos. Fuentes himself has said that literature is a universal
endeavor. As for Rulfo, he acknowledged the influences of
Faulkner and Knut Hamsun.

INTERVIEWER: Do you think that Mexican writers are different from other Latin American authors?

PONIATOWSKA: They definitely have a lot less fantasy than
Alejo Carpentier's *Explosion in a Cathedral* or García
Márquez's *One Hundred Years of Solitude.*

INTERVIEWER: Why do you think Latin American writers
have that ability to play with fantasy and reality?

PONIATOWSKA: Not all Latin American writers do, although
this is certainly true of Alejo Carpentier, Lezama Lima, Carlos
Fuentes, Mario Vargas Llosa, Octavio Paz, and Gabriel García
Márquez above all. So one becomes aware that the most fertile
ground or the gold vein—which a woman would destroy if she
were allowed in—is what they call fantastic realism and magic.

INTERVIEWER: Do you see something of this in Polish
literature?

PONIATOWSKA: Polish literature is very intense, it is a literature of great heroic zeal. Writers such as Brandys have an
overwhelming desire to be heroes and carry out exploits.

INTERVIEWER: Who are the writers who have influenced you?

PONIATOWSKA: I was born in France, and when I was fifteen
or sixteen, I read French Catholic writers primarily, like Léon
Bloy, Daniel Rops, Jacques Maritain and his wife Raïssa. I
also read Henri Bergson and Georges Bernanos and other
writers who were closely linked to Catholic thinking.

INTERVIEWER: What is the place of women in Hispanic
society and where would you like to see them?

PONIATOWSKA: Women are on the side of the oppressed
because they are a minority in the sense of access to any influential posts. The home is still considered their domain, but they
don't rule over anything else. Women writers have therefore
bewailed their situation and have believed that love was the
solution to life. That's why most of them to date are single or
divorced, or committed suicide. If you look at the number of
Latin American women writers who have killed themselves, the
list is a very long one: Alfonsina Storni drowned herself,
Antonieta Rivas Mercado shot herself in front of the altar of
Notre Dame, Rosario Castellanos electrocuted herself, and,
more recently, Violeta Parra and Alejandra Pizarnik killed
themselves, too.

INTERVIEWER: What do you think about feminism? Do you
consider yourself a feminist writer?

PONIATOWSKA: I think that feminism can be salvation. In
the first place, Latin Americans are very different from North
Americans or the French, because Latin American society is
so hierarchical that the needs of women in the upper classes are
very different from those of a worker or peasant. In Mexico, a
peasant woman tends to think of her son as an asset because he
is going to help plow the fields, while in the upper classes there
are fewer children because women have learned what family
planning is.

INTERVIEWER: Do you think women speak a different language from men?

PONIATOWSKA: I think they have a more extensive language than men because women have not yet given all they can give, as they are very insecure and don't believe their own words. When women finally cut loose, they'll give us a language which will flow like a river.

INTERVIEWER: Do you see some resemblance between your way of writing and that of Luisa Valenzuela?

PONIATOWSKA: No, I don't think so. I would like to write like Mercè Rodoreda in *La Plaça del diamant* (The Plaza of Diamonds).

INTERVIEWER: Why do you write and for whom?

PONIATOWSKA: I write for a spiritual family, I write so that the people of the world may communicate with me. I recently received a letter from a Japanese girl, and I have received mail from places as distant as Iran. So writing has allowed me to establish spiritual links with people over the years.

INTERVIEWER: Do you view writing as a social weapon or as a form of pleasure?

PONIATOWSKA: I think writing is like an instrument of love. Writing is a link established with other beings, over time and oceans, who identify with what you write.

INTERVIEWER: Do you think about the readers when you write?

PONIATOWSKA: No, I don't think about them, but readers and friends come through writing.

INTERVIEWER: Do you think about the critics?

PONIATOWSKA: No, never.

INTERVIEWER: Aren't you afraid to uncover crimes and reveal the truth, as you have done so many times?

PONIATOWSKA: No, because, as I said, I have a tremendous lack of awareness or excessive candidness which has been preserved over time.

INTERVIEWER: Is writing redoing history, telling the history of Mexico in a given time, and could you be called the chronicler of your time?

PONIATOWSKA: I hope to reflect my time.

INTERVIEWER: And what is Mexico for you? Why do you identify so much with the Mexican people?

PONIATOWSKA: Because it is my country, it is in my guts, it beats within me, it is born within me, it is a country that I chose to love and never leave. I have had many opportunities to leave Mexico and teach in the United States or other countries, but I haven't done so because I think I should stay here.

INTERVIEWER: What impact do you think your novelistic and journalistic work has had on Mexican life?

PONIATOWSKA: It is very difficult for me to analyze it, although I do think I have had an influence on new journalists and writers because they have seen that it is possible to write in a very simple and natural fashion and be as accepted as when people wrote with clichés or formulas.

INTERVIEWER: Are you writing a book now?

PONIATOWSKA: *Nada nadie* has just come out, which is a book on the earthquake of September 19, 1985. My novel on Tina Morotti will also be published at the beginning of 1989.

INTERVIEWER: In *Hasta no verte Jesús mío* the character says: "The Supreme Being calls on us to cleanse our souls, because He made us pure when He created us and in order to return to Him, we must be as He sent us." Are you religious?

PONIATOWSKA: I have a Catholic upbringing; I studied at the Sacred Heart Convent in Philadelphia for two years, which must have influenced me. Yes, deep down I am religious; I have a mother who is deeply religious and the faith of other people has always moved me.

INTERVIEWER: Since you are known for your interviews, how do you feel when it's your turn to be questioned?

PONIATOWSKA: Sometimes I feel intimidated or inhibited, I always think that my answers were pretty bad and I always would like to redo the interviews, but I am usually grateful that people are interested in me.

INTERVIEWER: What are you feeling at this moment?

PONIATOWSKA: Well, I think you prepared your questions very well, and I think maybe you are French because I heard someone speaking to you in that language. Perhaps we might have more affinity in person than over the phone, because I don't know what you look like, and although I can imagine to some extent, I can't really visualize you in depth. A gesture, an anxious look, the immediate environment, one's tastes, the shape of one's hands, are all of interest in doing an interview.

INTERVIEWER: Even though I don't know you personally, I think of you as courageous, sincere, romantic and tender because of your works. Who is Elena Poniatowska?

PONIATOWSKA: I am a romantic and an idealist, although that depends on how I feel in the morning when I wake up; sometimes I am ready to accept whatever comes, and other times I feel like hiding in the closet. I always hope that things will get better, that my next book will be a good, understandable one . . . so I am always optimistic about the future. I have a mother who is going to turn eighty and she looks like a woman of sixty-five, because even though her husband and only son have died, she has that ability to look to the future, she has a sort of faith in life.

Manuel Puig

Manuel Puig

Manuel Puig was born in December 1932, in General Villegas, a small town in the Argentine Pampa, twelve hours away by train from Buenos Aires. His novels are masterpieces of humor, violence and tenderness, and leave the reader spellbound.

The movie world has made a deep impact on his writings. When he was three years old, his mother would take him every afternoon at six to the only movie theater in town to see mostly American films that would make them live a world of fantasy. For this reason, when asked what he wanted to be when he grew up, he would answer: "a movie." His favorite stars were Ingrid Bergman, Joan Crawford, Marlene Dietrich, Greta Garbo, Rita Hayworth, Tyrone Power, Ginger Rogers, and Robert Taylor. Nonetheless, he also lived the world of reality and was the best student in his school.

In 1946, at the age of fourteen, he continued his education in a boarding school in Buenos Aires and experienced at first loneliness and cruelty away from home. In 1947, he discovered Freud, who left a deep imprint on his writings. He also read Gide, Hesse, Huxley and Sartre, and kept on going to the movies. In 1948, after seeing a French thriller directed by Henri Clouzot, he decided that he would become a film director and that he had to learn French, English and Italian—in his own words, "the languages of the cinema."

After graduating from secondary school in 1950, Puig began studying architecture, which he disliked, then philosophy. In 1953, he did his military service and worked as a translator. In 1955, after he received a scholarship from the Italian Institute, he went to Rome to study film direction at Cinecittà. In 1958 and 1959, he was in London and Stockholm, washing dishes to survive and writing film scripts. In 1960, he returned to Argentina to work as an assistant film director. In 1963, he was employed by Air France in New York and at the same time worked on his first novel. He has been living in Rio since 1980.

Manuel Puig is the author of countless novels, and his works have been translated into twenty-five languages. Among them: *La traición de Rita Hayworth,* 1968 (*Betrayed by Rita Hayworth,* 1971); *Boquitas pintadas,* 1969 (*Heartbreak Tango,* 1973); *The Buenos Aires Affair,* 1973 (*The Buenos Aires Affair,* 1976); *El beso de la mujer araña,* 1976 (*Kiss of the Spider Woman,* 1979); *Pubis angelical,* 1979 (*Pubis Angelical,* 1986); *Maldición eterna a quien lea estas páginas,* 1980 (*Eternal Curse on the Reader of These Pages,* 1982); *Sangre de amor correspondido,* 1982 (*Blood of Requited Love,* 1983).

After its tremendous success, *Kiss of the Spider Woman* was made into a film directed by Hector Babenco, which had its world premiere at the 1985 Cannes Film Festival. William Hurt was named best actor for his performance as Molina.

INTERVIEWER: I would like this interview to resemble the questions and answers that Larry and Mr. Ramírez throw back and forth as they poke at each other's minds and souls. Do you think we can achieve this tour de force that you created with your characters in *Eternal Curse on the Reader of These Pages*?

PUIG: I don't know which part you want me to play. Perhaps that of the writer who clarifies all the question marks that the reading of my book has produced in you. So go ahead.

INTERVIEWER: When you were writing the conversation between Larry and Mr. Ramírez, with whom did you identify?

PUIG: Mr. Ramírez. I was fascinated by Larry, he was a real person. I met this guy in New York and somehow he became the symbol of the city for me. This was in 1976, when things in

Argentina had taken a turn for the worse. We had just gone through the experience of the horrible Isabelita and then the military junta took over and succeeded in doing the impossible: to be worse than Isabelita. So at that moment I thought, "Well, it seems like I'm going to be in New York forever. Am I going to adopt this city?" I loved it and hated it, but I didn't really understand the city. And suddenly I met this character and he became New York. He was mysterious, he was attractive and obnoxious at the same time, and I told myself, "If I ever get to understand this guy, I may one day understand New York." So I proposed to him to work on a novel, and we wrote *Eternal Curse* together.

INTERVIEWER: Why the title?

PUIG: Because the book deals with somebody who wants to find the truth or eternal blessing.

INTERVIEWER: Do you think the title shocked people?

PUIG: Yes. After the first edition in Spain, we had to cut the title to *Eternal Curse* because there were complaints. People were coming to bookstores saying that the full title (*Eternal Curse on the Reader of These Pages*) represented an aggressive attack on somebody passing by. That's how superstitious and stupid people can be.

INTERVIEWER: In 1965, when you first lived in New York, you worked for Air France at Idlewild. Twenty-three years later, I am interviewing you at the same airport, now called Kennedy. Did you think back then that you would become one of the most talked about novelists and that your works would be best-sellers and be translated into twenty-five languages?

PUIG: My first encounter with New York was a fantastic one. When you are starting, you have dreams of grandeur and also nightmares of total failure. I used to go from one extreme to the other: from thinking that I would never be published in my life to believing that I would be appreciated because I had something valuable to offer. Being satisfied with my work was always the main thing for me. If recognition came afterward, that would be fine too.

INTERVIEWER: Do you feel differently now that you have achieved international recognition?

PUIG: I am very relieved, of course. I don't have to work eight hours a day at things that don't interest me. But you see, money hasn't come my way yet! I hope it will one day, and that is what may change me. I must admit that I have achieved a certain recognition, but it has come very slowly, and I have made lots of enemies for reasons I can't understand. Perhaps the ambiguity in my work, in terms of the roles that I point to at every level, makes some people nervous.

INTERVIEWER: Do you think that your childhood trips to the movies with your mother changed your life?

PUIG: They may have. My hometown was really stifling, and we felt the need to escape from that environment. Not only was there machismo all over the place, but there was also a total absence of landscape, just dry pampas all around us. So I needed something besides that. If it hadn't been films, I think I would have found it in literature. I mean reading, not writing.

INTERVIEWER: When did you first realize that you wanted to become a novelist?

PUIG: I found out after I had written the first chapter of my first novel. It was meant to be the preparation for a script. I wanted to write scripts and direct films. I thought films were a very pleasant field of work. They are not. Films are made under pressure, and I hate pressure; I cannot work under those conditions. I am too ambitious and too much of a perfectionist, and I am also very self-critical. So I wasn't really cut out for the movies. In films, you need a big ego to impose yourself. If you are not that kind of person, your collaborators don't believe in you and don't follow your orders. When I discovered that I could write, it was the biggest relief, because in whatever kind of work I am involved, I like to have the time to redo things, if they need redoing.

INTERVIEWER: How did you come to incorporate films and even soap operas into your writings?

PUIG: Well, they were a part of the concerns of my characters, and they were integral to my story. I grew up among people who were mesmerized by films; all my generation in some way was influenced immensely by films, and so it wasn't something I could escape if I wanted to talk about average people.

INTERVIEWER: When you were little and you were asked what you wanted to be, you replied, "A movie." What would you say now that you are a novelist if you had another chance to do something else, what would you want to do?

PUIG: I like writing. I would take any art that is done by oneself. What I love about literature is that you do it alone, and you have the opportunity to revise. I don't like my work to become a torture, as is the case with film directors. I see them arriving on the set saying, "My goodness, all the problems I have to solve!" I want my days to be placid and, if possible, productive. I like to create beauty, if I can.

INTERVIEWER: You never thought of being a psychologist, since you do work with the mind and with the soul?

PUIG: I wouldn't have minded doing that, and it's still a possibility.

INTERVIEWER: How is a novel born?

PUIG: Always with the need to understand something that is extremely important to you. When I started to write *Eternal Curse,* I wanted to know more about New York; when I started to write *Blood of Requited Love,* I wanted to know the secret of that maze. The energy in the end was all generated by anguish. My first novel reflected my need to understand how I was when a child, while *Heartbreak Tango* was an attempt to come to terms with the society that surrounded me then. In *Betrayed by Rita Hayworth,* I was writing more about misfits in that society. Then I felt like writing about the people that were more integrated into it.

INTERVIEWER: What is the role of recollection or memory in your work?

PUIG: It was very important in the first two books because I

was talking about my childhood in my hometown. Then I started
to deal with more contemporary subjects.

INTERVIEWER: Why are the first and last pages of *Betrayed
by Rita Hayworth* identical?

PUIG: Because there is a return to the past. The novel starts
with the character as a baby boy. In the last chapter, he is a
baby again, but it's another character's point of view.

INTERVIEWER: What made you write *Kiss of the Spider
Woman?*

PUIG: Around 1972, discussions on feminism became more
frequent in Argentina. I was totally in agreement with this
process. I was concerned, however, that people were only talking about the inconveniences of being oppressed women, and
never of the advantages, since there had to be some for such an
unnatural situation to last for centuries. I believe that in a war,
one should never underestimate the enemy's weapons; therefore, I wanted to know what those weapons were. So I had an
enormous desire to question some women and find out what
could make them both happy and oppressed. I wanted to find
such a woman, to turn her into the heroine of my next novel. I
have always tried to base my characters on real life.

INTERVIEWER: When you say that it is important to know
the enemy's weapons, do you consider women the enemy?

PUIG: No, absolutely not. The enemy is repression, the
enemy is that sort of society where women are oppressed. In
other words, the enemy is accepting the role of being oppressed.
So I wanted to know what the advantages of that role were,
because there had to be some. There were horrible drawbacks,
but there must have been some incentives for women to accept
that situation. I wanted to find out what those incentives were,
and that's why I was interested in listening to the voices of
oppressed women. But in 1972, I didn't find one single woman
who was completely satisfied with her role as an oppressed
being, and so I could not continue with the project. Although I
didn't find a female voice, I did discover an effeminate one, a

certain type of homosexual with a feminine fixation who would still defend the traditional state of things. Since it was impossible for him to get married, this homosexual could still find solace in the role of a defenseless being vis-à-vis a "strong" man who would protect him. I remembered terrible things from that period of the forties when women expressed themselves in such terms as "I cannot love a man if I do not fear him a little when he embraces me." In other words, eroticism was absolutely associated with domination, and people thought this was a completely natural state of affairs. It could be an unjust situation as far as women were concerned, but it was the voice of nature speaking and it had to be listened to. So I had no other choice but to work with a homosexual protagonist. I hadn't wanted a character like that, as I thought the average reader in our repressed and absurd society at that time knew very little about what it meant to be a homosexual (people know more about it now, although still not enough). So, when I wrote that novel I had to do all sorts of very curious things like placing explanatory footnotes at the bottom of many pages.

INTERVIEWER: What was your reaction upon seeing your novel *Kiss of the Spider Woman* in film?

PUIG: Negative.

INTERVIEWER: Why?

PUIG: Because the average spectator who had not read the novel would think the movie was progressive and liberating. But compared with the book, the movie is reactionary. In the book, the character of Molina is full of joy and life, and that's missing in the movie. William Hurt created a fascinating character, but not the one in my novel. Hurt created a neurotic and tortured character who has nothing to do with Molina, who was a very joyful person, among other things, and who did not feel the Calvinistic guilt that was attributed to him in the picture. In spite of all this, given the fact that homosexuality has always been ridiculed and reduced to putrid characterizations in movies, the film can be considered both progressive and liberating.

INTERVIEWER: What has been the reaction of women to the book?

PUIG: Excellent. They understand the novel the best because it is really a long discussion on the nature of submission and people's need for it.

INTERVIEWER: Have homosexuals reacted positively to the book?

PUIG: Very well, everything's been very good.

INTERVIEWER: Who are the narrators in your novels?

PUIG: Sometimes there is a third person, but very seldom. The sound of my own voice is not my main concern. I am not so concerned with creating a code of my own. I've been hurt a great deal by older writers; I won't give names, but I must say I despise them. These bitchy writers said I had no voice. I don't give a damn about a voice of my own; I care about the voices of people, of a generation, of a class. I am a part of that. Believe me, they say that sopranos and tenors are temperamental, but I can assure you that some Latin American writers are just as bad. But this sort of behavior is not limited to our continent: there are writers everywhere who, in spite of their great artistic sensitivity, can debase themselves through callous comments.

INTERVIEWER: Sometimes the music of your own voice joins in the music of your characters. Do you feel more at ease when you are describing men as characters or women, or is it the same for you?

PUIG: It depends. I have heard critics say, "He's at his best with just men as in *Kiss of the Spider Woman,*" and also, "He's at his best with female characters."

INTERVIEWER: How do you feel about it yourself?

PUIG: It depends on how close I get to the people.

INTERVIEWER: Some of your women characters are very striking, they are very impressive.

PUIG: One of my beliefs has been to focus on the truth of women. I hope that has been recognized by women. I wrote *Pubis Angelical,* which is a feminist novel, if there is such a thing.

INTERVIEWER: Why the title?

PUIG: *Pubis Angelical* has to do with the bad relationships the female protagonist has had with men. She needs them, but she has never gotten along with them. In some way, she has always been cheated or humiliated or underestimated. And she sees her sex as a means of degradation. So one fantasy that she has toward the end of the book is that she is sexless like the angels.

INTERVIEWER: How did feminists react to the book?

PUIG: There was a very strong feminist group in Mexico when I was living there. It was a difficult time. I showed them *Pubis Angelical,* and they said, "We are not going to endorse this book because your character is not a role model." They wanted a strong woman to show them what to do. I think that was very stupid on their part. What the book tries to show is how difficult it is for a sincere woman to deal with the values of the past. Meanness and stupidity grow like weeds.

INTERVIEWER: *Pubis Angelical* and *Buenos Aires Affair* have elements of the thriller and the detective story. Why did you approach those genres?

PUIG: Because I am interested in storytelling techniques. I always try to sustain my stories with suspense devices. I want to give pleasure and amusement to the reader at the same time that I try to tell him something.

INTERVIEWER: Do you have a favorite among your works?

PUIG: No.

INTERVIEWER: Not even *Betrayed by Rita Hayworth?*

PUIG: No, no, no. I have no favorite. But, generally speaking, I try to defend my least successful novels. These are usually my latest, because my novels are never received very well initially, not even *Kiss of the Spider Woman.* The only one of my books to be an immediate commercial success in Argentina was *Heartbreak Tango* and for the wrong reasons.

INTERVIEWER: Why "wrong"?

PUIG: Because it was seen as a caricature and mockery of

the middle class, which it was absolutely not.

INTERVIEWER: How do you feel when you finish a novel?

PUIG: It depends. If I have already started another project, it is a great relief to have finished one thing and move on to the other. But when there is no other project, I feel a terrible emptiness.

INTERVIEWER: What is more important to you—the character, the book, or both?

PUIG: Sometimes the character is important and dominates everything, as the mason of *Blood of Requited Love.* Then in *Heartbreak Tango,* it's a chorus of voices; there are at least six leading characters.

INTERVIEWER: Do you feel any special affection for any one of your characters?

PUIG: After being with them for two or three years, I would rather have others come to know them.

INTERVIEWER: The characters are people that actually exist?

PUIG: Always. And they reveal themselves to me mostly through their talk. I always write about people that I love and care for. Somehow, I am seduced by their voices, and I want to know more about them and listen to what they have to say.

INTERVIEWER: And who dominates whom? Does the author dominate the characters, or the characters the author?

PUIG: I think it is important that there be a good relationship. I have to respect the characters' reality, I cannot violate it. I have to depict the characters as they are. At the same time, their voices allow me to engage in a formal artistic experiment. The characters have to permit me to play a little aesthetic game which compensates me for the bitter part that comes when I have to deal with any form of reality.

INTERVIEWER: What is your relationship with the people on whom you base your characters?

PUIG: Generally speaking, people are very pleased with the attention they get, with seeing themselves as leading characters in a work of fiction.

INTERVIEWER: Do they recognize themselves in your work?

PUIG: Well, they have no other choice.

INTERVIEWER: Do you keep them at a distance or are you their friend?

PUIG: It depends, every novel has been different.

INTERVIEWER: You don't change reality at all?

PUIG: I take the mason's speech in *Blood of Requited Love* as a verbal code. For me, his words are notes, and I want to write music with those notes. I could also say that his words are colors and textures that I want to reproduce in my work somehow. I am more interested in the spoken word than the written word. I am not as concerned with creating a prose. I want to play with the music of people's voices.

INTERVIEWER: Do you take notes when you write?

PUIG: I take no notes. My books are notes. I am kidding. I elaborate things quite a lot. Sometimes my novels seem as if they were pieces of real-life conversations. But I am not interested in the least in a purely realistic approach. I want to recreate reality to understand it, to illuminate it, but always in terms of an aesthetic elaboration. That is, if I reproduce the voice of the mason, at the same time I am reworking it and stressing its musical and pictorial qualities.

INTERVIEWER: Do you play with reality and fantasy, as other writers do?

PUIG: Totally. I think one of the problems writers, readers, and teachers share is that in our society, in order to survive, we are forced to play roles. To be able to communicate with people, we have to find a tone of voice, we have to force our own being. To create an articulate character who is able to communicate with others, we learn to express ourselves with a code. What happens is that after a while we forget that what we are playing with is a character. We start to believe that the character is the same as the person, and we begin to cater to the character's needs and forget about those of the person.

INTERVIEWER: What do you mean by person?

PUIG: Your own self.

INTERVIEWER: So you end up identifying with your own characters?

PUIG: Yes! On the other hand, satisfying the needs of the characters may lead you to agonizing experiences. A terrible dissatisfaction may result when your characters are fulfilled and you are not.

INTERVIEWER: What do all your characters have in common?

PUIG: I don't know, ask the critics.

INTERVIEWER: Do you like critics?

PUIG: When I talk about critics, I talk about the ones who write for newspapers and magazines. Then there are the other kinds of critics, the academic people, who work on a different level. They have always supported me. And I am talking about academics at universities who teach and write essays. I don't respect the quickie review.

INTERVIEWER: Do you think all your characters search for identity and desire to escape from mediocrity?

PUIG: That is something very typical of Argentina. We are a very young nation. The bulk of the population is comprised of the descendants of immigrants who came at the beginning of this century. We don't even have one century of history.

INTERVIEWER: Reading your novels is like suddenly being forced into a conversation. Why do you always find that oral dialogue, and even written dialogue, have such vital force?

PUIG: I am interested in and entranced by the voices of people, especially those that let you into the fascinating world of the collective unconscious.

INTERVIEWER: Allen Josephs of the *New York Times Book Review* has said of you, "Puig spins a fascinating web of words, capturing the reader's attention with his uncanny ability to develop part of a character solely through dialogue." Did you ever consider being a playwright?

PUIG: I've written plays, but only recently. First of all, I adapted *Kiss of the Spider Woman* for the stage. It has never played in New York, although it has in other cities of the United States as well as in many other countries. After that I wrote a play that is called *Under a Mantle of Stars,* then another one, a two-character play about an old lady and her middle-aged nurse, called *Mystery of the Rose Bouquet.* I also have a musical comedy about Gardel.

INTERVIEWER: Do you like poetry?

PUIG: I am interested in music and painting, and what is poetry? Poetry is the music and the color of words.

INTERVIEWER: Do you feel part of the Boom?

PUIG: No!! There were people in the Boom that were really quite mean to me. I can't understand that, because in literature there is space for everyone. Just the other day, I read a work by a young American author who had written about Puerto Ricans. I was dazzled. Each time I read a book that I like, I feel good, I feel that literature is alive, I feel stimulated. When I see young writers, I don't have the urge to crush them because I don't see them as a threat.

INTERVIEWER: Do you see any resemblance between you and any other Latin American writers?

PUIG: I am not jealous of young writers. Now that I am fifty-five, I could start to become like an old bitch who resents the young, but I don't feel that way at all. The people who were very good to me were the critic Emir Rodríguez Monegal and the writer Juan Goytisolo. They always defended me, even when other prominent writers thought I was being frivolous.

INTERVIEWER: Why is violence such an integral part of your work?

PUIG: Because I hate it. I see aggressiveness as very unnecessary.

INTERVIEWER: How has censorship affected you?

PUIG: A lot, because I have been published through all of Argentina's disasters. Repression in Argentina made me lose all my readers there. In fact, when *Kiss of the Spider Woman* appeared, no one bought it. That book was not read in Argentina almost until the movie came out, because the junta and the post-junta managed to discredit me so that I no longer had a name and no one knew me or was interested in my work. *Kiss of the Spider Woman,* which had been the subject of intense discussions outside my country, was completely ignored in Argentina. Censorship originated a silence around my name, a fact which was taken advantage of by people in the press who opposed me.

INTERVIEWER: And do you think that because of the censorship you had to invent a series of masks?

PUIG: No, absolutely not, because since I didn't live in Argentina, I continued to write freely.

INTERVIEWER: Wouldn't you like to return to General Villegas, the small town in which you were born in the Argentine Pampa?

PUIG: Argentina is my country. It's my language. I spent some of my happiest years there as a child, from 1940 to 1944, when I was eight to twelve years old. But I wouldn't like to go back there now and be the center of attention. What I enjoy is being an observer with eyes that capture things and a pair of ears that listen.

INTERVIEWER: That's what being a writer is!

PUIG: Yes, but now that I am famous and a special person, I can no longer afford the luxury of being an observer or a pair of ears.

INTERVIEWER: What does living in Brazil mean to you?

PUIG: Brazil is to me like Miami is to old New Yorkers. It has the sun and a good climate, and the people are very sweet, but it is not my country. I have enjoyed being there since 1980. I have worked enough and I think I deserve a geographical haven.

INTERVIEWER: Who is Manuel Puig?

PUIG: I must say that, at this moment, he is a very tired person who has been up since eight and has been unable to stop for even five minutes the whole day. I would like to be a person,

not a writer. I always say the same thing: if you keep close to
yourself, you have a chance to grow, while characters sometimes don't have that opportunity. I think I must go now.

*(Boarding announcement: Ladies and Gentlemen, we have a
new departure time for flight 102 to Rio: it is now departing at
9:45 at Gate 1.)*

Ernesto Sábato

Ernesto Sábato

The novelist Ernesto Sábato was born in Rojas, a small town in the province of Buenos Aires, Argentina, on June 24, 1911, where he lived a sheltered childhood. In 1924, as an adolescent, he moved to La Plata, capital of the province of Buenos Aires, to begin his secondary studies at the Colegio Nacional. There he went through moments of despair, giving full vent to his extraordinary nightmarish imagination: "I found myself alone and unprotected, far from my mother. . . . I spent long hours agonizing and crying." While a student, he discovered in the world of mathematics a sense of order which brought peace to his anguished inner spirit. In 1928, he attended the Institute of Physics at the Universidad Nacional in La Plata and decided to become a scientist. In 1937, he received his doctorate in physics.

In 1938, Sábato was granted a fellowship to study atomic radiation at the Joliot-Curie Laboratory in Paris. During that period he was drawn into the surrealism of André Breton and his friends, and he became attracted to the world of the arts. He worked by day at the laboratory and by night he gathered with the surrealists at the Café du Dôme. A fierce critic of his own work, he wrote his first novel, *La fuente muda* (The Silent Well), and burned it. Other manuscripts have undergone the same drastic fate along the years. At the onset of the war in 1939, the grant to study radiation was transferred to the Massachusetts Institute of Technology in Boston. From 1940 to 1943 Sábato taught quantum theory and the theory of relativity at the Universidad Nacional in La Plata, and physics at the Instituto del Profesorado in Buenos Aires. At the same time, he began writing for *Sur,* Argentina's prestigious literary magazine owned by Victoria Ocampo. He also wrote for *La Nación,* one of the leading Buenos Aires papers.

In 1943, before officially abandoning science to devote himself fully to writing, he took refuge in the hills of Córdoba with his wife Matilde and their four-year-old son Jorge. In 1945, he gave up his scientific career because of his open opposition to Perón's régime.

It was in that same year that he became recognized exclusively as a writer and that his first work appeared, *Uno y el universo* (One and the Universe), 1945, which won the Buenos Aires Municipal Prose Prize.

Sábato is a writer who seeks truth and likes to think of himself as independent of any group. His first novel, *El túnel,* 1948 (*The Outsider,* 1950), attracted the attention of such prominent writers as Albert Camus, Thomas Mann and Graham Greene. It later appeared in English as *The Tunnel* in 1988. In 1961, Sábato published his second novel, *Sobre héroes y tumbas* (*On Heroes and Tombs,* 1981). The section of that book called a "Report on the Blind" is a most powerful encounter with the secrets of existence. His third novel, *Abaddón el exterminador* (Abaddon the Exterminator), 1974, won the French Prize for Best Foreign Book.

Sábato is also known for his numerous essays. Among them: *Hombres y engranajes* (Men and Machinery), 1951; *Heterodoxia* (Heterodoxy), 1953; *El escritor y sus fantasmas* (The Writer and His Ghosts), 1963; *Itinerario* (Itinerary), 1969; *Apologías y rechazos* (Apologies and Rejections), 1979; *Robotización del hombre* (The Robotization of Man), 1981; *Páginas de Ernesto Sábato seleccionadas por el autor* (Pages from Ernesto Sábato Selected by the Author), 1983. His works have been translated into twenty-one languages.

Sábato never left his country during the many years of dictatorship and was never afraid to condemn the horrors imposed by both the Left and the Right. In 1983, the democratic President Raúl Alfonsín appointed him to head the National Commission on Missing Persons. The document submitted by that Commission, which is known as "El informe Sábato" (The Sábato Report), came out in 1984 as a devastating revelation of "the greatest and most savage tragedy" in the history of Argentina.

In 1984, Ernesto Sábato was awarded the Cervantes Prize and the Gabriela Mistral Prize, created by the Organization of American States. He has been named Chevalier de la Légion d'Honneur by the French Government. The Gran Cruz al Mérito Civil was bestowed upon him by the Spanish Government, while Colombia awarded him the Cruz de Boyaca. In 1989, he won the Jerusalem Prize.

For the past decade, Ernesto Sábato has devoted much of his time to painting. An exhibition of his work was shown at the Centre Pompidou in Paris in the spring of 1989. At the same time, a symposium on his literary work was held in Paris as part of a tribute to him.

INTERVIEWER: Your theoretical writings and the tone of your novels might lead one to think that you are a romantic. Isn't this so?

SÁBATO: Those theoretical writings are essays on the dehumanization of man that science and technology have produced, and I do make a defense of romanticism in the deepest sense of that term, as it was used by the great German philosophical movements of the eighteenth century. Of course, I was not talking about the insipid romanticism that has dominated a good part of our literature.

INTERVIEWER: Your existence has been tumultuous and even contradictory.

SÁBATO: Why "even"? Just leave it at contradictory.

INTERVIEWER: All right, let's say it that way. I was referring to your having been a scientist and then turning to literature, and more recently to painting. What motivated you to make these curious changes?

SÁBATO: My mother was a reserved and stoic woman, but

fundamentally a very tender person, while my father was very strict during our youth. Perhaps that's why my childhood was a very sad one, plagued with nightmares, sleepwalking, anxiousness and melancholy. This situation became even worse when I was sent from my village to La Plata to do my secondary studies. I missed my mother, and at the same time I felt dirty, guilty, and imperfect. I longed for an order that I did not possess, and then I had a tremendous revelation when our math teacher showed us the first geometrical theorem. I didn't know it at the time, but I had just discovered the Platonic world, a world of ideal, pure, incorruptible and eternal objects. That discovery was crucial in my life because, although I continued with my precarious attempts at painting and literature, that mathematical world took me over, as it was devoid of the defects that tormented me, or put another way, the attributes of what we perhaps could and should call the "nocturnal universe." I can state that my entire existence has been a struggle between the forces of light and purity and those of darkness and impurity. This conflict grew over the years as I realized what a danger science posed for mankind. The ghosts of the unconscious thus grew stronger and stronger. Who were they, and what did they want? I still don't clearly know. I was aware, however, that these ghosts were part of the unconscious world and that it was impossible to avoid them, even when the Platonic ether made me forget them for a time. Sooner or later, they began to dominate me completely until they expressed themselves fully in my writing. That's how I began to write *La fuente muda,* a tribute to a famous poem by Antonio Machado, when I was working at the Curie laboratories in Paris before the war. As I have done with the great majority of my work, I burned that book, saving only a few fragments which I published in *Sur* magazine many years later.

INTERVIEWER: Why burn it? Wasn't it enough to throw it in the wastepaper basket?

SÁBATO: No, I never liked doing that. I always burned what didn't satisfy me.

INTERVIEWER: The purifying fire?

SÁBATO: Yes . . . (*He smiles and stares thoughtfully*)

INTERVIEWER: You seem to be fascinated with fire. In *On Heroes and Tombs,* for instance, Alejandra's final tragic act—following the shooting of her father—is to set fire to the belvedere and burn herself alive. So in those years preceding the war, while you were working as a physicist, you began writing your first novels?

SÁBATO: Yes, I worked at a laboratory during the day, and at night, I met with my surrealist friends at the Café du Dôme in Montparnasse. Like a good housewife who is a prostitute at night. (*He laughs*)

INTERVIEWER: Was the Dôme the café of the surrealists?

SÁBATO: Not only surrealists, but artists in general. Many great people used to frequent that place, from Joyce and Picasso to Breton and his friends. When I returned to that café ten or fifteen years later out of curiosity, I almost died: it had become a perfectly bourgeois café.

INTERVIEWER: What brought you to surrealism?

SÁBATO: The attraction toward the opposite of what I was doing. I have always been subject to contradictory impulses.

INTERVIEWER: How did you reach that point?

SÁBATO: Through the Argentine Ernesto Bonasso, a friend of Domínguez, the surrealist painter of the Canary Islands, who was very well known not only for his paintings but for having gouged an eye of the Rumanian painter Victor Brauner.

INTERVIEWER: Domínguez appears in your last two novels.

SÁBATO: Yes, and I have also narrated the eye incident in *Abbadón el exterminador.* That incident caused extensive discussions within the surrealist movement because it was tied to the issue of premonitions, which interested them. Brauner had painted several self-portraits in which his eye was depicted as torn out, long before the event actually occurred. When I arrived in Paris, I became a very good friend of Domínguez, who was one of the first people to encourage me to paint.

INTERVIEWER: What other artists and writers frequented the café?

SÁBATO: Almost all the surrealists. I met Tristan Tzara, Esteban Francés and André Breton himself. I also met Matta, when he was still unknown, although he was already a magnificent painter. Much later, we met again in Paris and had long conversations about that time when we were still unknown youths.

INTERVIEWER: Why did you abandon science?

SÁBATO: It wasn't an easy, linear thing: there was a period of five or six years from my time at the Curie laboratory to 1943 when I returned to Argentina and stopped being a professor. I went off to live in a cabin in the Córdoba sierra with my wife Matilde and our four-year-old son Jorge. There was neither electricity nor running water and we had to bathe and wash in the river, because it was the only way we could afford to live with the few pennies that I earned through my articles.

INTERVIEWER: So you were a scientist for only five or six years?

SÁBATO: Yes, but I was already writing intensely. I could feel a growing conviction that my destiny would lie in literature, especially fiction.

INTERVIEWER: Why "especially fiction"?

SÁBATO: Because even though I have written many essays, I don't consider that a significant activity. Essays are a daily activity written with the head, not because of reasons of the heart, as Pascal would have said. Fiction, meanwhile, translates the obscure world of the unconscious and has nothing to do with reason. The greatest truth of an author can be found in his creative writings, because his immersion in the unconscious is revealing of great truths. It is the same with dreams: one can say anything about them except that they are lies.

INTERVIEWER: That reminds me of something you wrote in *Hombres y engranajes* in 1951: borrowing Shakespeare's words, you said life could be "a tale told by an idiot, full of sound and fury." Do you still feel that way?

SÁBATO: Basically yes. But that does not mean that fiction expresses only the abysms of the soul, because characters in novels also think, just as all human beings do. Only delirious people can affirm that there should be no ideas in novels. There can be, and in a primary sense, there always are. There can be pure ideas, although they are usually personified in the characters, who are an intertwined mixture of pure mind and passions, dreams and visions, just like humans. How can we conceive the greatness of Dostoyevsky, Proust or Thomas Mann without ideas? If I remember correctly, in *The Magic Mountain* there is a heated discussion between Naphta and Settembrini on good and evil. Some idiot, whose name I cannot remember, criticized *The Brothers Karamazov* for being a theology treatise in the form of a dialogue.

INTERVIEWER: Who said that?

SÁBATO: I cannot remember the names of idiots. Memory should be used only for important things.

INTERVIEWER: The characters in your novels always reason.

SÁBATO: Most of them do, except for two characters who are paranoid: Castel in *The Tunnel* and Fernando Vidal Olmos in *Abaddón el exterminador*.

INTERVIEWER: In various essays, you have said that writing fiction is a form of catharsis, a way of freeing yourself of certain obsessions.

SÁBATO: I am less sick than before, that's for sure. I think if I wrote a dozen more books, I would be an acceptable person. But this is true with all authors, not just me.

INTERVIEWER: What obsessions drove you to write the three novels you have published?

SÁBATO: I don't know . . . the need to communicate with others as a result of recurrent loneliness . . . the night and its shadows, blindness . . . the existence or lack of existence of God . . . the desire for the Absolute and purification . . .

INTERVIEWER: They are something more than psychological

problems, then?

SÁBATO: Of course, they are metaphysical problems, but they take a psychological form in fiction. That's the difference between a philosophical treatise and a novel.

INTERVIEWER: I would almost say that they are religious problems.

SÁBATO: Yes, in the ultimate sense of that word.

INTERVIEWER: Do you believe in God?

SÁBATO: I think my novels can give you an answer, although naturally it will be contradictory, ambiguous and hard to explain. A religious person is someone in anguish with the problem of God, not necessarily believing in His existence. Many men and women—St. Teresa of Lisieux, for instance— had many doubts and later became saints. I give little credence to rational proofs of God's existence, so I differ with St. Thomas. Many distinguished thinkers, like Tertullian, have said that God's presence cannot be established through logic, but only through intuition. Why should such a mysterious being as God be ruled by pure reason? If this were the case, how can we reconcile God's omnipotence and infinite virtue with the horrible death of a child from leukemia? This would require convoluted theodicies. That's why I think fiction is more appropriate to deal with the supreme problem, since it involves not only logic but myths, visions, dreams, symbols, and everything that can be classified as magic or mythical-poetic thinking.

INTERVIEWER: On one occasion, you said that literature is not a pastime but a way to investigate the human condition, and, following your comments, the relation between man and the Absolute.

SÁBATO: No, I do not deny that literature can be a pastime, or any number of other things. The novel, in particular, can do anything, as long as it has its own characters.

INTERVIEWER: You once said that the author finds himself through his characters.

SÁBATO: I may have written something like that, but also in reference to certain novels to which I feel closest. Yes, there is what might be described as an existential dialectic between the author and the characters, and among the characters themselves. It is a fight between antagonists that takes place in our deepest selves and which is manifested in novels and dreams. That's why fictions are cathartic and curative: they free the Furies, who cannot be ignored and even less made the objects of ridicule, except at the cost of very severe penalties. Dostoyevsky asserted that God and the devil wage a fight for man's heart. Of course, I am referring to that type of fiction I mentioned earlier.

INTERVIEWER: In that case, no single character can represent the author.

SÁBATO: Ibsen confessed that all his characters came from his heart. Flaubert, meanwhile, who is considered a model by many "objectivist" writers, said roughly the following: "My characters affect me and pursue me, or rather it is I who dwell in them." He also said that he was Madame Bovary, which is an exaggeration, but significant nonetheless. There were also pieces of Flaubert's soul in the pathetic Bovary, in Rodolphe and even in the grotesque pharmacist. Flaubert's basic romanticism, which is expressed in the most tragically ridiculous way in *Madame Bovary,* also becomes its very opposite, because it ends up manifesting itself in people whom we might call "love atheists." In reference to that dialectic that I mentioned before, an author can give rise to characters who are fanatical atheists. I am thinking of Dostoyevsky and other writers known for their piety or kindness who nevertheless created characters who were mean and merciless. I would have to add, to the shame of many authors, that in these cases the writer not only experiences surprise at the unexpected behavior of his characters, but also a twisted satisfaction.

INTERVIEWER: Do you base your characters on yourself or on other people?

SÁBATO: I create portraits and caricatures based on people I have known, but I must add that these characters are neither central nor decisive in my work.

INTERVIEWER: Are there any characters to which you are particularly attracted?

SÁBATO: (*He stares and smiles*) Yes, I have preferences. In my case, I like people who live in the countryside, and are full of candor, innocence and warmth.

INTERVIEWER: I think you are referring to the servant Hortencia Paz and Humberto D'Arcangelo in *On Heroes and Tombs.*

SÁBATO: Yes, of course, but also to Carlucho, the illiterate anarchist of *Abaddón,* and the truck driver Bucich. These very modest beings comfort me and allow me to go beyond the other characters, who are terrible and perverse.

INTERVIEWER: Like Fernando Vidal Olmos?

SÁBATO: Of course. But all my characters, both good and bad, are a part of me. The horrible confession that comes out of the novel is what purifies the author.

INTERVIEWER: Did you ever consider being a psychologist?

SÁBATO: No, why should I? I have enough with my works of fiction.

INTERVIEWER: Did any psychoanalyst ever try to treat you?

SÁBATO: Yes, several times. During the time of the Café du Dôme and the surrealist movement, one of the founders of the psychoanalytic movement, Dr. Celes Cárcamo of Argentina, wanted to treat me. I was then twenty-seven years old and a perfect specimen for practical scholarly psychoanalytic research.

INTERVIEWER: And what did you reply?

SÁBATO: No, because I had already decided to write novels, which are a more redemptive and cheaper form of therapy.

INTERVIEWER: Is there some connection between Alejandra in *On Heroes and Tombs* and María in *The Tunnel?*

SÁBATO: I don't think so. María is a rather passive character, while Alejandra is violent and active.

INTERVIEWER: Why does your character Sabato in *Abaddón* turn into a bat with human dimensions?

SÁBATO: I don't know. By the way, do you see how mistaken people can be when they call that work an autobiography? And I mean autobiography in the common sense of the word. That transformation never happened to me.

INTERVIEWER: Can an author know his characters well?

SÁBATO: No. The character is an emanation, a hypostasis of the author, which as it begins to walk and to live becomes as mysterious as any human being, and achieves almost complete independence from the person who created it. When one writes a novel, very frequently the character can go one way or another: reason tells us one thing and intuition says something diametrically opposed and unexplainable. In these cases, if one wants to create a real character and not a puppet, one has to follow one's unexplainable intuition. Sometimes, this decision can repulse the author, but he has no choice lest he falsify reality. Many times people come up to me—like you in this instance—and ask me to clarify what my characters are doing, and if I reply that I cannot say anything beyond what is in the book, they may think I am a liar. For instance, they ask me if Hunter is truly María's lover: how can I possibly know that? María's ambiguity is part and parcel of her personality, producing a mystery that even the author can't figure out.

INTERVIEWER: I was going to ask you, precisely, why Juan Pablo Castel has to kill María.

SÁBATO: Because my instinct as a writer dictated that move.

INTERVIEWER: Do you believe in telepathy as does Alejandra in *On Heroes and Tombs?*

SÁBATO: Yes, I believe deeply in telepathy.

INTERVIEWER: Why do you have such a negative view of blind people?

SÁBATO: I don't refer to them in the strict sense of the word. Can anyone imagine that the blind of Buenos Aires actually live in sewers? It is a myth associated with shadows, caves and underground passages.

INTERVIEWER: Can you tell me something about the fictional "report on the blind" in *On Heroes and Tombs?*

SÁBATO: Everything I had to say is written in that "report."

INTERVIEWER: Why do parks, squares and statues play such an important role in your novels? Is it to give a sense of reality?

SÁBATO: I don't know. Obsessions, like certain dreams, are hard to explain. All this belongs to the poetic realm; it is neither logical nor clear, but rather ambiguous and resistant to explanations.

INTERVIEWER: How many books have you left unpublished?

SÁBATO: I have burned most of them, as I told you. I am very self-destructive. On the other hand, if one can write one book that withstands the test of time, one can be happy. I don't know if I have achieved that, but in any case, I wouldn't have made the situation any better by writing more books for the sake of money. Under this criterion, Agatha Christie would be more important than Shakespeare, and Corin Tellado than Cervantes. I don't believe in overproductivity. Even in the case of important authors, only two or three books can be saved out of the many they wrote. Lope wrote thousands of plays, but who reads more than his two or three masterpieces?

INTERVIEWER: What do you feel upon reading translations of your books?

SÁBATO: If I don't know the language, I am perfectly happy: translations into Japanese, Finnish or Hebrew seem perfect to me. I begin to suffer, however, when I read translations into French or some other language that I know. Philosophically speaking, any literary translation is impossible. The only perfect translations are those involving mathematics: Pythagoras' theorem can be translated from Greek to German or Spanish without losing anything because scientific terms are unequivocal. A hypotenuse is always a hypotenuse, irrespective of language. The languages of life and art, on the other hand, are open to various interpretations. An "operation," for instance, can be something mathematical, surgical or financial.

INTERVIEWER: What is poetry for you?

SÁBATO: It is the language of the world that does not respond to logic. When I say poetry, I do not mean thoroughly unpoetic verses like "Happy birthday to you." Poetry is art, generally speaking, it is the peak of art. So there is poetic painting, poetic music, and poetic novels.

INTERVIEWER: Why do you resort to poetry when you deal with the issue of death?

SÁBATO: Because it is the only tool that we have to deal with death and all other great metaphysical issues.

INTERVIEWER: What led you to painting?

SÁBATO: It was one of my passions as an adolescent, together with literature. But one cannot do everything, and for various reasons—especially having to do with the terrible inner conflicts I have been talking about—I decided to devote all my energies to novels. I have always thought that Van Gogh could have saved himself had he written novels. All his psychic and metaphysical anxieties could not be expressed through painting alone, however great it was.

INTERVIEWER: Why have you taken up painting only recently?

SÁBATO: Because my sight is beginning to deteriorate and I have a sacred horror of blindness. The size of my paintings allows me to do something I can't with letters. (*He rises as if the interview had come to an end.*)

INTERVIEWER: Let me ask you one more question: why do you consider "progress" sinister and of debatable value?

SÁBATO: No, I didn't mean that. I am only referring to the terrible consequences that modern technology has had on mankind. This has led to the most terrible alienation ever, by ossifying and robotizing man. Furthermore, the progressive movement, in the sense of the Enlightenment and positivism, did the most atrocious thing it could have done by proscribing and ridiculing magical thinking and overrating logical thinking.

The anxiety of modern man is tied to the development of Greek consciousness; in fact, the latter is "modern" consciousness insofar as it advances down the road of civilization. But the verb *to advance* is already an obscure sophism or at least a fallacy. We can now measure the extreme price man has paid for this progress that circumscribed the archaic potential of the unconscious. Artists and adolescents are the ones who feel this limitation the most, causing a general neurosis, collective hysteria, psychosomatic diseases, violence and drugs. Until recently, the East was protected by its great mystical traditions which insured harmony with the cosmos. The brutal and unrestrained invasion of Western technology, however, has produced devastation in the East. Japan, for instance, will soon face a massive psychological and spiritual crisis. The growth of rationalism has led to the increasing alienation of men of flesh and blood. It is natural that the artist, whose creation deals with man concretely, should have rebelled against this. That's why I believe that fiction in our times is a definite expression of the great crisis we are undergoing, and an attempt to redeem humanity.

Luis Rafael Sánchez

Luis Rafael Sánchez

Luis Rafael Sánchez was born in 1936 in Humacao, Puerto Rico. A leading playwright and short-story writer, his first novel, *La guaracha del macho Camacho,* 1976 (*Macho Camacho's Beat,* 1980), brought him immediate world renown and placed him alongside the writers of the "Boom."

Sánchez began his writing career as a dramatist. He received his Bachelor's Degree in Drama and Theater and was an actor in radio plays and on stage. His first play, *La espera* (The Waiting), premiered in 1959. His plays have been produced by the Experimental Theater of the Puerto Rican Ateneo and were presented in the theater festivals held by the Puerto Rican Institute of Culture. He acknowledges the influence of the Italian commedia dell'arte on his work and that of such leading figures as Brecht, Ionesco, Jarry, Lorca, Pirandello and Tennessee Williams. In the following interview he said that he would like his play "to bridge the gap between spectacle and spectators." His latest plays, *Quintuplets* and *Bel Canto,* premiered in New York in 1989.

Luis Rafael Sánchez would like to be considered a chronicler of Puerto Rican reality. His narrative work, as well as his plays, have magically captured what he called a decaying culture dominated by American advertising, comic strips and pop music. His main preoccupation is to see Puerto Rico as a Latin American country, capable of standing on its own two feet. In his own words, "I would like to see it become a modern republic with full rights for all, a model for every small nation."

Among his plays are the following: *Los angeles se han fatigado* (The Angels Are Exhausted), 1960; *La farsa del amor compradito* (The Farce of Purchased Love), 1960; *La hiel nuestra de cada día* (Our Daily Bitterness), 1962; *La pasión según Antígona Pérez* (Passion According to Antígona Pérez), 1968; *Parábola del andarín* (The Parable of the Runner), 1979. His first narrative work appeared in 1966 with his book of short stories *En cuerpo de camisa* (In Shirt-

253

sleeves). His latest book, *La importancia de llamarse Daniel Santos* (The Importance of Being Called Daniel Santos), simultaneously came out in 1988 in Mexico and the United States. It is a narrative work that goes beyond literary genres and is a composite of elements from the novel, short story, and essay.

Luis Rafael Sánchez was the recipient of a 1979 Guggenheim grant, a guest scholar at the Woodrow Wilson Center in Washington in 1983, a guest writer for the city of Berlin in 1985, and distinguished visiting professor at the City College of New York in 1988. He has been a professor of literature at the University of Puerto Rico for the past twenty years. His works have been translated into several languages.

INTERVIEWER: You are a playwright, storyteller, essayist and novelist: with which genre do you feel most at ease?

SÁNCHEZ: I am always asked that question when I am interviewed. I would say that I feel most comfortable with the genre that I am working with at a particular moment. But I cannot deny that dialogue comes very easily to me. I have a certain amount of training as an actor and I believe I have control of dramatic dialogue and a good ear for what an actor can say on the stage.

INTERVIEWER: Can one be all these things at the same time?

SÁNCHEZ: I believe they are forms that an author chooses to express the same things. Other Latin American writers do it with ease, such as Carlos Fuentes and Mario Vargas Llosa. Manuel Puig has dabbled in the theater, and Gabriel García Márquez's first play recently opened in Buenos Aires to mixed reviews. In Puerto Rico, René Marqués wrote plays, prose and essays. I think it can be done.

INTERVIEWER: How would you describe the differences between a story and a novel?

SÁNCHEZ: That division into genres seems pretty precarious and superficial to me. Some things are more reflective and more appropriately told in an essay, while others are meant to be heard out loud by the public. So the difference between a story and a novel is that in a story what you want to do is communicate a quick and fleeting impression, while a novel is more prolific and extensive.

INTERVIEWER: Your work is permeated with poetry: do you write poetry, strictly speaking?

SÁNCHEZ: No, it's the only thing I dare not attempt in terms of literature, although in life I am not afraid to do anything.

INTERVIEWER: When did you first realize that you wanted to write?

SÁNCHEZ: As an adolescent.

INTERVIEWER: And how did it happen?

SÁNCHEZ: I can't tell you specifically how it happened, but I believe I always had the desire to reorder my outlook on reality and with that desire came the need to write.

INTERVIEWER: Is writing a difficult exercise?

SÁNCHEZ: I think I suffer from a neurosis of perfection. I correct too much and sometimes I despair, and people despair waiting for me to deliver something I promised. I don't know whether I do this out of dissatisfaction or insecurity.

INTERVIEWER: What does writing mean to you, and why and for whom do you write?

SÁNCHEZ: Well, you just asked several questions, probably enough in themselves for an entire book. Writing allows one to have alternate, vicarious and improved experiences, which are not available in real life. What fascinates me about literature is that it makes the creation of a fantasy world possible, and it permits desire and everything that is usually repressed to flourish. I feel somehow that I don't write so that my friends will like me more, as García Márquez says, or because I can do nothing else, as some pretentious people have said. I write because I would like to leave an imprint behind of what it was like to be a Puerto Rican in our day and age, particularly in light of all the problems we have because of our ties with the United States. For whom do I write? For anyone who will read me; I really don't have specific readers in mind.

INTERVIEWER: Don't you think about the reader or the spectator when you write?

SÁNCHEZ: When I write plays I always think of the audience. I would even say that in all my plays I try to situate the writer so that a real spectator will immediately be able to tell where the author stands. From my first play to my most recent one, I have always wanted to reserve a special place for the spectator, so I keep him in mind along with the characters and the action when I write a play.

INTERVIEWER: Speaking of theater, do you see the influence of Pirandello in your work?

SÁNCHEZ: His influence is definitely there, as well as that of Bertolt Brecht, to name the two most significant figures to revolutionize twentieth-century theater. My prose also shows the influence of the great master Valle Inclán, in terms of his enthusiasm for dramatizing emotions and developing them to their utmost. In fact, in my plays there is an almost visceral expression of emotions which has to do with Pirandello, as you pointed out, and also a little bit with Valle Inclán, as I said.

INTERVIEWER: What about the picaresque novel?

SÁNCHEZ: I hadn't thought of that, but perhaps. One never knows where sources come from, whether they are distant cousins or brothers.

INTERVIEWER: Do you think an author should write for a social purpose or for pleasure?

SÁNCHEZ: I prefer to write for pleasure, but without forgetting that which is pleasurable should also contain a lesson, in the broadest sense of the word, not in its didactic or pedantic meaning. I would perhaps dare to say that my work has a definite social content, although it is not socially restrictive or demagogic. It is a product which is meant to be consumed by society.

INTERVIEWER: Are your two major concerns denouncing social injustices and creating your own literary language?

SÁNCHEZ: I am more interested in creating my own world and a language that is recognizably mine: that is my priority as a writer, and not out of verbal egoism, but because I want my view of reality to predominate so that everything else may follow.

INTERVIEWER: Do you have other concerns?

SÁNCHEZ: Yes, I wonder if literature is truly useful the way masonry is, for instance. Another literary concern I have is that the writers not give in to excess or exhibitionism in their desire to be in the limelight. It worries me when authors do not consider themselves working people like everyone else.

INTERVIEWER: Where do you find your characters and are they all alienated people like the beggar who pretends to be blind in your short story "La maroma" (The Acrobat)?

SÁNCHEZ: I find them in the street, first of all. My characters are almost always reflections of things I have lived through or people I have observed. Almost all of them are outsiders or transgressors. I didn't base the beggar in my short story on anyone in particular, but I have known many people who lead their lives by pretending to be blind, sick or disabled.

INTERVIEWER: What's more important for you: the character, the story, the language, or the book?

SÁNCHEZ: In some way, those four things come together to create a single reality. I am always interested in the story and how it is told. I would even say that an oft repeated joke is more effective if one tells it in a richer, more varied and detailed fashion. That's why I am so enthusiastic about Milan Kundera's novelistic art, because he tells a story so well.

INTERVIEWER: What made you start your career as a playwright?

SÁNCHEZ: I studied theater at the university, so that genre was closer to my experiences. I have been an actor in radio plays as well as on the stage, so it was easy to translate those experiences into writing.

INTERVIEWER: Do you see the influence of the commedia dell'arte on your theater?

SÁNCHEZ: Definitely. My first improvisations as an actor were based on that genre. In fact, the commedia dell'arte is present as the substrate of my play *La farsa del amor compradito.*

INTERVIEWER: Do you continue to write plays?

SÁNCHEZ: Yes, one of the reasons I am in New York is that the Intar Theatre is reading my next play, *Bel canto.* This is the North American way to do things: I present the play at a workshop, then they read it, I continue working with the actors, Rabassa translates it, and the play will finally premiere in 1989.

INTERVIEWER: Has Quevedo influenced your work?

SÁNCHEZ: He is one of the classical writers who has impressed me the most for his implacable view of reality. I don't know whether he has influenced me, but I can say that I am very enthusiastic about his work. I revere his conception of the writer as destructor and creator.

INTERVIEWER: Have you been influenced by journalism?

SÁNCHEZ: I don't know if journalism has influenced me intellectually, although perhaps the sensationalist press has. What has definitely influenced me has been films, but I think this is true of all writers, particularly Latin American ones. Most of us had our first sexual experiences at the movies, and we got our sentimental education through popular songs and films, especially Mexican ones.

INTERVIEWER: What do you think of the Boom?

SÁNCHEZ: For me, the Boom was made up of only four writers: García Márquez, Vargas Llosa, Fuentes and Cortázar. All the other authors usually included in the Boom were figures of great importance who were added to the movement. It was really an extraordinary force in opening up the literary riches of Latin America to the outside world. It seems to have come to an end with the publication of García Márquez's *The Autumn of the Patriarch.* The Boom appears to have been a homogeneous movement, and when differences began to spring up it exploded into a thousand pieces, which was a healthy result. Nowadays, each writer is following his or her way of understanding reality without taking into account the directives of the Boom in terms of its political and conceptual outlook on Latin American reality. I think the situation is far more interesting now because it is more complex and diverse.

INTERVIEWER: Nevertheless, do you see some resemblance between your work and that of the writers of the Boom?

SÁNCHEZ: I feel very close to all the authors of the Boom in the sense that they opened avenues that we later traveled with ease. I understand the passions of Manuel Puig, Cabrera Infante and Carlos Fuentes for the movies, and the enthusiasm of Carlos Monsiváis, that splendid Mexican writer, for his country's popular songs. I have always been struck by that.

INTERVIEWER: Is your sense of humor similar to that of Cabrera Infante?

SÁNCHEZ: I think there is a type of Caribbean humor that is very specific to Colombia, Cuba, the Dominican Republic and Puerto Rico. We all drink from the same fountain. Our humor is very sharp, piercing, aggressive and mocking, and never complacent. Because of this, my humor is close to that of Cabrera Infante and García Márquez. It is drawn from the same world of mulatto, half-breed countries where two worlds coexisted: that of the white who rules and that of the black or mulatto who is ruled. As the Mexican Ruiz de Alarcón tried to show in his writings, the mulatto servants always managed to protest even if the only way they could do this was by mocking in low tones.

INTERVIEWER: Do you write in Puerto Rican, rather than in Castilian Spanish, in the same way as Cabrera Infante used to say he wrote in Cuban?

SÁNCHEZ: Yes, in order to make street language respectable. It is a language that appears and disappears very quickly, and it has no literary prestige. I wanted to make a compilation of this fleeting and fragile language, I wanted to give it Puerto Rican citizenship.

INTERVIEWER: Which of your books do you like best?

SÁNCHEZ: Always the one I am in the process of writing.

INTERVIEWER: Do you have a favorite writer?

SÁNCHEZ: I have many: I mentioned Kundera, and I might also add Heinrich Böll. The way García Márquez constructs his prose fascinates me, and I marvel at Carlos Fuentes's ability and willingness to tackle new realities. In fact, my favorite writers are those who are willing to take risks and do things that they haven't done in previous books. Among North American authors, I must mention Norman Mailer for his willingness to fail, if necessary, in attempting to discover new realities.

INTERVIEWER: In *The Passion According to Antígona Pérez*, you rewrite history. Why do you give Greek myths a new dimension and convert them into Christian and Latin American myths at the same time?

SÁNCHEZ: I wanted to recover in my work the great recurrent theme of twentieth-century Latin American literature, which is the issue of the dictator and the oppression he perpetrates. I thought Antigone, because of her capacity to give of herself and her enthusiasm for fraternity, would be the most appropriate myth to recover. It is a myth that has so much prestige in various traditions that I felt the need to reestablish it in a fictitious Latin American republic. I really thought that in Antigone one could recognize the great Latin American conflict, that of fraternity and fratricide.

INTERVIEWER: Why did you choose a woman as a leading character and spokesperson for your ideals and your fight against any form of dictatorship?

SÁNCHEZ: In the first place, because the character was already there, I was appropriating an old myth. Also because throughout history women have suffered a certain amount of rejection and marginalization, and I thought it was a way of vindicating what Antigone stood for and, by the same token, the place of women in Latin American society.

INTERVIEWER: What do you think of women?

SÁNCHEZ: Women in our continent are splendid and wonderful, and really worthy of several Antigones, not just one.

INTERVIEWER: What do you think of the work of Rosario Ferré?

SÁNCHEZ: I wrote a very enthusiastic review of her book *Papeles de Pandora* when it came out. She is part of a vanguard of Puerto Rican narrators which includes such valuable members as Ana Lydia Vega, Mayra Montero, Magaly García Ramis and Carmen Lugo Filippi. These women are appropriating the language that was traditionally the monopoly of men. Rosario's work has a double merit: in the first place, it is excellent independently of who wrote it, and in the second instance, it is written from a feminist perspective that seeks to demythify. It is an aggressive literature, and Rosario attacks not only with her pen and her typewriter but also with her sex, which I find very healthy.

INTERVIEWER: Do you consider yourself a Puerto Rican first or a Latin American?

SÁNCHEZ: For me it is the same thing, although some Puerto Ricans have differing views on the issue. For my part, I have always felt that the Puerto Rican experience is the Latin American experience—I have never felt like a stranger in any Latin American capital, whether it be Bogotá, Santo Domingo, Caracas, Mexico City, or Buenos Aires. To be Latin American means acknowledging the fact that we are a continent of halfbreeds and that our overall contribution to the world encompasses not only racial characteristics but also cultural ones. The ability to recognize that we are a composite of races allows us to focus our wills and our history to come up with new options for the world.

INTERVIEWER: Would you like to be known as a chronicler of Latin American reality?

SÁNCHEZ: Yes, that wouldn't bother me. I would always like to be seen as a chronicler of Puerto Rican reality. I am interested in talking about the small area that I come from, which is Puerto Rico. I would like to be permanently associated with what is Puerto Rican.

INTERVIEWER: What does it mean to be Puerto Rican?

SÁNCHEZ: To be Puerto Rican means to be a man who comes from a world in permanent conflict as the result of the presence of a powerful and dominant invading culture. At the same time, it also means to be a man with a long tradition as a Latin American vis-à-vis the invading culture. In short, to be a Puerto Rican means to be in constant conflict with what one is.

INTERVIEWER: What do you think of the preparations for the 500th anniversary of the discovery of America?

SÁNCHEZ: Sometimes I think they are like burlesque or kitsch, although I acknowledge that there are many things to celebrate. The celebrations, however, should be honest and should include not only what happened in the past but what remains to be done. I don't think it should be a celebration of what we have lived, but a promise of reconciliation, betterment and respect for the future.

INTERVIEWER: What remains to be done, then?

SÁNCHEZ: In the first place, it must be recognized that the conquest and colonization engendered moments of absolute horror. This must be acknowledged with great honesty. It is true that the Spaniards came to the New World with the obsessive idea of spreading the Catholic faith, but they did so at the cost of a great deal of blood, exploitation and persecution. This dark side of the conquest should also be recognized as well as more positive aspects. So what remains to be done is to understand that the relationship between the Old and the New Worlds is no longer one where the mother country dominates, but one where both parties have achieved equal footing and are willing to walk together shoulder to shoulder.

INTERVIEWER: Is the myth a sort of mask?

SÁNCHEZ: Of course. Every myth is an attempt to mask reality. In fact, demythification is nothing else than an act of unmasking.

INTERVIEWER: Is the corrosive humor present in your stories and novels another sort of mask?

SÁNCHEZ: I would like it to be a means of unmasking and revealing our faces such as they are, unshaven and without makeup, in their essential beauty or ugliness.

INTERVIEWER: Is humor also a weapon?

SÁNCHEZ: Definitely. I would like it to be seen as such in my work. I will even go further and say that throughout history, humor has always been a weapon. For instance, when one sees the potential humor in *La Celestina,* and in the works of Quevedo, Genet and Valle Inclán, one realizes that it has always been used as a weapon, in one way or another. I think humor is a very serious thing. In fact, I believe that making someone laugh is more difficult than making someone cry. That's why there are so many great dramatic actors, but so few comic ones.

INTERVIEWER: Is music another mask and weapon?

SÁNCHEZ: For Latin Americans, music is not a weapon, nor a mask. It allows us to dream, to express what we dare not say openly, to travel toward our inner world and free ourselves, even though it might be by closing our eyes as we hug our partners.

INTERVIEWER: What about dance?

SÁNCHEZ: Dance as well.

INTERVIEWER: Do you wear many masks?

SÁNCHEZ: Many. I think everyone wears them, although some better than others. I think social life requires a good set of masks.

INTERVIEWER: Are you wearing one now?

SÁNCHEZ: I think that whenever we do an interview, one of our masks comes forth, whether it be that of charm, eloquence or lucidity. I suspect I am wearing some mask or other.

INTERVIEWER: In 1976, your first novel, *Macho Camacho's Beat,* came out. How has your life changed since that book was published?

SÁNCHEZ: A lot. Too much. In fact, I have tried to explain that sometimes success is yet another form of failure. I never expected the novel would be received so well. It changed my life for it opened many new possibilities for furthering my work, such as grants from the Guggenheim Foundation, the Woodrow Wilson Center for Scholars in Washington and the city of Berlin.

INTERVIEWER: Reviewers have said that in *Macho Camacho's Beat* you "capture in a funny mirror of crazed humor, sex, frustration and despair an elusive image of Puerto Rico and all of colonized Latin America." What made you write that novel?

SÁNCHEZ: In the first place, a conviction that the violent, aggressive and confused world of Puerto Rico, of my Puerto Rico of today, had to be translated into literature. I thought the Puerto Rican experience was screaming out to be put in writing, so that's what I did. As simple as that.

INTERVIEWER: García Márquez said of *Macho Camacho* that it was "one of the best books I've read in recent years . . . an excellent demonstration of what can be done with a popular voice . . . of great artistic value." What do you think of that?

SÁNCHEZ: That's very kind of him. I have never met him, but I am aware of his interest in my work. In this interview I would like to thank him.

INTERVIEWER: Is *Macho Camacho* based on a story with the same name that you wrote in 1969?

SÁNCHEZ: Yes, I wrote that story when Mario Vargas Llosa came to Puerto Rico and said he wanted to dedicate a special issue of the Peruvian magazine *Amarú* exclusively to Puerto Rican literature. He asked me to write something and so *Macho Camacho* first appeared in Lima in an issue promoted by Vargas Llosa. Later on, I came to think that that story could be turned into a novel, and that's what I did.

INTERVIEWER: When did the song that you mention throughout your novel come out?

SÁNCHEZ: I invented it, there is no such "guaracha." I wanted the novel to be built around a particular rhythm which would lead the whole text. I wanted the readers to feel as if they were reading a musical score of Caribbean rhythms. Unlike what I say in that invented song, however, life is not so wonderful. There was a type of irony that I wanted to establish between the lyrics of the song and the reality outlined in the text.

INTERVIEWER: Has anyone actually composed music for that imagined song?

SÁNCHEZ: I was told that some Puerto Rican in California had set the "guaracha" to music, but I don't know whether this is true or not.

INTERVIEWER: Would you consider adapting *Macho Camacho* for the theater?

SÁNCHEZ: Miriam Colón of the Puerto Rican Traveling Theatre wanted to adapt it. But I said no, because I thought the story would lose a lot of effectiveness on stage. What was attractive about the text was reading it out loud to oneself. Recently, a television producer, Miguel Angel Alvarez, suggested that I adapt the novel for television, and I told him that I didn't think that would be a very good medium for the story either.

INTERVIEWER: Is *Macho Camacho* a declaration of freedom for the language?

SÁNCHEZ: Yes, definitely, I want it to be seen as that. I want language to characterize and become the main protagonist of a situation.

INTERVIEWER: And how did you come to master colloquial language?

SÁNCHEZ: I think that what has to be done is filter what one hears. Some people think this involves a mere transfer process, but it is not that, it requires sifting what one hears through a sieve and making it appear that what has been strained is the essence of the text. So it is a task that must be done very cautiously.

INTERVIEWER: How do you reconcile that colloquial language with cultured language?

SÁNCHEZ: In the case of *Macho Camacho* I did so by establishing a narrator who leads the whole text. It was difficult to do because I like proper, accepted and cultured Spanish, but in that novel I had to give colloquial language great leeway, to reflect how my characters speak.

INTERVIEWER: Who is the narrator in *Macho Camacho?*

SÁNCHEZ: Many people think the narrator of that book is the author, when in fact he is a fictitious character who leads the novel's vibrant, violent and outlandish language.

INTERVIEWER: Following the great success of *Macho Camacho,* have you written another novel?

SÁNCHEZ: I have a short unpublished novel called *Mr. Lili nos invita a su congoja* (Mr. Lili Invites Us to Share in His Distress), which I wrote in 1978 and have not wanted to publish. At that time, I was more interested in writing plays and essays, and I was not so concerned with novels. From 1980 to 1987, I worked on my new book, *La importancia de llamarse Daniel Santos* (The Importance of Being Called Daniel Santos), which came out in 1988. Daniel Santos is one of the most famous singers of popular music in Latin America. He sings about great loves and great passions with a sort of sentimental fierceness. And Latin America is reflected in his songs. I think our daily life is so pregnant with music that it appears everywhere, and writers cannot afford to leave it aside.

INTERVIEWER: When you write novels, do you elaborate them in your head for years and then sit down and write them, as García Márquez does?

SÁNCHEZ: I think all authors have their own methods, but they all share certain things in common, like obsessively thinking about certain topics until these mature sufficiently in their imaginations to be put on paper. Sometimes I take brief notes and fill yellow pages with small solutions and ideas that need to be developed and organized. For *Daniel Santos,* for instance, I wrote three long versions, rejecting each in turn. It is a narrative work which is neither a novel nor a short story.

INTERVIEWER: Is writing an obsession, then?

SÁNCHEZ: It is an obsession and a pain; I would even say it is a torture, because it is a beating one administers to oneself.

INTERVIEWER: Do you envision it as a solitary trip?

SÁNCHEZ: A terribly solitary and desperately lonely trip. In fact, during my stay in New York, I have been thinking that it is getting increasingly more difficult for me to write with people around. Every day, I need more real solitude to be able to write. I cannot see anyone, not even the maid who comes to clean, and this has become part of my way of writing.

INTERVIEWER: Nevertheless, you need to write?

SÁNCHEZ: Yes, it's like a life sentence, and I want to do it. In fact, as the years pass by and I have become older, I need to write more and more, and not metaphorically or falsely, but truly. I need to leave some writings behind, like a testament.

INTERVIEWER: You are also a teacher, aren't you?

SÁNCHEZ: Yes, but I wish I didn't have to teach, and I spend my time thinking how I could leave that profession. But I do it because it has to be done.

INTERVIEWER: Do you teach literature or writing?

SÁNCHEZ: Literature, unfortunately, and I say unfortunately because my literature tends to be a marginal and transgressive one, while in the classroom we have to work with literary models. So there is a tension between what I say in public and what I practice in private. Masks, you see? Masks everywhere.

INTERVIEWER: For some time, you had a column called "En puertorriqueño" (In Puerto Rican) in a San Juan newspaper.

SÁNCHEZ: It wasn't a column. I wrote articles periodically that were labeled "Written in Puerto Rican" because they dealt with the aberrant or contradictory situations which continue to take place in the Puerto Rican colony. I wrote the articles for a

leftist/progressive newspaper called *Claridad,* and they were
well received.

INTERVIEWER: What do you feel when you finish writing a
book?

SÁNCHEZ: First of all, great relief and an agonizing moment.
It is very hard for me to go back over what I have written because
I begin to see all sorts of defects. When a work is completed, I
am happy to be done with it, as I imagine any person who
finishes and publishes a book feels.

INTERVIEWER: What's your reaction upon seeing your plays
performed?

SÁNCHEZ: I see my plays as many times as I think I have to
out of solidarity with the actors, and that's it. A play of mine
was recently performed in Cuba, Venezuela and Colombia, and
I refused to accompany the actors because there comes a time
when the play begins to bore me, so I would rather stay in my
country doing something else.

INTERVIEWER: What is your relationship to the director, the
actors, the characters and the spectators?

SÁNCHEZ: I must have great faith in the director because it is
to him that I turn over the project. Actors are my favorite people
in the theater, and I think they are tremendously bold because
they dare to face the audience. After all, I remain at home, leaving these people to express my thoughts. As far as the spectators
go, it is becoming increasingly difficult for me to decide where
they belong in a play. I don't like the idea of the spectators
disappearing into the darkness for two hours. Every day, I ask
myself critically if we shouldn't find a new place for the spectators, and what I have tried to do in my plays is to bridge the gap
between spectacle and spectator, so that the two do not remain
separate. I want the spectators to be more dynamic and to
participate more actively in the plays.

INTERVIEWER: This is what the reader has done for the Latin
American novel, right?

SÁNCHEZ: Perhaps. What every playwright who has written

novels dreams is for his plays to have the complete freedom that novels do. But in the theater, that freedom is still restricted by a limited space.

INTERVIEWER: What is your relationship with your characters, who dominates whom?

SÁNCHEZ: The character always dominates. In fact, I think that one of the great traps of the theater is that the playwright thinks he has the right to give the characters all his biases and prejudices. I believe that one has to give the characters true freedom and autonomy, and that they have to dominate the author.

INTERVIEWER: Gregory Rabassa has done an excellent translation of *Macho Camacho* into English. What do you feel when you read your work in translation?

SÁNCHEZ: There is also a very good translation of that novel into Portuguese by Eliane Zagury. But I don't like to read my work, in translation or otherwise, because I become very tense.

INTERVIEWER: Has it also been translated into French?

SÁNCHEZ: No, it hasn't, for the trite reason that no translator could be found. If a translator could have been found who could handle the novel, it would have been translated long ago, but no one felt confident with Puerto Rican colloquialisms to do justice to the novel. Severo Sarduy, who works for a French publisher, tried to no avail to find a translator for that book. For my part, I am a bad reader of my works, I resent and reject them, whether in translation or not.

INTERVIEWER: What do you think of your own work?

SÁNCHEZ: One always thinks one could have done more, but I am satisfied with it.

INTERVIEWER: Before beginning this interview, you asked me what I would focus on: political or literary questions. If the focus had been political, what would you have said?

SÁNCHEZ: I think I would have said the same thing, because literature cannot be separated from politics or the experience of the artist. I wanted to know whether you were going to ask me about my work or about my country, but in my case it is impossible to separate the two. That's why I told you that I would like to be seen as a Puerto Rican writer willing to interpret a complex reality: that of the sweet and bitter country that is my own. I say bitter because sometimes things happen in Puerto Rico that I find absurd and which bother me. These happen as a result of our difficult relationship with the United States, which we cannot break off. I hate Puerto Rico when its people are blind to the reality that surrounds them. What a horrible thing to say, right? At the same time, I love my country deeply, because it has tried to rise above the circumstances, and it has overcome many things with great dignity. I love it and hate it at the same time, because I can understand its misery on the one hand, and its splendor on the other.

INTERVIEWER: Would you like Puerto Rico to be independent?

SÁNCHEZ: Yes, I passionately want that, but I see this as more and more unlikely every day. I want Puerto Rico to be independent, I would like to see it become a modern republic with full rights for all, a model for every small nation, and an example of what a poor, developing country can achieve.

INTERVIEWER: If you could give some advice to aspiring young writers, what would you say?

SÁNCHEZ: I would tell them that they should go ahead with that profession if they can accept that it involves a lot of work, sweat and revisions. But if they want to be writers to achieve so-called success and recognition, they should give it up, because being a writer involves a real commitment.

INTERVIEWER: What is reality and what is fantasy for you?

SÁNCHEZ: Reality is what one appears to be, fantasy is what one aspires to achieve.

INTERVIEWER: Who is Luis Rafael Sánchez?

SÁNCHEZ: A Puerto Rican who loves and hates his country at the same time, who believes arrogantly that he understands Puerto Rico more as the years go by, and who wants to live with a little peace. I think that as time goes by, one's aspirations intensify rather than decrease, and what I really want at this moment is to be profoundly at peace with myself, independent of all the false glamour of the literary world. I would like to write very serious literature, but for reasons other than those involving the desire for success. If success comes—as it has already in some measure—then that's fine, but that's not my goal.

Severo Sarduy

Severo Sarduy

Severo Sarduy was born in Camagüey, Cuba, on February 25, 1937. His work, whether in poetry or prose, brings out the exuberant feast of words typical of the tropics.

Sarduy began publishing his first poems at an early age in the local newspaper *El camagüeyano*. In 1955, when he was only eighteen, one of his poems appeared in *Ciclón*, Havana's leading literary journal, whose director was José Rodríguez Feo. A year later, he moved to Havana to start medical school. Sarduy, however, continued writing and, with the triumph of the Cuban Revolution, began publishing his work in two of the most important journals of the time, the *Diario Libre* and the *Lunes de Revolución*. Cabrera Infante was the first ever to write a review of one of his literary works.

After receiving a grant to study the history of art at the Ecole du Louvre in Paris, in 1959, Sarduy left Cuba for France, where he has been living ever since. In 1967, he became a French citizen. From 1966 to 1968, he also wrote for the now defunct *Mundo Nuevo,* the literary magazine published in Paris by Emir Rodríguez Monegal, which gave exposure to the writers of the "Boom."

Sarduy is perhaps one of the best-known Latin American writers in France and one who has contributed greatly to the translation of many Spanish and Latin American writers into French. As head of a collection at the Editions du Seuil, he has focused attention on many of his colleagues from the Hispanic world. His own works have appeared simultaneously in Spanish and in French and have been translated into twenty-five languages.

His works may be divided into novels, essays and poetry. Among his novels are the following: *Gestos* (Gestures), 1963; *De donde son los cantantes,* 1967 (*From Cuba with a Song,* 1972); *Cobra,* 1972 (*Cobra,* 1975); *Maitreya,* 1978 (*Maitreya,* 1987); and *Colibrí,* 1984. Among his essays: *Escrito sobre un cuerpo,* 1969 (*Written on a Body,* 1989); *Barroco* (Baroque), 1976; and *La Simulación* (Simulation), 1982. His poetic works include: *Big Bang,* 1974;

Daiquirí, 1980; *Un testigo fugaz y disfrazado* (A Fleeting Witness in Disguise), 1985; *El Cristo de la rue Jacob* (Christ in the Rue Jacob), 1987.

Sarduy is also well known for his scientific chronicles in the French press, symbolic remnants of the interest he acquired during his years as a medical student in Cuba. He is equally known for his radio plays, *Dolores Rondón,* 1965; *La playa* (The Beach), 1971, winner of the Prix Paul Gilson de la Communauté Radiophonique des Programmes de Langue Française; and *Récit* (Narration), a collage based on *Cobra* which received the 1972 Italia Prix Médicis étranger. *Para la voz,* 1978 (*For Voice,* 1985), collects his radio plays.

Sarduy's writings have been inspired by the baroque. In the following interview he repeatedly mentions the influence of Góngora and Lezama Lima on his work. He also stresses the importance of the plastic arts, whether painting, music or ballet (he recounts a prank he played on some publisher by sending as his biographical note that of Rudolf Nureyev). Sarduy is an experienced art critic and should also be recognized as a painter in his own right.

INTERVIEWER: Severo, have you been affected in any way by the perfect symmetry of the initials of your name, S.S.?

SARDUY: Yes, my book *Cobra* was determined by them in some measure since it is a book about a sacred serpent, "s.s." Given the constant religious overtones of my books, one might also think that the "s.s." stands for sub-sanctity. For obvious reasons and because I live in a house shaped by those events, I would prefer not to refer to any other possible interpretations of the initials "s.s." that have been given in this century.

INTERVIEWER: Why "sacred serpent"?

SARDUY: Because the book deals with a cobra which is tied to the East (particularly India) and which is linked to initiation rites of one sort or another. For instance, in Tantrism the sacred serpent is utilized to achieve a kind of balance or stability through certain sexual practices. This cobra is visualized as Kundalini, which is a sacred serpent that the ancient tantric masters believed ascended the vertebral spine of an initiate to his brain through a series of sexual exercises. In the brain a white flower would explode, symbolizing enlightenment. So the tantric model is one possible iconography of the sacred serpent. India, however, is replete with allusions to sacred serpents and cobras. In Nepal, some of the gods sleep in a nest of serpents. Generally speaking, serpents represent a good and positive power in the East, contrary to Western notions.

INTERVIEWER: Why are you so interested in the East?

SARDUY: I could give you autobiographical reasons. For instance, in Camagüey, Cuba, where I was born, I was very closely linked to the teachings of the Theosophical Society from the time of my adolescence. The Cuban Theosophical Society, like those in the rest of the world, underwent a schism following the dissolution of the Order of the Star by Krishnamurti, who was to fulfill the role of Maitreya, the teacher of the universe. This is a long story, which I have detailed in one of my books called *Maitreya,* appropriately enough. Maitreya's story is Krishnamurti's story, more or less, and the latter is the main character of that book. Krishnamurti was discovered by members of the Theosophical Society near Madras, at a place which I know well. He was then groomed to be the teacher of humanity. They brought him to the West, and educated him in London to play that role. But when he was old enough, he immediately dissolved the Order which was supposed to receive his teachings. So, to get back to my childhood, I grew up in a schismatic world triggered by Krishnamurti's dissolution of the Order. I started reading his works very early on, perhaps at the age of eleven or even younger. From that distant time to the present, I have had a constant thirst for the East.

INTERVIEWER: Is that why your novels represent a dialogue between East and West?

SARDUY: Yes, precisely. My books, however, represent not only a dialogue, but also what I believe to be the destiny of the entire world: the abolition of that dialogue. My works attempt to overcome the seemingly permanent contradiction between East and West. The identity of both cultures must be maintained at the same time that the gulf between them must be eliminated.

INTERVIEWER: Do you mean "eliminated" in the sense that the East is more important for you?

SARDUY: Not at all. Neither one is more important than the other. What is significant is what we could call the reflected images between both civilizations and among the various religions—what is important is to eliminate contradictions. That's why *Cobra* ends in Tibet, a Buddhist country, because Buddhism presupposes the eradication of contradictions. In that book, I was also interested in eliminating the contradiction between the sexes, which is as pervasive as that between East and West. That's why the central character of *Cobra* is a transvestite, because that type of person embodies both sexes and eliminates the contradiction between them. I don't want to sound pedantic, but I will mention a term devised by Hegel: *Aufhebung*. It refers to synthesis, to that cancellation of opposites. So *Cobra* works on both levels: the elimination of the opposites of East and West, and the eradication of sexual differences.

INTERVIEWER: Do you especially identify yourself with the character Cobra?

SARDUY: I identify with all my characters, but perhaps more with this one.

INTERVIEWER: According to Roberto González Echevarría,

in your work you speak of India to reclaim Cuba, by opposition with Columbus, who spoke of the new continent as if it were India.

SARDUY: Yes, everything that González Echevarría has written or said about my books is extremely sharp and intelligent, much more so than my own comments on my work. I am also going to respond to what might be called the anamorphosis of Cuban literature. In opposition to the rest of Latin America (including Brazil), when a Cuban wants to speak about Cuba, very frequently he speaks about something else. If a Mexican novelist is going to speak about Mexico, he will in all probability talk about the Mexican Revolution and the indigenous cultures of his country before Cortés. If an Argentine speaks about Argentina, he will probably write a book of sonnets, like Federico Urbach's *La urna* (The Urn). The works of Girondo and Borges also come to mind in this respect. When a Cuban writer wants to speak about his country, however, he will frequently refer to things that have no relation to Cuba. In Lezama Lima's *Paradiso,* for instance, the author talks about an imaginary university called Upsalón to refer to what is taking place in Havana under Machado's dictatorship. The characters in that book are called Fronesis, Foción and Cemí, thoroughly un-Cuban names, and Lima frequently alludes to Pythagoras, the pre-Socratics and Taoism in that work. The same is true of Virgilio Piñera: his book *Electra Garrigó* is a Greek tragedy in which he supposedly talks about Camagüey. In my very humble case, *Cobra* is a book which evokes India and which ends in the north of that country, but in which I speak about Cuba almost exclusively, in the tradition of Cuban literature. This process is what I have called an anamorphosis, and a good example of it is Holbein's *The Ambassadors,* a painting which looks like a seashell from the front and like a skull from the sides. This is what is also taking place in Cuban literature.

INTERVIEWER: You have just mentioned the name of one of your heroes, Lezama Lima. Do you think that if neither he nor

Góngora, another great master who influenced you, had existed, your work would have been different?

SARDUY: Yes, not only different but perhaps non-existent, because I write about concrete daily events, not abstract notions which I cannot put a handle on. For instance, when I wrote about Tibet, I was at Tibetan monasteries in Sikkim, Bhutan, Assam, Nepal and the north of India—in the ancient kingdoms of the Himalayas. I always write about what is right in front of me. But what is right in front of me is filtered or mediated by what Roland Barthes called "the paper code tradition," which is the age-old literary tradition that stretches from the Buddhists to Lezama Lima and beyond. Everything is filtered, transposed and metaphorized by this textual tradition.

INTERVIEWER: In addition to Góngora and Lezama Lima, do you also see the influence of Quevedo on your work?

SARDUY: Yes, especially in the poems. I have a book of poems called *Un testigo fugaz y disfrazado,* published in Barcelona by Edicions Libres del Mall, in which Quevedo's influence is very apparent, particularly in relation to the issue of death and the funerary aspects of the poems, but also in connection with the parodical and sometimes erotic allusions. There is a connection between love and death, a sort of bitterness or acidity, which comes directly from Quevedo, and also from Valdés Leal, who has deeply influenced my work.

INTERVIEWER: And what about the picaresque novel?

SARDUY: There are many picaresque characters in my novels: the Celestina is present throughout, as is the Lozana andaluza. José Rodríguez Feo's essay revealed that in *La lozana andaluza* the author, Francisco Delicado, speaks to his characters for the first time in history. This dialogue between author and characters is a device I resort to in my books. In fact, the characters criticize me, take me to task, and sometimes speak to me in a very disrespectful fashion, in the best picaresque tradition. They do not follow the designs or whims of an all-powerful author, but rather, they intervene directly in the narrative, which they modify, alter, parody, erase, change or correct according to their own inclinations. The characters, therefore, are alive as a dialectic force in the books. It is never the case that an almighty author deals with inert matter which he can manipulate. Rather, the characters in the book speak and decide their own destinies.

INTERVIEWER: Is the author present in the novel as a narrator?

SARDUY: In the work of the great Cuban writer Alejo Carpentier, the narrator is always the same, despite the baroque flavor of many situations, the exuberant decor, and the verbal luxury. In my own humble works, there is what might be called an exteriophony, which means that there are many voices, not just one. There is a fictional narrator, the voice of Severo Sarduy, the voices of the characters, and even the voice of the author's mother sometimes. It is a choral narrative situation, never a monophony.

INTERVIEWER: Who is the "we" that appears so frequently in your work?

SARDUY: That "we" frequently changes according to the situation. But what is important about it is that it is an articulation of a plural voice. At the carnival, particularly as it is conceived by Bakhtin, what is important is the plurality or polyphony of voices, or the fact that everyone is capable of speaking, laughing and parodying. To get back to the comparison with Carpentier, what is different about my work is that a monolithic voice gives way to a chorus of voices.

INTERVIEWER: Are your characters as powerful as their author?

SARDUY: Yes, and sometimes more so. On occasion, they insult me with words that I cannot repeat. The characters are interested in determining their own fate and narration, which they can do because they are the ones in charge.

INTERVIEWER: Where do your characters come from: your imagination or real life?

SARDUY: Everything I have written is strictly autobiographical, things I have lived through. I am a very limited author. In fact, I am so limited that I am incapable of inventing, I have never invented anything. There is a very small distance between what I have lived and what I write. A good example of this is a painting which has influenced me a great deal: Rembrandt's *The Night Watch*, a very famous group portrait which can be found at the Amsterdam museum. The realistic painting, which most likely depicts a group of cloth workers, has one special feature which could be taken as an example for all creative endeavors. In the midst of the picture, a young albino dwarf can be seen crossing with a dead chicken tied to her waist. This little girl changes the whole scene, because she doesn't belong there, at night, and with a chicken tied around her waist—children have never been allowed to play with dead animals. So her presence swings the balance from realism to fiction and the imaginary. My work tries to achieve the same effect: to move from mundane reality to fiction through a minor detail, which is what happened with Rembrandt's painting.

INTERVIEWER: Is that why there is always a female albino midget in your books?

SARDUY: It is an allusion to her, of course, but also to *Las meninas,* which is the absolute model of all enigma, representation and fiction as Foucault saw it. So the midgets are an echo of baroque artists such as Rembrandt and Velázquez, among others. Carreño's dwarfs can also be seen in the Prado museum, dressed up as Silenus and Faunus.

INTERVIEWER: Are the characters you create based on other people, or are they an extension of yourself?

SARDUY: Both. They are like *tableaux vivants* which come out of their paintings to accompany me through life. I frequently say that my immediate family consists of characters such as Carreño's obese midgets; they are a little like brothers or sons.

INTERVIEWER: Your books are really like a series of paintings, which reveal the influence of your studies in art history in Paris.

SARDUY: I do not consider myself a writer strictly speaking, in the sense of someone who could write a thriller, an autobiography or a screenplay. I see myself as a painter who uses words instead of paints and brushes. It is almost like a Zen Buddhist koan: how would you paint using only words and no colors? Lately, I have also been painting: I have had exhibits and even sold some of my paintings. Paradoxically, they are very reminiscent of a form of writing, but that is another matter.

INTERVIEWER: You started out studying medicine. Why, like Cabrera Infante, did you give it up?

SARDUY: I would say that I haven't stopped practicing it because I make my living as a science journalist with Radio France Internationale. Paris is one of the most expensive cities in the world, and I love to travel, and I could not meet my expenses through writing alone. The broadcasts I do are almost always on medicine, and I could even treat a patient if I had to. Another subject I address concerns the latest advances in astronomy, for which I also developed a passion in Cuba. I wrote the book called *Big Bang* on the subject. Medicine, biology, genetics, cosmology and astronomy are all constantly present in my work. Even *Cobra* is full of astronomical metaphors. The white dwarf, for instance, is no more than a star which has collapsed on itself, losing its gravitational stability to the point that it has imploded, as opposed to exploded. There are also gigantic red stars, traveling blue ones, black holes, and curved space. So the book is full of metaphors that do not come from any literary tradition, but rather from my own inventions based on current cosmological research, particularly from the United States.

INTERVIEWER: Is interpreting your work like holding a dialogue with poets and painters?

SARDUY: Yes, the root of everything is painting. I believe

that humanity and knowledge move along parallel tracks. There is a common episteme of our time, as Foucault said. In this sense, I believe that the first thing which moves forward is painting. Painting takes the lead and must be listened to, and I underline the words "listened to." For instance, in speaking of this century's episteme, we can say that the audible moment of a painter such as Mark Rothko has not yet arrived. Perhaps it will take another century before we can perceive his work in its entirety. We are barely beginning to visualize it and perhaps for the wrong reasons, like the beauty of the colors or the harmony of the proportions or even his own tragic life. I think that painting is so far ahead that we have to wait for architecture, music, science, mathematics and literature to catch up. The case of Rothko is a good example, because he cannot yet be heard, and once again I will emphasize the word *heard*.

INTERVIEWER: In *Cobra* you defined writing in many different ways. Could you add something to each of these statements? I'll begin with, "Writing is the art of the ellipsis."

SARDUY: Obviously, that is a reference to the baroque, to the astronomy of Kepler, where the planets are viewed as an ellipsis, contrary to Galileo's astronomy, where the orbits of planets are seen as circular. So there is perhaps a somewhat pedantic but hopefully humorous reference to Kepler's baroque and ellipsis and also Kepler's ellipse. Finally, I must also mention Góngora's baroque and his ellipsis. So there is a reference to the main components of the baroque, the ellipse and the ellipsis.

INTERVIEWER: Your second statement is, "Writing is the art of digressing."

SARDUY: Yes, as you can hear, when I speak or write I use digression and subordinate clauses a lot. I think I draw this from the Cuban mode of speaking, where everyone talks at the same time using digressions. Unlike the French and other people who speak in a linear fashion and develop a theme to its conclusion, Cubans speak with subordinate clauses and digressions, through a type of syntactic and verbal arborescence which leads them to a disordered view of the world and its problems. They also all speak at the same time, which tends to give a choral impression of their subject matter. I believe talking in this way helps to mediate the topic under discussion.

INTERVIEWER: Now the third statement: "Writing is the art of recreating reality. Let's respect it."

SARDUY: That statement is a little parodical, because it is a reference to figurative or representative literature. My books are not really immediately readable. One must make a little effort to enter into the story—it is not a photocopy of reality.

INTERVIEWER: You also say, "Writing is the art of restoring History."

SARDUY: When I say that in the book, I systematically begin to alter the history that I am dealing with. So, I am laughing at that precept, because as I utter it I begin to change history. I am not restoring it in the least, therefore, but rather varying and modulating it, according to a series of paintings.

INTERVIEWER: Another reference is the following: "Writing is the art of disordering order and ordering disorder."

SARDUY: Yes, that has a lot to do with Lévi-Strauss's notion of *bricolage,* or rebuilding an object on the vestiges or ruins of another. Lévi-Strauss held that all art is like *bricolage,* restructuring something from the remnants of something else. I think that very frequently art is precisely this: starting with a given situation, one begins to alter and play with the elements to build up a second order, a metaorder, metaobject and metalanguage. It is a secondary operation on the primary data of our senses and our lives, and even of our paintings and representations.

INTERVIEWER: You also say, "Writing is the art of correcting."

SARDUY: Yes, because writing involves playing with words and correcting. In fact, the page is corrected to such an extent that it looks like an enormous scar or tattoo. In some way, writing is like tattooing. Like a person applying a tattoo on a willing victim, the writer tattooes the skin of language with his motives, obsessions and compulsions. Under the hands of a great writer, dead and lifeless language is tattooed so that it becomes significant and vibrant, even violent.

INTERVIEWER: You also say, "Perhaps writing is like this: being able to invent life each time, destroying the past, spilled water, water under the bridge."

SARDUY: Speaking of inventing, something very funny happened: a Spanish magazine asked me for my biography, and since I think that my life and my ideas are rather dull, I copied the biography of one of my dancing idols, Rudolph Nureyev, from a dictionary on dance, and passed it off as my own. Dancing is another one of my obsessions. So I sent the biography, and to my considerable surprise another Spanish magazine thought it was true and used it in introducing me for an article I had written on sacred manuscripts. They said Severo Sarduy had performed with the greatest dance companies in the world.

INTERVIEWER: Why does dance always appear in your work, why does it attract you so?

SARDUY: Because I do my writing with my body, not with consciousness, intelligence, knowledge or culture. I write with my body as a whole, with every muscle, and with sex of course. So the body is present, and dancing is its epiphany. The ritual dances of India are very present in my works, as I have seen them performed many times in India. But Western classical and modern dances are there too. Nijinski and Nureyev have given the best lessons in writing. With them, the body ceased to be an inert, heavy, insignificant mass, and became a true ideogram and a symbol of pure expression, which has only happened two or three times in the history of dancing.

INTERVIEWER: Does the body turn into spirit when this happens?

SARDUY: I wouldn't use the word spirit, because it is very ambiguous. In my books, I have always refrained from referring to any notion of spirit, even when I was talking about Buddhism.

I think the concept of spirit can be very misleading in the context of Eastern religions, because in places like India there is no distinction between the body and the spirit: the dichotomy between sacred and profane is eliminated in reaching for the sacred. Daily life is sacred in India, as we can see when we look at workers from different castes going to the river, or washing their clothes or whatever. It is like witnessing a religious ritual, when in reality it is just a daily event. But the abolition of the distinction between sacred and profane has reached such a level that any menial task looks like a devotional exercise.

INTERVIEWER: Are you a Buddhist?

SARDUY: I can't say that, because it would sound a little strange and pretentious coming from a Cuban. I will say that I am very interested in Buddhism, as I am in the African religions of Cuba and Brazil. I am interested in the religious phenomenon per se.

INTERVIEWER: Why do you write and for whom?

SARDUY: I can tell you how I write; I could even give a course on it or write a thesis on how I use commas and adjectives. What I cannot tell you, however, is why I write. Many writers classify themselves in answering this question. Some say, "I write to change mankind," or, "I write to achieve a universal revolution," or, "I write to alter man's consciousness." And most of the writers who make these pretentious statements are traditionalists or reactionaries—extremely boring people. Other writers say they ply their craft to make money or become famous. But I distrust all these responses, because they categorize writers. I certainly don't write to make money, because I haven't earned a lot yet.

INTERVIEWER: Do you do it to restore freedom to writing and to ideas?

SARDUY: I am speaking to you from a little village in the French region of Oise, where Gothicism and impressionism first appeared. The French impressionist painters came from this area. The colors of the region, therefore, are unique, as well as the general atmosphere of luminosity or mist which can be found only in impressionist paintings. I am very sensitive to color, form, drawing, trees, animals, and a river that passes by my house. I would very humbly argue that I try to restore color. To use a contemporary image, a writer is like a TV set: he uses the antenna to receive images, and the channels to transmit them. So the writer cannot stop writing or painting. In the region of Oise, he has to transmit color and form; if he doesn't, he will go mad.

INTERVIEWER: Is the art of writing a voluptuous one for you?

SARDUY: Yes, inasmuch as voluptuousness requires immense effort, because achieving pleasure and ecstacy are the hardest tasks. I try to give my readers immediate pleasure through words, very similar to sexual pleasure, rather than providing them with an ideology, a knowledge, or a thesis on how to capture reality. In Tantrism, certain colors are held to be beneficial. Likewise, I believe that words can also affect the body of the person reading them, especially if they are well written and people know how to read them.

INTERVIEWER: Do words also affect the soul?

SARDUY: The word *soul,* like the word *spirit,* can give rise to dead spiritualism or to partial philosophies in the West, which have no strength either conceptually or expressively. So, I don't like to use those concepts.

INTERVIEWER: What do you feel when you write?

SARDUY: It is very difficult to bring oneself to write. There is always some excuse not to write, such as having a glass of water, taking a walk, eating or sleeping. It can be extremely frustrating, because sometimes I can spend an entire day searching for a particular adjective or expression. Sometimes it comes at night, and sometimes it never comes.

INTERVIEWER: Is writing a solitary trip?

SARDUY: Yes, a solitary trip where the characters can provide some company. But there are mute characters, and an author may spend his entire life with a character who does not speak. It's a little like the relationship with God: one can pray and pray for a long time and it is possible that God will not answer. It's almost a stroke of luck when a character appears with something to say. In my books, there are certain characters whom I have never managed to hear (I won't say which ones). On the other hand, there are others who spoke right away. So it's a little like a lottery.

INTERVIEWER: What do you feel upon turning in a completed work?

SARDUY: A book is like a living body. I let it take its own path, and I never read it or touch it again. In a way, Roberto González Echevarría or Ariana Méndez Ródena, among others who have written about my work, know my books far better than I. This does not mean that I don't understand the books of others. For instance, I consider myself a humble expert on Lezama Lima. But I forget my own novels because I never reread them. I do read the books of my friends on my works, however, although I stay away from doctoral theses on my work. If I read all the material written about me or reread my own books, I would never move forward. To be able to write, I have to forget everything I ever wrote, so that I can hear what the page has to say.

INTERVIEWER: You have said that the word is sometimes a paradise and sometimes a wall. What does it mean to you now?

SARDUY: Well, it was Roland Barthes who said I am in a paradise of words and that I want more of them each time. According to him, I am trying to create a sort of Jesuit paradise through words, and I think this is true. I try to create an atmosphere which will welcome, involve, fascinate and almost hypnotize the reader. It's almost like butterflies hypnotizing us through the designs on their wings, or life mesmerizing us with the beauty of its colors, volutes and arabesques. This hypnosis is writing, so words are a paradise. They fascinate in the same way that a peacock does when it shows off its colors. It's like a sexual attraction.

INTERVIEWER: You have also said, "The page is like a hall, the book is a palace, writing builds structures of symbols, the letters are repeated."

SARDUY: Where did I say that?

INTERVIEWER: In *Big Bang*.

SARDUY: I think *Big Bang* makes a lot of references to the Islamic world, because I wrote it in Iran and the north of Africa. That passage you just read evokes Islamic architecture for me, especially that of Isfahan. It's a very beautiful passage.

INTERVIEWER: And what relation do the pages have between them?

SARDUY: I think they are like spheres. There is a very persistent prejudice which insists that the page is an object with only two dimensions. In reality, the page has three dimensions, because it has depth. When writing, it is very important to keep the idea of a sphere in mind, and avoid thinking in two-dimensional terms, which is what painters have tried to avoid doing. The page has depth and perspective; it never works on just one level.

INTERVIEWER: Is that why in *Big Bang* the page not only has a written message but also a pictorial one?

SARDUY: Yes, the point is to achieve a pictorial representation, where the word representation includes abstraction, as in the works of Franz Kline or Mark Rothko or more recent American painters.

INTERVIEWER: Your prose is poetic, but it also has the elements of an essay, right?

SARDUY: I started as a poet and I am finishing as one (if I am finished), because that's what I am mostly writing these days. Poetry is the model for all writing. I am also working on a novel, but even with novels, the goal is for the narrative prose to have the conceptual clarity and formal beauty of poetry.

INTERVIEWER: What geometric forms would you give your books?

SARDUY: Polyhedrons, of course, because they are the

representative forms of the Renaissance, and the most complex spheres as well. I'll do anything to escape two dimensions.

INTERVIEWER: When you say Isabel the Chaotic One or Juana the Logical One, are you playing a game?

SARDUY: No, I am not, it is done in all earnestness. For personal reasons, I am very interested in Judaism and Islam. In the context of these two traditions, Isabel the Catholic is not a very endearing figure. So I call her the Chaotic One, and thereby vindicate the Jewish and Muslim traditions to which I feel so close.

INTERVIEWER: Since we are nearing the 500th anniversary of Columbus's discovery, do you have any comment on that celebration?

SARDUY: Yes, we are definitely reaching the 500th anniversary of a fiction. All of America is a fiction: the fiction of the East, the Renaissance, Marco Polo, Columbus and the Catholic Kings. We are definitely living the dream of the Admiral and explorer. And the dream has become a nightmare. So all of us who search for the meaning of America have to try to attenuate or control this nightmare. In my humble case, I do this through writing.

INTERVIEWER: What about the American Indian?

SARDUY: I am thinking of him above all, and of all other minorities of Latin America, because unfortunately this continent is made up of them. Everyone is alienated and perhaps that's why there are conflicts, because all these minorities are attempting to assert their autonomy and expression.

INTERVIEWER: Do you identify with surrealism, structuralism or "action writing," or are you unconnected to any movement?

SARDUY: My life was marked by French structuralism, because when I first arrived in Paris it had just begun. I was lucky enough to take courses and become friends with Roland Barthes, one of the leaders of the structuralist movement. I also studied with Jacques Lacan, and I met François Wahl, with whom I now live. So I have definitely been touched by structuralism, although I would say that its influence on me today is less obvious. I am also very interested in the French surrealist movement, which I consider one of the most significant of this century.

INTERVIEWER: Do you compare yourself to any of the writers of the Boom?

SARDUY: If we consider that Lezama Lima belongs to the Boom, which is debatable, then he would be the one I am closest to, perhaps too close. I am a good friend of the writers of the Boom, I enjoy their work, but I don't see much resemblance between my books and theirs.

INTERVIEWER: But do you believe in the Boom?

SARDUY: Yes, I believe in the Boom, but I believe more in the post-Boom.

INTERVIEWER: What does it mean to be a Cuban, write with tropical vibrations, and live in Paris?

SARDUY: It's all the same, because even though I live in France, when I write it is as if I were in Cuba, sleeping on a hammock and having a guarapo, a tropical drink.

INTERVIEWER: Who is Severo Sarduy? Does he wear as many masks as his characters?

SARDUY: From the Buddhist viewpoint, the question has no meaning, because the subject doesn't exist; it is a fiction or illusion. Many writers complain that they are anxious, melancholy, and that they have lost their roots and their sense of identity. And laughingly I reply, "So what?"

Luisa Valenzuela

Luisa Valenzuela

Since childhood, Luisa Valenzuela has been exposed to literature. Her mother, Luisa Mercedes Levinson, was a well-known writer; her father, Pablo Valenzuela, was a physician. Among the close friends who visited their home was Jorge Luis Borges.

Born in Buenos Aires, Argentina, she started working as a journalist at the age of fifteen in *Quince abriles,* a magazine created by Rafael Alberti's wife María Teresa León and their daughter Aitana. She later worked for *La Nación,* a noted Buenos Aires newspaper. Since then, she has become one of the best-known Latin American writers of short stories and novels, and most of her works have been translated into English.

In 1969, Luisa Valenzuela was granted a Fulbright scholarship to take part in a writing workshop at the University of Iowa. In 1979, she was invited as writer-in-residence at Columbia University. She has been living in New York ever since, with frequent visits to Mexico, where she enjoys writing, and to Argentina. In 1980, she became writer-in-residence at the Center for Inter-American Relations and held many writing workshops throughout the Hispanic communities of greater New York. In 1983, she was a Guggenheim Fellow of the New York Institute for the Humanities. She is also a member of the Freedom to Write Committee of the PEN American Center. She has conducted a Creative Writing Workshop at the Writing Division of the English Department of New York University and participated in several seminars in NYU's Spanish Department.

Luisa Valenzuela is the author of numerous books, including *Hay que sonreír,* 1966, and *Los heréticos,* 1967 (translated into English as *Clara: Thirteen Short Stories and a Novel,* 1976); *El gato eficaz* (Cat-O-Nine-Deaths), 1972; *Aquí pasan cosas raras,* 1975, and *Como en la guerra,* 1977 (translated into English as *Strange Things Happen Here,* 1979); *Libro que no muerde* (The Book That Does Not Bite), 1980; *Cambio de armas,* 1982 (*Other Weapons,* 1985); *Donde viven las águilas* (Where Eagles Dwell), 1983; *Cola de lagartija,* 1983 (translated in the same year as *The Lizard's Tail*); *Crimen del otro* (Crime of the Other), 1989.

The *Review of Contemporary Fiction,* with John O'Brien as its editor, dedicated a whole issue to Luisa Valenzuela in the fall of 1986.

The Argentine writer Julio Cortázar said of her work, "Luisa Valenzuela's books reflect our present, but they also contain much of our future; there is a true light, a true love and a true liberty in each of her pages." And the Mexican novelist Carlos Fuentes pointed out that "Luisa Valenzuela is the heiress of Latin American literature. She wears an ornate baroque crown and yet she walks barefoot." The *Village Voice* has said of her use of language: "Valenzuela plays with words, turns them inside out, weaves them into sensuous webs. She uses them as weapons, talismans to ward off danger and name the unnameable."

The interviews that follow were held on three separate occasions: in 1980, 1983, 1988, all in New York. The first two were held prior to Argentina's return to democracy.

Part 1

INTERVIEWER: Borges said that he worked with a few themes which he carried over from work to work. Do you find that each novel or short story that you write is a total break from the previous work, or is each new book a modified version of the same theme?

VALENZUELA: I think it is both. The style, I feel, usually changes. I am always looking for different things to say and new ways of saying them. But there are small, or perhaps big obsessions, that come back again and again in a writer's work. One of my obsessions is with heresies, that very subtle point where any religion falls into heresy. Practically all living religions are heresies of the original dogma, and I find them marvelous because a human being should not be dogmatic at all. And there is also the theme of a search that comes back again and again in many of my works. I am still waiting to know what I am searching for.

INTERVIEWER: Many of your characters are searching for identity. Will you explain why?

VALENZUELA: The Argentines are searching for an identity. We have a very undefined identity, which is also part of our charm, in a way. Because we are half European and did not have a great Indian culture from our past to support us, we do not believe in the past so much. But I do not know whether we even believe in the present, that is the trouble. At the same time, we are very literary people.

INTERVIEWER: Do you think of yourself as a novelist or a short-story writer?

VALENZUELA: I think of myself as a writer. I don't like to put labels on things. I would just say that writing is a hard way of life. I don't like it too much. I do not think I like it too much.

INTERVIEWER: Then why do you write?

VALENZUELA: It is a necessity and it is a great joy when writing is going on very well. When you are really doing fine, writing is fabulous, but there is all this inner struggle, and the inner fight of knowing you are not writing enough, and you are not doing it well enough. So, sometimes short stories come to me and sometimes a novel grows on its own.

INTERVIEWER: When you start writing do you know whether it will be a short story or a novel?

VALENZUELA: Yes, although my first novel started out as a short story and turned into a novel, which surprised me very much. But now I know perfectly well what it is going to be at the outset, because the rhythm of a story is far different from that of a novel.

INTERVIEWER: Could you describe your style, or is that difficult for you?

INTERVIEWER: My style changes, it is a search for my own voice. The trouble is that the search never ends because one's voice is always changing. Voice is everything, language is everything, so I think the only way we can express ourselves is through this voice. It can be exterior or interior, but what is really important for me is language. I usually play with it a lot and mostly let it play with me.

INTERVIEWER: You have said that your novels are "an active dialogue with the reader." Do you think of the reader when you write?

VALENZUELA: When writing, I think of myself as a reader. I enjoy it and surprise myself. I cannot write when I am not surprised, so I hope to do the same to the reader. I am always trying to present different possibilities and sufficient ambiguity in writing, so that the reader can add his own level of reading to the work.

INTERVIEWER: Are your characters figments of your imagination or are they derived from your personal experiences?

VALENZUELA: It is a cross between both. The experience might trigger an imaginative character. I seldom use myself as a character, although now I am trying to. But it is very hard because stories derived from my real life have no element of surprise for me. I am trying to be very much in touch with what we call reality, so I can allow it to grow on its own and not limit it to what I know for sure.

INTERVIEWER: You have given seminars on the art of writing in many universities and also in Hispanic communities. Have you learned from your students?

VALENZUELA: You always learn a lot. Borges used to say that parents learn from their children, and as he never had children he learned from Bioy Casares. I learn a lot from my students. I do not think you can teach anybody to be a good writer. That is not only a natural gift but also a great struggle in which you have to look and fight all the time. But you can teach people this act of freedom, which writing is all about. And you receive that freedom at the same time as you give it. More than anything else, I would tell young people to say everything, to be very courageous about it and not to censor themselves.

INTERVIEWER: Could you discuss the importance of disguise, mask, and change of identity in your works?

VALENZUELA: They are especially important in *Strange Things Happen Here*. I think that we are always using masks, we are never ourselves. You were laughing at me when I was trying to fix my hair before we started the interview, but that is my mask and I was trying to show a good face. The knowledge of our masks and the possibility of interrelating with others through these masks and disguises is very important. We are wearing them because we never have real access to our unconscious desire. The minute we become conscious of it, we lose it. So, the only way to reach certain strings of that desire is by wearing a mask.

INTERVIEWER: Did you start writing because of your mother, Luisa Mercedes Levinson, who was an author in her own right?

VALENZUELA: I started writing in spite of my mother's career. There were many writers who came to our home, so I wanted to be a painter or a mathematician or something completely different. One day, I decided it would be very easy to write a short story which could be as good as any written by my mother's friends. I then wrote my first story and everything started growing on its own.

INTERVIEWER: Are you a feminist writer?

VALENZUELA: I am against labels. I am a feminist in the sense that I am fighting for women to have all opportunities and freedom. What we women writers are looking for is a woman's language. We were never allowed to express ourselves in a very free way. So when women started writing they used an everyday pattern of speech which had been imposed on them by men. And I know there is a woman's language, which is very visceral and very strong, and not at all this nice, rhythmic sort of thing which men tried to make us believe is women's speech.

INTERVIEWER: So you think women write differently from men?

VALENZUELA: The difference is very subtle. It is not a different way of writing, it is a different approach to language. Language is sex, an idea which we never want to recognize.

INTERVIEWER: What is women's place in Latin American literature today?

VALENZUELA: Women's place is unfortunately the place society will allow us to have, for the time being. There are very fine women writers such as Clarice Lispector, who was an extraordinary writer and should have been part of the Boom. She belonged to the same generation as Cabrera Infante, so why was she not included in the Boom? Because she was a woman.

INTERVIEWER: Can you explain how rebellion and freedom are vital parts of your works?

VALENZUELA: I hope they are. Freedom is a search. We do not usually have it, but we are looking for it. We try to express it by showing our own inner freedom whenever we can. And the rebellion must be there constantly. If we forget to be rebels we are no longer writing, we are not being artists. If we repeat what has already been done or said, it is worthless.

INTERVIEWER: Has censorship affected your writing?

VALENZUELA: When I wrote *Strange Things Happen Here*, it was a moment of great violence in Argentina, and I was fighting to be able to say what was going on without being censored. That was a rather unconscious challenge, but it was there. So I managed to do something very positive for my style of writing, because that book became a metaphor for everything that was going on at the time. I was really playing my game then.

INTERVIEWER: Why did you write *El gato eficaz,* which

deals with death?

VALENZUELA: Before I started writing that book I made a very serious statement. I said, "I never think about death, death does not worry me at all. It is something that is there, of course, but I believe I am immortal, I do not care about death." But then I wrote a whole book about it because I do care, as everyone does. Life and death are like a game, with the deadly things being sort of lifelike and the living things as if they were dead—not deadly, not dangerous, but sleepy.

INTERVIEWER: You said in *He Who Searches*, "It is like nighttime, night is another country, a chest of mirrors, a nest of sparrows, night is the possibility of entering through the other door." Would you say that this quotation is symbolic of all your writing?

VALENZUELA: It is symbolic of all writing in general. I had not thought about it, but now that you suggest it, "the possibility of entering through the other door" could be a definition of writing. I was thinking of night all the time I was writing that book. I had to write it at night, although I usually write during the day.

INTERVIEWER: Carol Cook said, "There is something more to Valenzuela's art than just mastery. I think she may be divinely inspired." Are you religious? Do you believe in divine inspiration?

VALENZUELA: I am religious in a very strange way, so I do not know very well whether this divine inspiration comes from above or below.

INTERVIEWER: And what is below?

VALENZUELA: Who knows? And what is above? I do not believe in inspiration at all. I believe in something much more reasonable: the unconscious mind of the writer and of everyone else. That conscious or unconscious possibility of writing is what I call inspiration.

INTERVIEWER: Who are the writers who have influenced you the most?

VALENZUELA: I think everyone has influenced me. Every writer influences all the others. Even the most horrible things I have read have influenced me. It would be a cliché to list the writers I care for most. However, I will mention Borges, Cortázar, and Bioy Casares. But I greatly enjoy other writers. I loved Carlos Fuentes's *Terra Nostra.* I started using it as a puzzle of time and space. We are all discoverers. That is why I also love the last of Carpentier's books, *El arpa y la sombra* (The Harp and the Shadow), which is the story of Christopher Columbus. He really did not discover a new world because he already knew there was a world there. Writers are like that. We feel as if we were discovering new lands, but we have in fact already heard of them from other writers. We are just making our humble explorations. Nevertheless, the trip can be full of risks, and we have to create our lies and our deceptions well so as to make the story worthwhile.

Part 2

INTERVIEWER: Luisa, you are cosmopolitan and at the same time very Latin American. How do you reconcile living outside Argentina and yet manage to hold on to your indigenous roots?

VALENZUELA: I think roots come from many parts. A good sense of perspective is the most important thing for me, because I think that when one is involved in a situation, one can't always see it very clearly. My first revelation in this respect came when I was in Iowa in 1979. It was then that I discovered that Argentina really was a Latin American culture, steeped in Latin American tradition. We Argentines have always believed we were so European, which is absolutely not true.

INTERVIEWER: Speaking of you, Carlos Fuentes once said, "Luisa Valenzuela is the heiress of Latin American literature. She wears an ornate baroque crown, and yet she walks barefoot." Do you feel a responsibility as the heir to your continent?

VALENZUELA: I think it is far too generous of Carlos to say something like that. I don't believe one assumes responsibilities in that sense—we are always heirs to our continent. It is not a question of living up to that legacy, but rather a matter of looking it squarely in the face. I think there is some degree of courage required in facing things as they are, because many ugly truths must be faced as well. I write as an attempt to learn what is beneath the surface. In this sense, my continent is a little confusing, but all the more interesting because of it.

INTERVIEWER: You began writing as a journalist who managed to infiltrate places where women had never been allowed. Now that you are a novelist, do you carry your experiences as a journalist into your work?

VALENZUELA: I think one is inseparable from the other. The journalist I once was, and still am, continues to influence the way I look at my surroundings—it has taught me many things. Thanks to journalism, I have learned how to synthesize, how to narrate a story as concisely as possible. This is something which I have carried over into my books, to the occasional dismay of my readers, who say they have to read every page twice because there is too much information on it. Journalism has also taken me to vastly different worlds from the ones I was used to. I was a *redactora estrella* (star reporter) for a popular magazine, so I was sent to boxing matches, world soccer championships, and the like. This gave free expression to a very vital part of my character. Ironically, I have chosen a very quiet and sedate profession, writing fiction, which contradicts this need to run free.

INTERVIEWER: Can you say something about the interplay of fantasy and reality, the third dimension you have created in your work?

VALENZUELA: I have a feeling that reality is much wider than what we see. I think everything is real; what happens is that we label as real only the most evident things. We have limited the boundaries of reality too formally. In the final analysis, everything that goes through our minds is real, including dreams, poetry, and a whole gamut of elements which we do not usually associate with reality. We are like horses with blinders, and the only thing I try to do is to take the blinders off and see all sides of reality, the known as well as the dark aspects of reality, which people call fantasy. Cortázar was very aware of this, and he used to refer to the pataphysical idea of worlds complementary to this one. I think he was very correct, obviously. We are immersed in a reality which there is no need to limit. When we do so, it is out of ignorance, pure and simple.

INTERVIEWER: Do you think the woman as a writer has a responsibility to other women?

VALENZUELA: I don't agree with that use of the term "responsibility." If a woman writer felt she had a direct responsibility, the result would probably be a messy confusion in her writing and her actions. Responsibility must be intrinsic; it must come together with a profound and basic ideology. If this is the case, then when a person acts those inner tenets will express themselves either directly or indirectly. Obviously, since we are women, we speak to other women, but we direct ourselves to anyone who may be willing to listen.

INTERVIEWER: You have said, "I strive so that my stories may be ambiguous, so that they say more than what is apparent." Why do you like to carry that ambiguity to art?

VALENZUELA: Because I don't think a written work ends with the last word. There is never a last word. When someone reaches that point, the dialogue with the author is only beginning. Then suddenly the reader is acting and creating a new reading. Every reading represents a new awareness of the work. I am very concerned that there be different possibilities and an array of mythical, political or other foundations.

INTERVIEWER: In an interview you held in Buenos Aires in April of 1983, you said, "I think my literature is vibrant and my life is literary." Could you explain this a little?

VALENZUELA: As far as saying that my literature is vibrant,

that is a wish—I would like it to be so. There is not the slightest doubt, however, that my life is literary. It is very difficult for me to separate life and literature. I live through certain situations which I know I am propelling; it is like someone who pushes against the wall to reach another reality. I try to force certain situations to their extreme to see what lies behind them. One always tries to break the toy to see what is inside. In the same way, I want to take life apart to see what is inside. My experiences as a writer are all my life. I don't ever stop writing, even when I am walking or riding the subway. Writing is a sort of screen separating me from the rest of the world, even to the extent of making me miss some part of real life. Then again, real life is writing too, so I don't know.

INTERVIEWER: Your mother, Luisa Mercedes Levinson, was a writer. Do you see some likeness between your work and hers?

VALENZUELA: I don't see any likeness; we speak with very different voices. During the last years of her life, however, we were beginning to approach similar themes. We viewed them from different angles with our own very personal perspectives, but we did share some obsessions, and I think this is fascinating. For instance, we were both drawn to landscapes. In *The Lizard's Tail,* I describe marshes and miasmas, landscapes which are somewhat putrefied, if not completely. This is something which is present in the work of my mother as well. She dealt with the theme of the embalming of Eva Perón, as I had also. She hadn't read my novel on the subject nor had I read hers. When she read me part of her book, I noticed there were certain subterranean similarities between our works, although nothing direct. There is an intertextuality which runs in the family.

INTERVIEWER: Susan Sontag has said of *The Lizard's Tail:* "Luisa Valenzuela has written a marvelously free novel, full of wit about sensuality and power, death and history, the 'me' and literature." How did you come up with the idea for this fascinating story about the Minister López Rega, whom you call "the

Sorcerer," and who has made his presence felt here this morning through a violent storm?

VALENZUELA: That sorcerer sometimes throws us a curse or two. Unfortunately, there is an intimate relationship between us, appearances notwithstanding. For that very reason, it is "the 'me' and literature," as Susan said. I wanted to narrate the story of this man who began sowing terror in Argentina. All of a sudden we were caught up in the heart of Latin American sorcery, embodied by the Minister of Social Welfare under Perón. He had really been a witch doctor and had published books on sorcery, talismans and love potions. When Perón died and Isabel ascended to power, he became the force behind the throne. That's when I began asking myself how we could have fallen into the hands of a sorcerer and his black magic, we who thought we were so European. So I wrote this book to answer that question. I wanted to write it from my point of view, but I realized it was far too negative and critical, and that is not literature. Literature is precisely the freedom to let the matter speak through you, so I decided to let the sorcerer speak, and he did me in. Suddenly, the sorcerer was a madman, a crazed, omnipotent messiah, like all people who have been tempted by power, but he also had a certain pull to him. That was when I withdrew and inserted myself into the novel as a character. I wanted to attempt to counter the force of this man, who even in black and white, even in print, had a vitality all his own, as well as a fascination with horror.

INTERVIEWER: Why did you turn to myth to describe the years of repression in Argentina?

VALENZUELA: Because I think it is a very powerful dialectic situation. If we don't look at things through myths, the structure of our deepest unconscious, we are not going to understand them. Because events spring from myths, a person acts in accordance with myths in real life. This was something that Freud understood clearly. If we do not use myths to gain perspective and understand why something happened, we would

not even realize it took place. If I had done a straightforward
narrative, I would have been unable to understand what
occurred during those years. Using myths gave me an added
dimension and the possibility to delve more deeply, to use the
metaphor, which is the only thing which can really teach us.

INTERVIEWER: Why do you write?

VALENZUELA: I write because I can do nothing else—I think
any writer would tell you the same thing—and because I want
to learn. I want to know, but I don't know what I want to know,
so in order to get a taste of the pudding, I write.

INTERVIEWER: You have an impressive collection of masks
in your home. Why?

VALENZUELA: The mask in itself is man's only artistic
element which is truly reflective of him, and even greater than
him in some ways. The men or women who don masks take on
the spirits represented by them. Masks are really mediators
between the world of spirits and the world of humans.

INTERVIEWER: How did you come up with the strange
notion of the sorcerer's third testicle, which he wears as a mask?

VALENZUELA: These are intuitions one has. I always
pictured that man dressed as a woman, a transvestite. And he
quite obviously wanted absolute power, like Nero, Caligula,
and, to some extent, Perón also. The sorcerer was power-
crazed, he hid nothing. He had to have both sexes, he had to
be androgynous. So I gave him that embryonic cyst because
I wanted the novel to be realistic. The cyst is his twin sister
Estrella, who did not develop in the mother's womb, and whom
he wants to impregnate in order to be the sole master of the
world. These ideas come by free association.

INTERVIEWER: Why are you so drawn to magic?

VALENZUELA: Because I think it is a part of life. It comprises
all the activities of the right hemisphere of our brain, to put it as
scientifically as possible. There is a facet of the mind that we
call magic for lack of a better word, which I think is fascinating
in all its expressions and insightful about things we don't know

how to explain.

INTERVIEWER: Why do you like to play with symbols and metaphors so much?

VALENZUELA: Because they help us understand. Because we need to grasp the full scope of language. I think this a great contribution of the latest wave of Latin American literature— a reappraisal of language, of the sort the French are so fond of engaging, an analysis of the metaphorical and metonymical structure of language. It is thanks to this freedom one gives to words that imagination grows, and that the spectrum of ideas becomes so much broader, because it is the very words which are guiding you to take the next step.

INTERVIEWER: Do you conceive of literature as a game or a weapon?

VALENZUELA: As a weapon *and* as a game, but not in the derogatory sense of that word. I think games are among the most important components of life. This is the *homo ludens*— it is this meaning which we are rescuing now, through that game of imagination and invention which is going on in physics with the work of microphysicists. A nebulous poetical area remains wherein one can invent and be wrong and continue inventing . . . because nothing is as real as it seems.

INTERVIEWER: What are some of the recurrent themes in your work?

VALENZUELA: That is very difficult for me to say. It is for the critics to discover and resolve them. I think masks have been there since the beginning, like cats and critters of that nature, although I believe this is all a bit limiting. I think my work is constantly changing, but the obsessions remain.

INTERVIEWER: What do you feel upon seeing your name in the North American press mentioned in the same breath as the writers of the Boom, like Fuentes, Vargas Llosa and Cortázar?

VALENZUELA: I am happy I guess, although we should all be there, not just me. Because there are a number of writers of my generation who should be on that list as well, there is a long way to go yet.

INTERVIEWER: You have said, "New York is the most surrealist place on this earth." Why are the ideas for your books born here, and why do you have to isolate yourself from New York to be able to write?

VALENZUELA: I said that about New York to counter that "surrealist" label North Americans apply to Latin American literature. I don't believe in those tags, I don't think Latin American literature is surrealistic. Surrealism is something very precise and limited, it is the exaltation of madness. Our literature is very rational in certain respects. New York is a completely crazy city, full of contradictions and superimposed elements—people don't see that here because they don't focus on that reality, but we Latin Americans do see it. This is greatly stimulating, but I must isolate myself before the city swallows me up. I need to return to Spanish, to surround myself with it, and that's why I often travel to Mexico. The language spoken around me is very important.

INTERVIEWER: So you consider Mexico a second home?

VALENZUELA: In the same way that New York is a second home. I have a lot of second homes.

INTERVIEWER: Are you a poet?

VALENZUELA: We are all poets. We all have a little bit of the poet, the doctor, and the madman in us. I am a poet and a doctor and a madwoman. But I write very little poetry, although I did recently. It is the facet of my craft in which I indulge the least, although there is a certain poetry to my prose.

INTERVIEWER: How did you meet Julio Cortázar?

VALENZUELA: I met him by accident in Mexico and then I saw him again at a convention in Frankfurt. It was there that we became close friends. He was an extraordinary human being.

INTERVIEWER: What about Jorge Luis Borges?

VALENZUELA: I have known Borges since childhood, as he was a close friend of my mother's. They even wrote a story together called "La hermana de Eloísa" (Heloise's Sister).

They laughed a lot when they wrote it; it was truly fantastic, and it was a sort of apprenticeship in the joys of writing for me.

INTERVIEWER: Along with María Teresa León, Rafael Alberti's wife, and their daughter Aitana, you were part of the magazine *Quince Abriles* in Buenos Aires.

VALENZUELA: I began writing in that magazine by doing an interview with Mirtha Legrand, the well-known Argentine actress. I was a pretty awful writer then, but by the time I was seventeen I was much better.

INTERVIEWER: What makes up the creative process which takes you from the idea for a novel to the finished product?

VALENZUELA: It consists in the happiness of continual discovery. It is a question of surmounting obstacles, because the conception one has of a novel can be very limited and imprecise. When I conceive a novel in very narrow and specific terms, it is very difficult for me to write, and it doesn't take off. What is important, therefore, is to have certain steady elements, and then give the characters a free rein, so that the novel begins to write itself.

INTERVIEWER: What kind of relationship do you have with your characters? Do you lead them or do they lead you?

VALENZUELA: I try never to have power struggles with anybody, not even with my characters. They lead me because I want them to be as alive as possible. They start growing on their own and they even go against my feelings on occasion. That's when I feel I am writing well, when I can express my unconscious thoughts without needing a mask. Either the characters have become the mask or there is a part of my unexpressed self which is able to say, "That's true," without it necessarily being my personal truth.

INTERVIEWER: How do the characters come alive?

VALENZUELA: By forcing you to do things you don't want. When an author tries to tell her characters what to do, that's when the book is going badly. On the other hand, when the characters are so well defined that they act of their own volition, that's when the novel works.

INTERVIEWER: How do you come up with the titles for your novels?

VALENZUELA: Don't even talk to me about that, forget it! Either one chooses the title at the outset, or it becomes a horrible torment afterward. This happened with *The Lizard's Tail,* for instance. I think I may have told you that the novel used to be called *El brujo Hormiga Roja, el señor del Tacurú, amo de tambores, dueño de la Voz, patrón de los desamparados, serruchero mayor, alto sacerdote del dedo, y su hermana Estrella* (The Red Ant Sorcerer, Master of Tacurú, Owner of the Drums, Patron Saint of the Forsaken, the Great Sawer, the High Priest of the Finger and His Sister Estrella). They thought the title was a little long.

INTERVIEWER: I wonder why . . .

VALENZUELA: What I meant to do was to put the first title in large letters, followed by all the others in small print, so that the entire cover would be filled. They objected to this, however, especially with the English version, and since it came out first, I had to search frantically for a new title. A distant cousin of mine had lent me a book when I told him I was writing about certain events which take place in the Province of Corrientes, in the marshes of Iberá. The book referred to a whip made of knotted leather called *Teyú cuaré* (lizard tail whip) in the Guaraní language. It was used in that province in the late nineteenth century to punish people. I thought lizard tail was a very good name, so I used it. Later, I discovered that there was indeed a class of lizards called whip-tail lizards, so everything is interconnected. I then dabbled a little into the mythology of the lizard and found out that it is the direct relative of the dragon, whence the original egg, and androgyny, spring.

INTERVIEWER: You work with the themes of censorship, exile, and human rights. What does freedom mean to you?

VALENZUELA: Everything. Creating is impossible without freedom. I find it sinister to say that censorship is good for literature because it stimulates the imagination of writers. Censorship castrates, and in the long run the castration is total.

INTERVIEWER: Did you revise and correct *The Lizard's Tail* extensively?

VALENZUELA: Yes, for purely literary reasons; it wasn't a question of censorship. There are things I didn't think myself capable of saying, which astonished me as I reread the book. This happens when I get caught up in the thrill and ecstasy of writing—when I look at the words afterward, some of them seem very harsh, especially the scenes dealing with torture.

INTERVIEWER: Can you speak about your book *Other Weapons* a little?

VALENZUELA: It is a story about a woman who has been tortured to such an extent that she has a complete loss of memory. The story, which is more of a novel really, develops as she recovers snippets of her memory. The title indicates a change from weapons of torture to sexual weapons. I had to reread the story many times, because it is a very precise tale requiring a lot of polish, and each time was more painful than the last. Finally, when they sent me the proofs to the book, I could read it no longer. In fact, I haven't read the translation either for the same reason. Had I realized how difficult it would be to face the novel's elements of eroticism, horror, and death, I would have censored the tale completely.

INTERVIEWER: Do you feel more comfortable as a novelist or as a storyteller?

VALENZUELA: That's very difficult to answer. Speaking in a literary sense, I like the short story more than the novel. It is very hard to put together a collection of stories. With each story one has to start anew, whereas a novel, if it is already on track, flows of its own volition. It is a great pleasure when this happens, and situations become more complex and unpredictable —and then, all of a sudden, everything is set straight again.

INTERVIEWER: What is your reaction upon reading your works in English?

VALENZUELA: It is a very amusing reaction, because the spirit of the books changes dramatically. The only time when I really got concerned about carefully analyzing a translation was with *The Lizard's Tail.* In English, this book sounded much more baroque, unexpectedly. English is not as flexible a language as Spanish in this respect. When something in Spanish is a little twisted, somewhat removed from daily experience and yet not baroque, in English it becomes something really strange and distant. So I had to rewrite many parts, and I had quite a bit of fun doing it.

INTERVIEWER: Since we have been speaking so much about your country's history, could you say something about that most enduring Argentine myth, Evita Perón?

VALENZUELA: I think Eva Perón was not born spontaneously, she is a fruit of the veneration of her people. There is a dialectic relationship in the structured dialogue between the people and this madonna, who is a prostitute. It is the soul of every desire of man for woman, the prostitute and the virgin, the savior and the mother, all in one. How marvelous to have a character like that to observe directly.

INTERVIEWER: Since your characters all search for their own identity, even the Sorcerer, and since Luisa Valenzuela appears among those characters, who is Luisa Valenzuela?

VALENZUELA: Like any of us, I wonder what it is to be human, where we came from, where we are going, who we are. I think I am a person who is conscious of seeking. The only thing in which I am slightly different from other people is that I know that I seek, which is very frustrating because at times I know I am looking for something that is not there. That search is the elusive part of desire, to find out what is behind that which does not exist. Do you like that definition?

Part 3

INTERVIEWER: You have mentioned to me in a previous interview that some of the themes in your work are heresies and a
quest, and you have even said, "I am still waiting to know what
I am searching for." Did you find out the answer to your quest?

VALENZUELA: Fortunately, I haven't, because I suppose
that the day I find the answer to that, I will stop writing, or
worse still, I will be dead. I think that life is a search for the
reason of the quest, or what you are after. So the interesting
thing is simply to keep on going. I don't think I'll ever find an
answer. I don't think there is an answer.

INTERVIEWER: What is Argentina to you now that it has
recovered its freedom?

VALENZUELA: That is a very difficult question because
Argentina is my homeland, of course, and in a sense it is my
home. But it's a home far away from home and I don't know if
I'll ever really want to go back to stay. I would like to go and
spend time there, however. Even if Argentina has found its
freedom, I don't find my freedom in Argentina, because I am
trapped by my own past. If you leave your homeland and then
you go back to it, it's never the same as what you left. You
haven't gone through that period of change, so you are not
altogether a part of it. It's just a place of nostalgia then, but
since I am not a nostalgic person, it's a non-place in a sense,
although it's also a place of comfort and reassurance.

INTERVIEWER: Does it mean that the need for freedom will
no longer be an essential part of your writing?

VALENZUELA: The need for freedom is an essential part
of my life; in a sense it is a part of everything. It's not a question of freedom or no freedom—I don't think freedom is that
superficial. Argentina has found democracy, and it's going
through a very good time, if you don't think of the economy.
But there is no internal freedom; there is too much pain, the
wounds are too deep. People are too subjected to rules, more

than rules, regulations, of course regulations of fashions and fads. So the search for freedom is an important part of my personality and I hope of everybody else's.

INTERVIEWER: Will there ever be another novel like *The Lizard's Tail* for you?

VALENZUELA: That I can't tell. I hope there will be, because I really enjoyed writing it, even if it was scary. It was a crazy, somewhat excessive Latin American baroque novel and it wrote itself in more than one sense, so I hope there will be some other. It will be very different, not only for historical reasons, but for personal ones.

INTERVIEWER: How was it received in Argentina?

VALENZUELA: It had very good reviews, but there was much more indifference than in the United States, because it was touching points that were too painful for the people to handle. It hurt them to have that truth shoved in their faces, and at the same time it was far too mocking, too full of humor. Argentineans have a very good sense of humor, but not in the British manner, so they don't like to be laughed at.

INTERVIEWER: Can you explain the importance of humor and irony in your work?

VALENZUELA: It is essential. I think humor is more important. Irony, however, is a necessary by-product, although we shouldn't be too proud of it. I don't think I would relate to anybody without a sense of humor, and I don't think I could keep on moving in life without it. When I am down, I remind myself of that and I perk up. Even when humor is not in my work, I have a feeling there is irony or cynicism or some biased way of saying things which could be more or less funny. Humor allowed me to break the barriers of censorship in more than one way, because not only was I evading the censors, wherever they were, I was forcing the reader to read me. Otherwise, he would have put the book down. The main reason for having a sense of humor in writing is to allow oneself to say things that otherwise one wouldn't dare even acknowledge. But they suddenly come out through jokes.

INTERVIEWER: Now that you can express that truth freely, does it mean that humor is going to be left out of your work?

VALENZUELA: The truth that cannot be uttered is not the truth that the censors, or the people or the government will punish you for expressing. The deep unspeakable thing is what you don't dare say, because it is your own dark side relating to other dark sides. So that is always there crouching somewhere inside you, trying to avoid being brought out in the open, and wanting to come out nevertheless. Humor, therefore, is always necessary and is unrelated to external freedom.

INTERVIEWER: What is the force that propels your writing?

VALENZUELA: I wish I knew, because then I would switch it on when I need to. I don't know.

INTERVIEWER: When I talk with you I always find that there is a special magic around you. Do you think that the world of the occult is watching over us?

VALENZUELA: I think that we are the world of the occult; it's not that it's watching over us, it is there all the time. So it is only that we refuse to see part of the reality that surrounds us.

INTERVIEWER: Why is it so important to you?

VALENZUELA: Because it is another vision. The South American Indians said that you have to learn to look twice, simultaneously. You have to learn the straightforward vision that encompasses everything that is out there and recognize it, and also the lateral vision that shows you the world of shadows. There is another world, there is a magical thinking which has lost all its charm. Scientists now speak of the lateralization of the brain. There is the right side of the brain too, and you have to think about it. It is as simple as that.

INTERVIEWER: But for you it is another dimension?

VALENZUELA: No, it is the same dimension that is absolutely embedded in the other; they are interlinked, you can't separate them, that is why I said it is not watching over us—we are part of that too. But we don't want to acknowledge it. That's why Americans think the Latin American novel is surrealistic when it is totally realistic!

INTERVIEWER: Are masks as important to you now as they once were? I see we are still surrounded by them.

VALENZUELA: Much less; most of them are in crates. They have been internalized. I have a friend who was speaking to me about the naked masks, and the naked masks in African art are invisible. So sometimes the dancer comes in and his face is showing, but you know he is wearing a mask because he is performing a certain ceremony, and that is a naked mask, an invisible mask. And now I am exploring these masks, which are much more abstract. But it is never a form of unmasking, because I don't believe in the possibility of being unmasked. I think we are like onions, there is always another layer behind it.

INTERVIEWER: Do you wear a mask?

VALENZUELA: We all do. Unfortunately, I don't think there is a way to avoid wearing a mask. I always recall Oscar Wilde saying, "Give me a mask, and I'll tell you the truth." So perhaps sometimes we want to don that other mask, the one that will allow us to really be ourselves and see our inner truth.

INTERVIEWER: And yet, when I talk to you, I feel that I know you and that there is nothing standing between us.

VALENZUELA: Because it is not a mask to disguise my feelings; I think it is not a dishonest mask, it is an honest mask.

INTERVIEWER: Is style more important to you than characters?

VALENZUELA: I wouldn't phrase it like that. In Joyce's words: "I am more interested in how you say it than what you say." Words and language are more important to me than anecdotes or situations. I am more interested in what is being said in spite of ourselves.

INTERVIEWER: Do you mean going beyond words?

VALENZUELA: No, words go so far that you can never reach them. I am more interested in going beyond the psychological possibilities of the character I am building. And suddenly the language this character is using really depicts a picture that is much more true to itself than what I was trying to do.

INTERVIEWER: Words in spite of ourselves.

VALENZUELA: Yes, language speaks through us, as they say nowadays. It says much more than we realize we are saying or want to say.

INTERVIEWER: Do you feel closer to the Spanish language being in New York, Buenos Aires, or Mexico?

VALENZUELA: I feel very close to language in Argentina, of course. You are touching an important point there, because perhaps I feel too close to language in Buenos Aires, and that is why I am always running away from it. Because if you are really immersed in the stew, you don't see the ingredients.

INTERVIEWER: Where do you write best?

VALENZUELA: In Mexico, which is midway between Buenos Aires and the United States, but now I manage to write well in my own country.

INTERVIEWER: Do you feel that there has been an evolution in your style?

VALENZUELA: I feel that there has been a real change in my style. It has evolved, because I think I have sharpened the instrument and I now use words as weapons more and more. But one cannot presume to dominate language, because that would really be a fascist pretension. I am allowing language to become more fluent. I have a feeling that every time I write, and write well, I see more clearly than before. Language is to me like a house, the home in which I feel most comfortable. Each brick is a particular word and has to be laid in an exact position to maintain the whole structure.

INTERVIEWER: Do you feel close to all your books?

VALENZUELA: Yes, I feel close to certain situations in them. I feel close to them when I write them. But I am also indifferent because I don't open them after they have been published.

INTERVIEWER: How do you feel during the actual process of writing?

VALENZUELA: When it is going well, I usually feel elated

and I think it is a great thing to do. Sometimes when I am tackling a very difficult subject matter, however, I feel I have to tear the book out of my system. Then I don't feel elated at all, except for the fact that I am working in a world with language, and that gives me great drive, great energy, even if I am telling horrible stories with horrible situations.

INTERVIEWER: Do you want to say something about your new novel, *Crimen del otro?*

VALENZUELA: It's a novel about a couple of Argentine writers living in New York. When one of them kills a woman, or thinks he has killed her, they get immersed in the darker side of New York with all its sadomasochism and weird characters. The book is a search for truth, for the reason why one of the writers committed this alleged crime, but it is also a search into language and the transvestism that language implies.

INTERVIEWER: Why is your work so powerful?

VALENZUELA: Because I have a sense of what should be said in spite of myself. It is also a trap because there are some very tender, sweet things that I love. This is when you start fighting the barriers of censorship again. The other day Susan Sontag asked me if I had a fascination with sadomasochism and I replied, "No, I don't," to which she said, "Well, it comes out in your books." After this conversation, I realized that it is not that I am fascinated by the dark part of our nature, but merely that I acknowledge it. Coming from a beautiful country which suddenly became the cradle of torturers, I cannot avoid acknowledging the existence of evil things and their power over people. I look for the horrible and put it out in the open, so that it will not come out of hiding at a moment when I don't want it to.

INTERVIEWER: Do you write for a purpose then?

VALENZUELA: I always think there should be a purpose, although I could also say, "No, I write for no purpose whatsoever." But then I start wondering, "What the heck do I write for anyway?" I write to shake people up. I used to think that I wrote to pull the rug from under the readers' feet and I would say, "This is the reality you see but there are also all these other possibilities and things going on at the same time." Even in the most banal and innocent statement, there are dark and somber aspects of human nature hidden.

INTERVIEWER: How do you feel when you part with your book?

VALENZUELA: When the book ends and suddenly "plop," it's over, I feel as if it had abandoned me. When I part with it and it's due to be published, I'm very scared to know that it is out for others to read, and then I don't want to read reviews. I don't know why one writes and goes through all that hassle.

INTERVIEWER: Now that we are approaching 1992, the year commemorating the 500th anniversary of the discovery of America, could you speak about your attitude toward that event?

VALENZUELA: I feel very ambivalent about the discovery of America. I'm here because of it, inevitably. On the one hand, I see the *conquistadores* coming forward in this continent of luxurious vegetation, with their armor plates, sweating and giving off this very bad smell—the Aztecs sniffed flowers just to avoid it. On the other hand, they were also courageous, they burned their ships and went forward in the middle of nowhere, looking for gold. Strangely enough, they were looking for wealth and getting crazy and suddenly they discovered the most marvelous wealth in the world, which was those landscapes. Then they started burning idols, which was a horrible thing to do. They were supposed to bring civilization, but instead they destroyed another culture. I think they were marvelous and abominable at the same time.

INTERVIEWER: And your attitude toward Columbus?

VALENZUELA: I like him better than others, of course, because he was much better than they and because he was so misunderstood. But my attitude toward Columbus is absolutely literary; it's similar to Carpentier's.

INTERVIEWER: What about Spain?

VALENZUELA: It is also ambivalent. I like Spain very much, but it doesn't belong to me. It is something that is absolutely alien to me, even though I am not Italian, as more than half of the Argentines are. I am of Spanish origin.

INTERVIEWER: Do you feel that you speak a borrowed language, as some writers from Latin America do?

VALENZUELA: Oh, no! I think I speak this marvelous Argentine language, whatever it is. I like it, I really enjoy it, I think it is very imaginative, it is full of jargon and slang which are my inner language. My father belonged to a very old Argentine family, which had settled there in colonial times. And yet I feel I am much closer to the American Indians than to the Spanish *conquistadores.* If I could choose, I would prefer to be an Aztec or a Mayan.

INTERVIEWER: What do you think of the native American languages and the literature of these people?

VALENZUELA: These pseudoprimitive languages were very interesting, and full of richness and subtlety. Just listen to the Nahuatl, which has such a beautiful ring to it. I have read *La crónica de los vencidos* (The Chronicle of the Beaten Ones), written by the Indians. It is a fantastic work, far more beautiful than the chronicles of the Spaniards. The Indians were poets, which is not to say that the Spaniards weren't, because they had these fantastic writers in the Golden Age. But the *conquistadores* were a mass of brutes, by and large. They were just a force of nature.

INTERVIEWER: Do you think that Latin Americans are living in a new golden age?

VALENZUELA: Are you pulling my leg, perchance? No, we are far from that. We are very impoverished by comparison with the Spanish Golden Age. We have to compete against all their great poets. We could never live a golden age, but we are trying. We are struggling our best to say our part, that is all.

INTERVIEWER: Is another Boom about to occur, and what is the future of the Latin American novel?

VALENZUELA: I don't know if the Boom hasn't become a myth, which would be dangerous. But it is true that it has always been mentioned as such. People are still reading the same old novels, however, and no new style of writing has come forth. So now we have to read novels when they come. The so-called Boom is an *entelechia*—it is something that has been made up. But it is true that it represents another approach to literature, and that is something I'm always analyzing and trying to pinpoint. It is another vision of reality. It probably comes from the Indians, it probably comes from that dual, simultaneous vision. It is really the attraction of opposite poles. It is a Heraclitean idea. Regarding the second part of your question, the future of the Latin American novel is the destiny of the lotus that can survive even in the most horrible, most polluted, darkest, swampy waters. Survive and flower, survive and bloom into a beautiful flower.

Mario Vargas Llosa

Mario Vargas Llosa

Mario Vargas Llosa, one of the leading figures of the "Boom," was born in 1936 in Arequipa, the second largest city in Peru, also known as the "White City." He completed his primary studies in Cocha-bamba, Bolivia, where his grandfather was posted as Consul. His secondary studies were undertaken at the well-known Leoncio Prado Military School in Lima, and in Piura. He later studied at the University of San Marcos where he got his first degree. While a student, he worked as news editor for a Lima radio station and as a journalist for *El Comercio,* one of Peru's foremost newspapers. In 1958, he received a scholarship to study in Spain. Thirteen years later, he obtained his doctorate from the University of Madrid with a thesis entitled *Gabriel García Márquez: Historia de un deicidio* (Gabriel García Márquez: History of a Deicide), published in 1971 in Barcelona.

During his sixteen years of voluntary exile in Europe, he experimented with literary techniques, acquired self-discipline and learned what it meant to be a Latin American. In 1974, he decided to return to Lima with his wife Patricia. He has said that he needed to feel the vitality of the everyday language of Peru and to relive the Peruvian experience. He now divides his time between London, where he finds peace to write, and Lima, his inspiration for writing.

A first-rate novelist, playwright, literary critic and journalist, Vargas Llosa achieved international recognition at an early age. In 1959, he was granted the Leopoldo Alas Award for his book *Los Jefes* (The Leaders). At the age of twenty-six, he received the 1962 Biblioteca Breve Prize and the 1963 Crítica Prize for his novel *La ciudad y los perros,* translated as *The Time of the Hero* in 1966. This was the first time that such an award was conferred on a Latin American. His next book, *La casa verde,* 1966 (*The Green House,* 1968), received the Crítica Prize in 1976 and the Rómulo Gallegos International Literature Prize in 1979. In 1985, he was the recipient of the first Ritz Paris Hemingway Award for his epic historical novel *La guerra del fin del mundo,* 1981 (*The War of the End of the World,* 1984). In 1986 he received the prestigious Príncipe de Asturias Prize.

Among his other works are the following: *Conversación en La Catedral,* 1969 (*Conversation in The Cathedral,* 1975); *Pantaleón y las visitadoras,* 1973 (*Captain Pantoja and the Special Service,* 1978); *La orgía perpetua: Flaubert y "Madame Bovary,"* 1975 (*The Perpetual Orgy: Flaubert and Madame Bovary,* 1986); *La tía Julia y el escribidor,* 1977 (*Aunt Julia and the Scriptwriter,* 1982); *La señorita de Tacna* (The Lady from Tacna), 1981; *Contra el viento y la marea* (Against Wind and Tide), 1983; *Historia de Mayta,* 1984 (*The Real Life of Alejandro Mayta,* 1986); *La chunga* (The Joke), 1985; *¿Quién mató a Palomino Molero?,* 1986 (*Who Killed Palomino Molero?,* 1987). His recent novel *El hablador* (The Storyteller), 1987, illustrates the reality of fictitious life, with its dreams, which is an integral part of real life. This novel refers to a tribe in the Amazon, the *Manchingueras,* who await with religious fervor the coming of the storyteller. His latest work, *Elogio de la madrastra* (Praise of the Stepmother), 1988, is an erotic novel that he considers a diversion.

INTERVIEWER: The great Mexican writer Octavio Paz has said, "Without Brazil, we Latin Americans are half body and half spirit." In your novel *The War of the End of the World,* why did you choose to focus on the populist uprising that occurred at the end of the nineteenth century in the northeast of Brazil?

VARGAS LLOSA: I think a writer doesn't choose his themes, they choose him, and this is what happened to me with that particular work. One day I read an extraordinary book called *Os sertões,* by Euclides da Cunha. It was the first book written on the Canudos conflict, a few years after this civil war occurred in the northeast of Brazil. Very few times has a book moved and shaken me internally as much as this essay in which Euclides da Cunha attempts to explain what happened in Canudos. It is an adventurous and fascinating story from the point of view of the human beings who lived it and the problems that it raised. As to why I found in this story something tremendously relevant to contemporary Latin America, I think one could see in it, as in a laboratory, a series of attitudes and problems that all of our countries have faced throughout their histories and which many of them, including my own, continue to live with today. I think all of these reasons finally stimulated me to write this novel on the subject of Canudos.

INTERVIEWER: It has been said of this particular novel that it is "a moral and political parable on the human condition. *The War of the End of the World* is not only a great book by Mario Vargas Llosa, but also a fundamental book in the literary history of the twentieth century and in the universal history of the novel." How did you succeed in turning an episode in the history of nineteenth-century Brazil into a universal event?

VARGAS LLOSA: I didn't want to write a novel completely faithful to what happened in Canudos. My interest, therefore, was not in reproducing a historic event based on what happened in Brazil. I wrote a novel—that is to say, a free and imaginative version—separate from its purely historical roots. Basically it's a fiction, an invention into which I have thrown not only what I found out about the history of Canudos but also a great deal of my own experience and the experiences of my own society and my own country. At the same time, I have tried to present that history through a language that would deregionalize it and give it a non-local, non-provincial dimension.

INTERVIEWER: In the novel, one of the characters is a journalist. Why do you insist on his myopia so much—is it that journalists lack a sense of perspective?

VARGAS LLOSA: The character is myopic for several reasons,

one of them being that he is based on Euclides da Cunha. This Brazilian writer was an intellectual who went to Canudos as a journalist during the fourth expedition. He was a man who was physically very weak and sickly, and I have given my character some of these traits. However, I think that the myopia of the journalist in the novel is not only a physical myopia but also an intellectual one. During a great part of the story, at least, the journalist doesn't really see what's happening, not only because he is nearsighted and has lost his glasses but because he has barriers, prejudices of an intellectual and ideological nature that prevent him from understanding what is happening. The same thing occurred to Euclides da Cunha with the events of Canudos. He also did not see what was happening and he wrote articles that contributed to poisoning the atmosphere in Brazil vis-à-vis the events. But unlike some other intellectuals, da Cunha, and I think the character in the novel as well, succeeded in learning the lesson and moving beyond it. They mastered those prejudices and limitations that prevented them from understanding reality, thereby accepting the message of this reality. Later, they wrote something that is like a confession and a rectification of their own errors and prejudices in judging reality.

INTERVIEWER: What was your reaction upon reading *The War of the End of the World* in English?

VARGAS LLOSA: I don't really read the works in English. In general, I help the translators with their work. In this case, Helen Lane sent me lists of words, many questions on certain turns of phrases and some expressions, and then I collaborated as much as I could to make sure the translation was accurate. I think she is a magnificent translator, but I don't reread my books once they are written, neither in English nor in Spanish.

INTERVIEWER: Why not?

VARGAS LLOSA: Because, once I publish a book, I have worked on it to the point where I am so saturated by the story that I prefer not to look at it again.

INTERVIEWER: How do you explain the fact that, in Latin American novels, literature almost always mixes with politics, religion, and sex?

VARGAS LLOSA: Well, all generalizations are always a little dangerous. I don't know if this is true of other novelists, but I do think that in my own novels political themes do appear fairly frequently, one way or another, due to the type of novel I attempt to write. These are novels with a sense of mission, we might say, which strive to show an integrated vision of society. I try to write about a world on several levels of experience, and on some level politics would of course play a very important role, as well as sex and religion and diverse institutions that are intimately tied to people's daily experience. I think this happens with other novelists, although there are certain Latin American writers with much more specialized concerns in some very specific areas.

INTERVIEWER: You are a researcher, a literary critic, even a historian. As a novelist, how do you reconcile facts with imagination, history with myth?

VARGAS LLOSA: With the Canudos affair there was one element that facilitated my work as a novelist, and it was that the history of Canudos is full of legends and myths. Historically, we know about the Republican side of Canudos. Everything that refers to the military expeditions and what Republican Brazil finally decided to do with Canudos on the basis of those documents is available. But on the other side, the rebel faction, the faction of the counselor and his followers, there is virtually no information. There is only testimony gathered after the defeat at Canudos, so there is an entire facet of the history of that event that is freed to the imagination, to pure fantasy. I received much help with this from the natives of the region where the war occurred, in the interior of Bahia, where they still think and talk about the Canudos event. So, for me, the history has been mainly a starting point that I have created, taking many liberties and into which I have introduced many half-truths.

INTERVIEWER: In *Aunt Julia and the Scriptwriter,* how did you manage to bring together the delirious and imaginary world of Pedro Camacho with the real world?

VARGAS LLOSA: My idea for the novel was precisely a story where a purely fantastical, purely imaginary, purely unreal world would coexist with a normal world with purely objective experiences. I wanted to show how the two are intimately linked, how that fantastical dimension really has its roots in experiences that are very normal, even sordid.

INTERVIEWER: The narrator of that work is named Mario. Why did you feel the need to insert yourself in your book and live among your characters?

VARGAS LLOSA: The character who bears my name came to me at the end. At first, I wrote a novel exclusively about Pedro Camacho, the writer of radio plays. The first version of *Aunt Julia* was going to be written through his plays, but I later had the feeling that a story told in this way would be too unreal, it would appear to be a mere play on fantasy and imagination, and then the story would lose its roots in objective reality. I therefore decided that, as a counterweight to the unreality embodied by Pedro Camacho, I would introduce a narrator, in some way representing me, who would narrate with complete objectivity in exactly the opposite way to Pedro Camacho. This established a vivid experience which lay somewhere between that extreme unreality and the extreme reality of the narrator named Mario, setting up a truthful means which maintained a middle road between pure fantasy and realism.

INTERVIEWER: When did you think of that work and come up with that idea?

VARGAS LLOSA: Perhaps the most remote idea occurred to me when I was working for a radio in Lima in the 1950s, an era when radio plays were very popular and had a large audience. As I saw the world of radio theater close up, the people who wrote it, the people who acted in it and those who listened to it,

I got the idea to write a novel on the popular world of radio theater.

INTERVIEWER: Where do you find the characters that people your novels? How do you situate yourself in relation to them, and who dominates whom?

VARGAS LLOSA: I believe that a great number of my characters spring from my experiences, the people I know, the people I see, or people about whom I hear stories. Perhaps the prime matter for a character always comes through these personal experiences. Later, logically, there is fantasy and imagination. There are characters who are invented, although a majority of them are a combination of both things, a sort of hybrid of fantasy and reality. There is a famous reply that Proust gave to someone who asked if his characters were real or invented. I don't remember the exact words, but it went something like this: This character has the eyes of so and so, the mouth of someone else, the way of thinking of yet somebody else, the physical appearance of a fourth person, and some characteristics which I did invent. I think all literary characters are a hybrid into which one puts as many memories as fantasies, things which have been taken from here and there.

INTERVIEWER: But who is stronger, the author or the characters?

VARGAS LLOSA: The author invents them, gives them a certain dynamism, and the characters begin to live and establish relations between themselves. A story then begins to acquire its own laws and one has to obey them to a certain extent. These norms undoubtedly contribute to creating a relationship between the characters and the author.

INTERVIEWER: On one occasion, you said that the writer should work like a peon. What does that work consist of? Don't you believe in inspiration?

VARGAS LLOSA: I think literature is basically a task, an effort, something that requires concentration, which demands patience and perseverance. In my case, at least, inspiration is born of hard work. Of course, I believe in inspiration; there are days when I work with much more concentration, much more creatively than others. But this trance state, what the romantics called inspiration, is something that, in my case at least, does not come naturally. It is something that is created through perseverance and assiduity. That is why I have referred to the effort aspect of literature. I don't think that there is only effort, however; I also believe that there is intuition, that predictive faculty. But if this is not accompanied by discipline and work, it does not do one much good.

INTERVIEWER: A majority of writers do not know how to analyze their own works. Do you think you are capable of being your own critic?

VARGAS LLOSA: No, I think I'm in the majority. I believe a writer does not have sufficient detachment from what he has written to be able to analyze and judge it objectively. For me, a text is also a context. It reveals what is underneath, where the materials come from, so I do not think I would be a good reader of my own works.

INTERVIEWER: You once said, "To burn incense is the task of sacristans, and for me a writer is the antipode of a sacristan." Do you see the writer as having a mission, or is writing a diversion, an entertainment?

VARGAS LLOSA: I don't think the two are incompatible. Writing can be a lot of fun, it can be something fascinating, something which can elate, and at the same time it also fulfills a critical function. It is one of the functions of literature to show the deficiencies of reality, the distance between what men would like to be and what they really are. Desire does not enter into this space, and reality is the space which literature occupies. At least for me as a reader, the literature that has interested and helped me the most is precisely that in which I discover the limits of reality, all the things in which reality is deficient or insufficient. This is the type of literature that I would like to write.

INTERVIEWER: When did you first feel your calling as a writer and decide to fulfill that responsibility?

VARGAS LLOSA: I began to feel that literature was very important to me when I was a student. I took to reading when I was a very young boy. Discovering literature was a very significant event in my life. Books enriched my existence immeasurably. I also began to write for fun when I was very young, but it is only when I was a university student that I realized literature was my calling. This was probably during my first years at the university, when I was sixteen or seventeen years old.

INTERVIEWER: You have written a book on *Madame Bovary*. How did you come to be acquainted with that work and take such a liking to it?

VARGAS LLOSA: I have great admiration for Flaubert, primarily because I think he was a great writer. I think that *Sentimental Education* and *Madame Bovary* are the most beautiful novels ever written. I also think that Flaubert as a writer interests me as much as his books. Flaubert was a man who built his talent on the basis of an almost superhuman effort. The first things that he wrote, for instance, did not in the least reveal a brilliant writer. It was through effort, perseverance, and insistence that he finally managed to educate his talent. He also gave the novel artistic status, which it had not had prior to that. He manipulated prose in such a way that he transformed it into an artistic object, something which up to that time had almost exclusively been the domain of poetry. This is another aspect that I find extraordinary in Flaubert—he wrote realistic novels about a sordid world which was not very poetic, and yet he wrote with a prose which is the very negation of that sordidness and opacity, a prose which is extraordinarily rich and varied. This is the type of literature that I would have liked to have written, and this is why Flaubert is one of the writers with whom I identify most.

INTERVIEWER: More than with Cervantes?

VARGAS LLOSA: These comparisons are always a bit

capricious. Cervantes is an extraordinary writer and *Don Quixote* is a masterpiece, and a very important manual for a novelist to follow. Happily, we need not choose between the two—we can keep them both.

INTERVIEWER: You are a great admirer of *Amadís de Gaula* and *Tyrant le Blanc*. Do you plan to write a chivalry novel someday or have you already done so?

VARGAS LLOSA: I think *The War of the End of the World* is my chivalry novel. It is an adventure novel, but it is also a novel that has its roots in a concrete reality, although some of the men within it have extraordinary, uncommon destinies. Perhaps the subject of Canudos fascinated me, among other reasons, because it allowed me to write the sort of novel I had been wanting to since I discovered the literature of chivalry.

INTERVIEWER: You write novels, plays, and literary criticism. In which genre do you feel most comfortable?

VARGAS LLOSA: The novel, without a doubt. It is the most practical and richest of genres. It has the greatest possibilities, although I also like the other genres. Above all else, I detest specialization in literature. I don't think, therefore, that it is incompatible for a novelist to write plays or stories, because I believe the other genres are complementary, and that, in some way, they feed on the seeds that I leave in my novels. The stories and plays I have written are really extensions of my novelistic world.

INTERVIEWER: What role does poetry play in your world?

VARGAS LLOSA: Like everyone else I think, I wrote poetry when I began writing as a youth. I even got some of my poems published, which I am now ashamed of having written because they are so awful. But at some point I realized that my calling was really narration, although I still remain an avid reader of poems.

INTERVIEWER: You are one of the most important figures of the Boom. Do you see the novel as a genre at a crossroads?

VARGAS LLOSA: For many years prophets and know-it-alls

have said that the novel was at its end, that it was decadent, that it was an already dying genre. I am not that pessimistic. I think the novel is showing many signs of vitality and that very creative novels are being written and are finding an audience. This must mean that they are giving that audience something. In the last few years, this has happened not only in Latin America but also in some countries of central Europe where there has been very interesting novelistic flowering, reminiscent of what happened in Latin America twenty years ago. I think the novel specifically, and literature in general, still have plenty of life in them.

INTERVIEWER: In writing your novels, do you intend them as social criticism or do you want to stimulate a change in your reader?

VARGAS LLOSA: When I write a novel, I'm interested in telling a story that will be persuasive and convincing. I want to make the novel alive and truthful. That is perhaps my main concern. However, I imagine that as I write, logically, I instill in my fiction some of my concerns, be they social, political, moral, cultural, because one writes with all of one's personality. Moreover, I think that a novel is not only entertainment but also gives its readers a sensibility of sorts to understand certain problems, perhaps even a critical perspective on these problems. I think these are by-products, however. The fundamental thing is basically the creation of a work which, through its language and technique, will impose itself on the reader as a valid artistic object.

INTERVIEWER: Do you think of the readers as you write?

VARGAS LLOSA: Yes, I think the readers are always present in an unconscious manner as one decides which techniques to use to tell a story. As it unfolds, as it transposes itself to the objective readers, one tries to be constantly aware of how they will react to the things that are being told and the way in which they are being told. Yes, in that sense, I am aware of the readers. I am not, however, aware of them as something concrete. I write so that reading will be concrete and determined, but the readers are undoubtedly there, because I do not think one writes for oneself. Writing is always done with the idea of communicating to someone else.

INTERVIEWER: You once said you did not like novels with a moral. Nevertheless, you approach history with a great moral and idealistic sense. How do you explain this?

VARGAS LLOSA: I think morality is distinct from morals. Morals are very clear instructions that accompany a novel like a sort of label. Certainly, I dislike this, but I also do not think that it is possible that in writing a novel there should not be a very great margin for interpretation in it. Many times, the ideas that one puts in a novel are not the only ideas present in the novel when it is finished. One does not write with ideas alone but also with intuitions and instincts, purely irrational, spontaneous elements which can sometimes give the artistic product ideological connotations that one could not foresee. In this sense, I do not think that a novel should be a mere explanation or illustration of a moral or political theory, although the novel should unquestionably have moral and political implications.

INTERVIEWER: How do you manage to master narrative technique and express yourself as if you were talking with friends?

VARGAS LLOSA: I think that the effectiveness of technique is directly related to invisibility. For a technique to be effective, it should not be perceived as a technique by the reader. Only its effects should be felt, otherwise the technique becomes the central character of the story, although this is fine in a novel which basically wants to tell a story in that way. But for me, the anecdote is very important in a novel. In that case, technique is at the service of the characters and the story. In other novels, the characters and the story are at the service of a technique or a way of telling, which is what the novelist fundamentally wants to show. This happens with many experimental authors these days, although I am not one of them.

INTERVIEWER: Your novel *Conversation in The Cathedral*

is a powerful critique of the dictatorship under General Odría. What motivated you to write a chronicle of that era of Peruvian politics?

VARGAS LLOSA: The dictatorship of Odría profoundly marked my generation: those Peruvians who passed from childhood into adolescence and later into manhood between 1948 and 1956. We grew up and became men in a society which lived a narrowly defined experience, with many liberties sacrificed to the repressive system, with a massive administrative goal of inverting many values. This experience marked me as a Peruvian and as a human being. One fine day I decided to turn it into literature and to show through fiction the way in which an experience of this sort can harm and corrupt an entire society.

INTERVIEWER: In your novels, particularly *Captain Pantoja and the Secret Service,* you stress machismo, and a code of manliness dominates. What do you think of feminism?

VARGAS LLOSA: It deserves to be backed in its struggle for equal rights, since it responds to a great need. It also has its radicalisms, however, which I find a little dangerous. I think it is important that men and women continue to be men and women. I do not believe that concepts of men and women are merely cultural and will disappear with equality between both sexes, because I think the difference is essentially based on domination. Among other factors, this is important because it makes love and passion possible, as well as all the things that in some way enormously enrich the lives of humans. This could be threatened if the very notions of man and woman disappeared, as some feminists would like.

INTERVIEWER: If you were such a beloved and spoiled son, how is it that you discovered pain, violence, and evil so early?

VARGAS LLOSA: I don't know if in this I have been different from the vast majority of human beings. I think it was as I entered adolescence that the paradise that we all have in childhood was shattered. I then discovered that life was much more complex and that it had a dark side. An event which was decisive for me in this respect was entering the Leoncio Prado Military School in Lima in 1950 when I was fourteen years old. That experience made a deep impression on me because I discovered a series of things that had been unknown to me until then. These experiences allowed me to write my first novel, *The Time of the Hero.*

INTERVIEWER: You lived outside Peru for many years, in Madrid, Barcelona, Paris and London. What advantages did this voluntary exile have for your work?

VARGAS LLOSA: I think that the years I lived in Europe helped me in many respects. First of all, they gave me a broadened education, a comprehensive perspective which helped me understand the things in my own country. I think they allowed me to discover that I was a Latin American. Europe made me understand that what is Peruvian, Bolivian or Chilean are all facets of the unified experience which is Latin America from the cultural and historical points of view. I discovered this in Europe, not in Peru. I also think Europe gave me the discipline to work. It was there that I discovered that literature is basically a task, a discipline and an effort. It also gave me a non-provincial perspective on literature. In all respects, I think that my exile was a very beneficial experience for me.

INTERVIEWER: How have you managed to keep street language alive or, more accurately, the use of localisms or Peruvianisms?

VARGAS LLOSA: I lived in Europe many years, but at some point I began to feel that being absent from my country and my own culture was impairing precisely what is most important in a writer, which is language. And it was probably for these reasons that I decided to return to my country, because after all I write about things that are intimately tied to the Peruvian experience, which is something fundamental for me. When I returned in 1974, I had been living abroad for sixteen years, although I had been back many times for vacations. This is why I decided to live once again in my country. I think it was the right decision, because reinserting myself in all the problems of Peru not only gave me new themes and new materials for my writing but also renewed that vitality of language which I think is fundamental for a writer.

INTERVIEWER: Who is Mario Vargas Llosa?

VARGAS LLOSA: Well, a man does not know his own face. They say that when he looks at himself in the mirror, he does not know what he is like. Others can see one with objectivity, but one cannot see oneself. I think a writer is basically what he writes, and what he has written is the most important part of him. In the end, it is all that will remain of what he was. Everything else is transient and circumstantial, and of that nothing will remain. In the final analysis, what matters about a writer are his books and nothing else.

Selected Bibliography

I. Works by the Authors

ISABEL ALLENDE

De amor y de sombra. Barcelona: Plaza & Janés, 1984. (*Of Love and Shadows.* Trans. Margaret Sayers Peden. New York: Knopf, 1987.) Novel.

La casa de los espíritus. Barcelona: Plaza & Janés, 1982. (*The House of Spirits.* Trans. Magda Bogin. New York: Knopf, 1985.) Novel.

Eva Luna. Barcelona: Plaza & Janés, 1987. (*Eva Luna.* Trans. Margaret Sayers Peden. New York: Knopf, 1988.) Novel.

GUILLERMO CABRERA INFANTE

Arcadia todas las noches. Barcelona: Seix Barral, 1978. Essays.

Así en la paz como en la guerra. Havana: Revolución, 1960. Short stories.

Exorcismos de esti(l)o. Barcelona: Seix Barral, 1976. Essays.

La Habana para un infante difunto. Barcelona: Seix Barral, 1979. (*Infante's Inferno.* Trans. Suzanne Jill Levine and the author. New York: Harper & Row, 1984.) Novel.

Holy Smoke. New York: Harper & Row, 1985. Non-fiction.

O. Barcelona: Seix Barral, 1975. Autobiography.

Tres tristes tigres. Barcelona: Seix Barral, 1965. (*Three Trapped Tigers.* Trans. Donald Gardner and Suzanne Jill Levine with the author. New York: Harper & Row, 1971.) Novel.

Vista del amanecer en el trópico. Barcelona: Seix Barral, 1974. (*A View of Dawn in the Tropics.* Trans. Suzanne Jill Levine. New York: Harper & Row, 1978.) Novel.

JOSÉ DONOSO

Casa de campo. Barcelona: Seix Barral, 1978. (*A House in the Country.* Trans. David Pritchard with Suzanne Jill Levine. New York: Knopf, 1984.) Novel.

El Charleston. Santiago: Nascimento, 1960. (*The Charleston and Other Stories.* Trans. Andrée Conrad. Boston: Godine, 1977.) Short stories.

Coronación. Santiago: Nascimento, 1957. (*Coronation.* Trans. Jocasta Goodwin. Knopf, 1965.) Novel.

Cuatro para Delfina. Barcelona: Seix Barral, 1982. Novellas.

Cuentos. Barcelona: Seix Barral, 1972. Short stories.

La desesperanza. Barcelona: Seix Barral, 1986. (*Curfew.* Trans. Alfred MacAdam. New York: Weidenfeld & Nicolson, 1988.) Novel.

Este Domingo. Santiago: Zig-Zag, 1966. (*This Sunday.* Trans. Lorraine O'Grady Freeman. New York: Knopf, 1967.) Novel.

Historia personal del "boom." Barcelona: Anagrama, 1972. (*The Boom in Spanish-American Literature: A Personal History.* Trans. Gregory Kolovakos. New York: Columbia University Press, 1977.) Criticism.

El jardín de al lado. Barcelona: Seix Barral, 1981. Novel.

El lugar sin límites. Mexico: Joaquín Mortiz, 1967. ("Hell Has No Limits," in *Triple Cross.* Trans. Suzanne Jill Levine. New York: Dutton, 1972.) Novella.

Los mejores cuentos. Santiago: Zig-Zag, 1966. Short stories.

La misteriosa desaparición de la marquesita de Loria. Barcelona: Seix Barral, 1980. Novel.

El obsceno pájaro de la noche. Barcelona: Seix Barral, 1970. (*The Obscene Bird of Night.* Trans. Hardie St. Martin and Leonard Mades. New York: Knopf, 1973.) Novel.

Tres novelitas burguesas. Barcelona: Seix Barral, 1973. (*Sacred Families: Three Novellas.* Trans. Andrée Conrad. New York: Knopf, 1977.)

Rosario Ferré

El acomodador: una lectura fantástica de Felisberto Hernández. Mexico: Fondo de Cultura Económica, 1986. Criticism.
El árbol y sus sombras. Mexico: Fondo de Cultura Económica, 1989. Essays.
Los cuentos de Juan Bobo. Río Piedras, PR: Huracán, 1982. Short stories.
Fábulas de la garza desangrada. Mexico: Joaquín Mortiz, 1982. Poetry.
Maldito amor. Mexico: Joaquín Mortiz, 1986. (*Sweet Diamond Dust.* Trans. the author. New York: Ballantine, 1989.) Novel.
El medio pollito: siete cuentos infantiles. Río Piedras: Huracán, 1976. Children's stories.
Papeles de Pandora. Mexico: Joaquín Mortiz, 1976. (*The Youngest Doll and Other Stories.* Trans. the author and Diana Vélez. Norman: University of Oklahoma Press, forthcoming.)
Sitios a Eros: siete ensayos literarios. Mexico: Joaquín Mortiz, 1980. Essays.

Carlos Fuentes

Agua quemada. Mexico: Fondo de Cultura Económica, 1981. (*Burnt Water: Stories.* Trans. Margaret Sayers Peden. New York: Farrar Straus Giroux, 1980.)
Aura. Mexico: Era, 1962. (*Aura.* Trans. Lysander Kemp. New York: Farrar Straus Giroux, 1965.) Novel.
Las buenas conciencias. Mexico: Fondo de Cultura Económica, 1959. (*The Good Conscience.* Trans. Sam Hileman. New York: Ivan Obolensky, 1961.) Novel.
La cabeza de la hidra. Mexico: Joaquín Mortiz, 1978. (*The Hydra Head.* Trans. Margaret Sayers Peden. New York: Farrar Straus Giroux, 1978.) Novel.
Cambio de piel. Mexico: Joaquín Mortiz, 1967. (*A Change of Skin.* Trans. Sam Hileman. New York: Farrar Straus Giroux, 1968.) Novel.
Cervantes: o, la crítica de la lectura. Mexico: Joaquín Mortiz, 1976.

(Don Quixote: or the Critique of Reading. Austin: University of Texas, 1976.) Criticism.

Constancia and Other Stories for Virgins. Trans. Thomas Christensen. New York: Farrar Straus Giroux, 1989.

Cristóbal nonato. Mexico: Fondo de Cultura Económica, 1987. *(Christopher Unborn.* Trans. Alfred MacAdam. New York: Farrar Straus Giroux, 1989.) Novel.

Cuerpos y ofrendas. Madrid: Alianza, 1972. Short stories.

Una familia lejana. Mexico: Era, 1980. *(Distant Relations.* Trans. Margaret Sayers Peden. New York: Farrar Straus Giroux, 1982.) Novel.

Gringo viejo. Mexico: Fondo de Cultura Económica, 1985. *(The Old Gringo.* Trans. Margaret Sayers Peden and the author. New York: Farrar Straus Giroux, 1985.) Novel.

La muerte de Artemio Cruz. Mexico: Fondo de Cultura Económica, 1962. *(The Death of Artemio Cruz.* Trans. Sam Hileman. New York: Farrar Straus Giroux, 1964.) Novel.

Myself with Others: Selected Essays. New York: Farrar Straus Giroux, 1988.

La nueva novela hispanoamerica. Mexico: Joaquín Mortiz, 1969. Criticism.

Orquídeas a la luz de la luna: comedia mexicana. Barcelona: Seix Barral, 1982. Play.

La región más transparente. Mexico: Fondo de Cultura Económica, 1958. *(Where the Air Is Clear.* Trans. Sam Hileman. New York: Ivan Obolensky, 1960.) Novel.

Terra Nostra. Mexico: Joaquín Mortiz, 1975. *(Terra Nostra.* Trans. Margaret Sayers Peden. New York: Farrar Straus Giroux, 1976.) Novel.

Todos los gatos son pardos. Mexico: Siglo Veintiuno, 1970. Play.

El tuerto es rey. Mexico: Joaquín Mortiz, 1970. Play.

Zona sagrada. Mexico: Siglo Vientiuno, 1967. ("Holy Place," in *Triple Cross.* Trans. Suzanne Jill Levine. New York: Dutton, 1972.) Novella.

Isaac Goldemberg

Hombre de paso/Just Passing Through. Trans. David Unger and the author. Hanover, NH: Norte, 1981. Poetry.
Tiempo al tiempo. Hanover: Norte, 1984. (*Play by Play.* Trans. Hardie St. Martin. New York: Persea Books, 1985.) Novel.
La vida a plazos de don Jacobo Lerner. Lima: Libre 1, 1978. (*The Fragmented Life of Don Jacobo Lerner.* Trans. Robert S. Picciotto. New York: Persea, 1976.) Novel.

Juan Carlos Onetti

Los adioses. Buenos Aires: Sur, 1954. Novel.
El astillero. Buenos Aires: Fabril, 1961. (*The Shipyard.* Trans. Rachel Caffyn. New York: Scribner's, 1968.) Novel.
Cuando entonces. Madrid: Mondadori, 1987. Novella.
Cuentos secretos: Periquito el aguador y otras máscaras. Montevideo: Marcha, 1986. Short stories.
Cuentos completos. Buenos Aires: Corregidor, 1974. Short stories.
Dejemos hablar al viento. Barcelona: Bruguera, 1979. Novel.
Jacob y el otro: un sueño realizado y otros cuentos. Montevideo: Oriental, 1961. Short stories.
Juntacadáveres. Montevideo: Alfa, 1964. Novel.
La muerte y la niña. Buenos Aires: Corregidor: 1973. Novel.
Novelas cortas completas. Caracas: Monte Avila, 1968.
La novia robada y otros cuentos. Montevideo: Alfa, 1968. Short stories.
Para una tumba sin nombre. Montevideo: Marcha, 1959. Novel.
El pozo. Montevideo: Signo, 1939. Novel.
Presencia y otros cuentos. Madrid: Almarabú, 1986. Short stories.
Requiem por Faulkner y otros artículos. Montevideo: Arca, 1975. Essays.
Tan triste como ella y otros cuentos. Montevideo: Alfa, 1963. Short stories.
Tiempo de abrazar y los cuentos de 1933 a 1950. Montevideo: Arca, 1974. Short stories.
Tierra de nadie. Buenos Aires: Losada, 1941. Novel.

La vida breve. Buenos Aires: Sudamericana, 1950. (*A Brief Life.*
Trans. Hortense Carpentier. New York: Viking, 1976.) Novel.

NICANOR PARRA

Antipoemas: antología (1944-1969). Barcelona: Seix Barral, 1972.
(*Anti-Poems.* Trans. Jorge Elliot. San Francisco: City Lights,
1960; *Antipoems: New and Selected,* edited by David Unger.
Trans. Lawrence Ferlinghetti et al. New York: New Directions,
1985.)
Artefactos. Santiago: Universidad Católica de Chile, 1972.
La cueca larga y otros poemas. Santiago: Universitaria, 1958.
Hojas de Parra. Santiago: Ganymedes, 1985.
Nuevos sermones y prédicas del Cristo de Elqui. Valparaíso:
Ganymedes, 1979.
Obra gruesa. Santiago: Universitaria, 1969. (*Emergency Poems.*
Trans. Miller Williams. New York: New Directions, 1972.)
Poema y antipoema a Eduardo Frei. Santiago: América del Sur,
1982.
Poemas y antipoemas. 1954; rpt. Santiago: Nascimento, 1971.
(*Poems and Antipoems.* Trans. Miller Williams. New York: New
Directions, 1967.)
Sermones y prédicas del Cristo de Elqui. Santiago: Universidad de
Chile, 1977. (*Sermons and Homilies of the Christ of Elqui.* Trans.
Sandra Reyes. Columbia: University of Missouri Press, 1984.)
Versos de salón. Santiago: Nascimento, 1962.
(With Pablo Neruda.) *Discursos.* Santiago: Nascimento, 1962.

ELENA PONIATOWSKA

¡Ay vida, no me mereces! Mexico: Joaquín Mortiz, 1985. Criticism.
De noche vienes. Mexico: Grijalbo, 1979. Short stories.
Domingo 7. Mexico: Océano, 1982. Non-fiction.
La "Flor de Lis." Mexico: Era, 1988. Novel.
Fuerte es el silencio. Mexico: Era, 1980. Non-fiction.
Gaby Brimmer. Mexico: Grijalbo, 1979. Non-fiction.
Hasta no verte Jesús mío. Mexico: Era, 1969. (*Until We Meet*

Again. Trans. Magda Bogin. New York: Pantheon, 1987.) Novel.
Lilus Kikus. Mexico: Los Presenteo, 1954. Novel.
Nada nadie. Mexico: Era, 1988. Non-fiction.
La noche de Tlatelolco: testimonios de historia oral. Mexico: Era, 1971. (*Massacre in Mexico.* Trans. Helen R. Lane. New York: Viking, 1975.) Non-fiction.
Palabras cruzadas: Crónicas. Mexico: Era, 1961. Nonfiction.
Querido Diego, te abraza Quiela. Mexico: Era, 1978. (*Dear Diego.* Trans. Katherine Silver. New York: Pantheon, 1986.) Epistolary novel.
Tina Modotti. Mexico: Era, 1989. Novel.
Todo empezó el domingo. Mexico: Fondo de Cultura Económica, 1963.

MANUEL PUIG

Bajo un manto de estrellas: pieza en dos actos. El beso de la mujer araña: adaptación escénica por el autor. Barcelona: Seix Barral, 1983. (*Under a Mantle of Stars: A Play in Two Acts.* Trans. Ronald Christ. New York: Lumen Books, 1985; *The Kiss of the Spider Woman: the Screenplay.* Adapted by Leonard Schrader. Boston: Faber & Faber, 1987.)
El beso de la mujer araña. Barcelona: Seix Barral, 1976. (*The Kiss of the Spider Woman.* Trans. Thomas Colchie. New York: Knopf, 1979.) Novel.
Boquitas pintadas. Buenos Aires: Sudamericana, 1969. (*Heartbreak Tango: A Serial.* Trans. Suzanne Jill Levine. New York: Dutton, 1973.) Novel.
The Buenos Aires Affair: novela policial. Mexico: Joaquín Mortiz, 1973. (*The Buenos Aires Affair: A Detective Novel.* Trans. Suzanne Jill Levine. New York: Dutton, 1976.) Novel.
La cara del villano: recuerdo de Tijuana. Barcelona: Seix Barral, 1985. Play.
Maldición eterna a quien lea estas páginas. Barcelona: Seix Barral, 1980. (*Eternal Curse on the Reader of These Pages.* Trans. the author. New York: Random, 1982.) Novel.
Pubis angelical. Barcelona: Seix Barral, 1979. (*Pubis Angelical.*

Trans. Elena Brunet. New York: Aventura, 1986.) Novel.
Sangre de amor correspondido. Barcelona: Seix Barral, 1982. (*Blood of Requited Love.* Trans. Jan L. Grayson. New York: Random, 1983.) Novel.
La traición de Rita Hayworth. Buenos Aires: Sudamericana, 1968. (*Betrayed by Rita Hayworth.* Trans. Suzanne Jill Levine. New York: Dutton, 1971.) Novel.

ERNESTO SÁBATO

Abaddón el exterminador. Buenos Aires: Sudamericana, 1974. Novel.
Antología. Buenos Aires: Librería del Colegio, 1975.
Claves políticas. Buenos Aires: Rodolfo Alonso, 1971. Essays.
La convulsión política de nuestro tiempo. Buenos Aires: Edicom, 1969. Non-fiction.
Itinerario. Buenos Aires: Sur, 1969. Essays.
Sobre héroes y tumbas. Buenos Aires: Fabril, 1961. (*On Heroes and Tombs.* Trans. Helen R. Lane. Boston: Godine, 1981.) Novel.
Tango: discusión y clave. Buenos Aires: Losada, 1963. Nonfiction.
Tres aproximaciones a la literatura de nuestro tiempo: Robbe-Grillet, Borges, Sartre. Santiago: Universitaria, 1968. Criticism.
El túnel. Buenos Aires: Sur, 1948. (*The Outsider.* Trans. Harriet de Onís. New York: Knopf, 1950; *The Tunnel.* Trans. Margaret Sayers Peden. New York: Ballantine, 1988.) Novel.
Uno es el universo. Barcelona: Seix Barral, 1981. Essays.

LUIS RAFAEL SÁNCHEZ

Los ángeles se han fatigado. San Juan, PR: Lugar, 1960. Play.
En cuerpo de camisa. San Juan: Lugar, 1966. Short stories.
Farsa del amor compradito. San Juan: Lugar, 1960. Play.
La guaracha del macho Camacho. Buenos Aires: Flor, 1976. (*Macho Camacho's Beat.* Trans. Gregory Rabassa. New York: Pantheon, 1980.) Novel.
La hiel nuestra de cada día. San Juan: Instituto de Cultura Puertorriqueña, 1962. Play.

La importancia de llamarse Daniel Santos. Hanover, NH: Norte, 1988. Novel.

O casi el alma: auto de fe en tres actos. Río Piedras: Cultural, 1974. Play.

La pasión según Antígona Pérez. Hato Rey, PR: Lugar, 1968. (*The Passion according to Antígona Pérez.* Trans. Charles Pilditch. New York: Studio Duplicating Service, 1972.) Play.

Quintuples. Hanover: Norte, 1985. Play.

SEVERO SARDUY

Barroco. Buenos Aires: Sudamericana, 1974. Essays.

Big Bang. Barcelona: Tusquets, 1974. Poetry.

Cobra. Buenos Aires: Sudamericana, 1972. (*Cobra.* Trans. Suzanne Jill Levine. New York: Dutton, 1975.) Novel.

Colibrí. Barcelona: Argos Vergara, 1984. Novel.

De donde son los cantantes. Mexico: Joaquín Mortiz, 1967. ("From Cuba with a Song," in *Triple Cross.* Trans. Suzanne Jill Levine. New York: Dutton, 1972.) Novella.

Escrito sobre un cuerpo: ensayos de crítica. Buenos Aires: Sudamericana, 1969. (*Written on a Body.* New York: Lumen, 1989.) Criticism.

Gestos. 1963; rpt. Barcelona: Seix Barral, 1973. Novel.

Maitreya. Barcelona: Seix Barral, 1978. (*Maitreya.* Trans. Suzanne Jill Levine. Hanover: Norte, 1987.) Novel.

Micro-opera de Benet Rossell. Barcelona: Ambit, 1984.

Para la voz. Madrid: Fundamentos, 1978. (*For Voice.* Trans. Philip Barnard. Pittsburgh: Latin American Literary Review Press, 1985.) Radio plays.

La simulación. Caracas: Monte Avila, 1982.

LUISA VALENZUELA

Aquí pasan cosas raras. Buenos Aires: Flor, 1975. (*Strange Things Happen Here: Twenty-six Short Stories and a Novel.* Trans. Helen R. Lane. New York: Harcourt Brace Jovanovich, 1979.)

Camio de armas. Hanover, NH: Norte, 1982. (*Other Weapons.*

Trans. Deborah Bonner. Hanover: Norte, 1985.) Short stories.
Cola de lagartija. Buenos Aires: Bruguera, 1983. (*The Lizard's Tail.* Trans. Gregory Rabassa. New York: Farrar Straus Giroux, 1983.) Novel.
Como en la guerra. Buenos Aires: Sudamericana, 1977. (*He Who Searches.* Trans. Helen R. Lane. Elmwood Park, IL: Dalkey Archive, 1987.) Novel.
Crimen del otro. Hanover: Norte, 1989. Novel.
Donde viven las águilas. Buenos Aires: Celtia, 1983. Short stories.
El gato eficaz. Mexico: Joaquín Mortiz, 1972. Novel.
Hay que sonreír. Buenos Aires: Americalee, 1966. (*Clara: Thirteen Short Stories and a Novel.* Trans. Hortense Carpentier and J. Jorge Castello. New York: Harcourt Brace Jovanovich, 1976.)
Los heréticos. Buenos Aires: Paidos, 1967. (Trans. in *Clara,* as above.) Short stories.
Libro que no muerde. Mexico: Universidad Nacional Autonoma de Mexico, 1980. Short stories.
Open Door. Trans. Hortense Carpentier and J. Jorge Castello. Berkeley: North Point, 1988. Short stories.

MARIO VARGAS LLOSA

Los cachorros. Barcelona: Lumen, 1967. (*The Cubs and Other Stories.* Trans. Gregory Kolovakos and Ronald Christ. New York: Harper & Row, 1979.) Novella and short stories.
La casa verde. Barcelona: Seix Barral, 1966. (*The Green House.* Trans. Gregory Rabassa. New York: Harper & Row, 1968.) Novel.
La ciudad y los perros. Barcelona: Seix Barral, 1963. (*The Time of the Hero.* Trans. Lysander Kemp. New York: Grove, 1966.) Novel.
Contra el viento y la marea (1962-1982). Barcelona: Seix Barral, 1983. Essays.
Conversación en La Catedral. Barcelona: Seix Barral, 1969. (*Conversation in The Cathedral.* Trans. Gregory Rabassa. New York: Harper & Row, 1975.) Novel.
Día domingo. Buenos Aires: Amadís, 1971. Novella.

Elogio de la madrasta. Barcelona: Tusquets, 1988. Novel.

Entre Sartre y Camus. Río Piedras, PR: Huracán, 1981.

García Márquez: historia de un deicidio. Barcelona: Seix Barral, 1971. Criticism.

La guerra del fin del mundo. Barcelona: Seix Barral, 1981. (*The War of the End of the World.* Trans. Helen R. Lane. New York: Farrar Straus Giroux, 1984.) Novel.

El hablador. Barcelona: Seix Barral, 1987. (*The Storyteller.* Trans. Helen R. Lane. New York: Farrar Straus Giroux, 1989.) Novel.

Historia de Mayta. Barcelona: Seix Barral, 1984. (*The Real Life of Alejandro Mayta.* Trans. Alfred MacAdam. New York: Farrar Straus Giroux, 1986). Novel.

La historia secreta de una novela. Barcelona: Tusquets, 1971. Criticism.

Los jefes. Barcelona: Rocas, 1959. (*The Cubs and Other Stories,* as above.) Short stories.

Kathie y el hipopótamo: comedia en dos actos. Barcelona: Seix Barral, 1983. Play.

La novela en América Latina: diálogo entre Gabriel García Márquez y Mario Vargas Llosa. Lima: Milla Batres, 1968. Criticism.

La orgía perpetua: Flaubert y "Madame Bovary." Barcelona: Seix Barral, 1975/Madrid: Taurus, 1975. (*The Perpetual Orgy: Flaubert and "Madame Bovary."* Trans. Helen R. Lane. New York: Farrar Straus Giroux, 1986.) Criticism.

Pantaleón y las visitadoras. Barcelona: Seix Barral, 1973. (*Captain Pantoja and the Special Service.* Trans. Gregory Kolovakos and Ronald Christ. New York: Harper & Row, 1978.) Novel.

¡Quien mató a Polomino Molero? Barcelona: Seix Barral, 1986. (*Who Killed Palomino Molero?* Trans. Alfred MacAdam. New York: Macmillan, 1987.) Novel.

La señorita de Tacna: pieza en dos actos. Barcelona: Seix Barral, 1981. Play.

La tía Julia y el escribidor. Barcelona: Seix Barral, 1977. (*Aunt Julia and the Scriptwriter.* Trans. Helen R. Lane. New York: Farrar Straus Giroux, 1982.) Novel.

II. Critical Works on the Authors

A. IN SPANISH

Achúgar, Hugo. *Ideología y estructuras narrativas en José Donoso (1950-1970)*. Caracas: Centro de Estudios Latinoamericanos Rómulo Gallegos, 1979.

Acker, Bertie. *El cuento mexicano contemporáneo: Rulfo, Arreola y Fuentes: temas y cosmovisión*. Madrid: Playor, 1984.

Alonso, M. Rosa, et al. *Agresión a la realidad: Mario Vargas Llosa*. Las Palmas: Inventarios Provisionales, 1972.

Alvarez-Borland, Isabel. *Discontinuidad y ruptura en Guillermo Cabrera Infante*. Gaithersburg, MD: Hispamérica, 1983.

Balkenende, Lidia. *Aproximación a la novelística de Sábato*. Buenos Aires: Plus Ultra, 1983.

Barradas, Efraín. *Acercamiento a la obra de Luis Rafael Sánchez*. Río Piedras, PR: Editorial Cultural, 1981.

———. *Para leer en puertorriqueño: acercamiento a la obra de Luis Rafael Sánchez*. Río Piedras: Cultural, 1981.

Barrera López, Trinidad. *La estructura de "Abaddón el exterminador."* Sevilla: Escuela de Estudios Hispano-Americanos, 1982.

Befumo, Delia Liliana, and Elisa T. Calabrese. *Acercamiento a "La muerte de Artemio Cruz" de Carlos Fuentes*. Mar del Plata, Argentina: Universidad Católica de Mar del Plata, 1972.

———. *Nostalgia del futuro en la obra de Carlos Fuentes*. Buenos Aires: F. García Cambeiro, 1974.

Belaval, Emilio S. *Los problemas de la cultura puertorriqueña*. Río Piedras: Cultural, 1977.

Boldori de Baldussi, Rosa. *Vargas Llosa: un narrador y sus demonios*. Buenos Aires: F. García Cambeiro, 1974.

———. *Mario Vargas Llosa y la literatura en el Perú de hoy*. Santa Fe, Argentina: Colmegna, 1969.

Campos, René Alberto. *Espejos: la textura cinemática de Rita Hayworth*. Madrid: Pliegos, 1985.

Cano Gaviria, Ricardo. *El buitre y el ave fenix: conversaciones con Mario Vargas Llosa*. Barcelona: Anagrama, 1972.

Carranza, Luján. *Aproximación a la literatura del mexicano Carlos*

Fuentes. Santa Fe, Argentina: Colmegna, 1974.

Catania, Carlos. *Genio y figura de Ernesto Sábato.* Buenos Aires: Editorial Universitaria de Buenos Aires, 1987.

————. *Sábato: entre la idea y la sangre.* San José: Editorial Costa Rica, 1973.

Cersosimo, Emilse Beatriz. *"Sobre héroes y tumbas": de los carácteres a la metafísica.* Buenos Aires: Sudamericana, 1972.

Coddou, Marcelo. *Los libros tienen sus propios espíritus.* Mexico: Universidad Veracruzana, 1986.

Collazos, Oscar. *Julio Cortázar y Mario Vargas Llosa: Literatura en la revolución y revolución en la literatura.* Mexico: Siglo Veintiuno, 1977.

Colón Zayas, Eliseo. *El teatro de Luis Rafael Sánchez: ideología y lenguaje.* Madrid: Playor, 1985.

Correa, María Angélica. *Genio y figura de Ernesto Sábato.* Buenos Aires: Editorial Universitaria de Buenos Aires, 1971.

Curiel, Fernando. *Onetti: cálculo infortunio.* Mexico: Universidad Nacional Autónoma de México, 1980.

Dellapiane, Angela B. *Sábato: un análisis de su narrativa.* Buenos Aires: Nova, 1970.

Durán, Gloria. *La magia y las brujas en la obra de Carlos Fuentes.* Mexico: Universidad Nacional Autónoma de México, 1976.

Durán, Manuel. *Tríptico mexicano: Juan Rulfo, Carlos Fuentes, Salvador Elizondo.* Mexico: Secretaría de Educación Pública, 1973.

Echevarren Welker, Roberto. *Manuel Puig: montaje y alteriadad del sujeto.* Santiago de Chile: Instituto Profesional del Pacífico, 1986.

Fernández, Castro Manuel. *Aproximación formal a la novelística de Vargas Llosa.* Madrid: Nacional, 1977.

Ferro, Roberto. *Juan Carlos Onetti: "La vida breve."* Buenos Aires: Hachette, 1986.

Figueroa, Alvin Joaquín. "La narrativa de Luis Rafael Sánchez. Texto y contexto." *Dissertation Abstracts International* 47, no. 4 (1986): 1309A-10A.

Frankenhaler, Marylyn R. *J. C. Onetti: la salvación por la forma.* New York: Abra, 1977.

Giacoman, Helmy F., comp. *Homenaje a Carlos Fuentes.* New York: Las Américas, 1971.

————. *Homenaje a Juan Carlos Onetti: variaciones interpretativas en torno a su obra.* New York: Las Américas, 1974.

————. *Homenaje a Ernesto Sábato: variaciones interpretativas en torno a su obra.* New York: Las Américas, 1973.

————, and José Miguel Oviedo. *Homenaje a Mario Vargas Llosa: variaciones interpretativas en torno a su obra.* New York: Las Américas, 1972.

González Bermejo, Ernesto. *Cosas de escritores. Gabriel García Márquez, Mario Vargas Llosa, Julio Cortázar.* Montevideo: Marcha, 1971.

González Echevarría, Roberto. *La ruta de Severo Sarduy.* Hanover, NH: Norte, 1987.

Gottlieb, Marlene. *No se termina nunca de nacer: la poesía de Nicanor Parra.* Madrid: Playor, 1977.

Guerrero, Gustavo. *La estrategia neobarroca: estudio sobre el resurgimiento de la poética barroca en la obra narrativa de Severo Sarduy.* Barcelona: Mall, 1987.

Gutiérrez Movat, Ricardo. *José Donoso: Impostura e impostación.* Gaithersburg, MD: Ediciones Hispamérica, 1983.

Hernández Vargas, Nelida, and Daisy Caraballo Abreu, comp. *Luis Rafael Sánchez: crítica y bibliografía.* Río Piedras: Seminario de Estudios Hispánicos Federico de Onís, 1985.

Jiménez Grullón, Juan Isidro. *Anti-Sábato o Ernesto Sábato: un escritor dominado por fantasmas.* Maracaibo: Universidad de Zulia, 1968.

Ludmer, Josefina. *Onetti: los procesos de construcción del relato.* Buenos Aires: Sudamericana, 1977.

Mardoqueo Reyes, Sixto. *Ernesto Sábato y su compromiso con el hombre.* Santa Fe, Argentina: Cuadernos de Arcién, 1982.

Martín, José Luis. *La narrativa de Vargas Llosa: acercamiento estilístico.* Madrid: Gredos, 1974.

Martínez Dacosta, Silvia. *Dos ensayos literarios sobre Eduardo Barrios y José Donoso.* Miami: Universal, 1977.

————. *El informe sobre ciegos en la novela de Ernesto Sábato, "Sobre héroes y tumbas": comentario crítico a la luz de las teorías de Segismundo Freud.* Miami: Universal, 1972.

Mayer, Marcos. *Ernesto Sábato: "Sobre héroes y tumbas."* Buenos Aires: Hachette, 1986.

Méndez Rodenas, Adriana. *Severo Sarduy: el neobarroco de la transgresión.* Mexico: Universidad Nacional Autónoma de México, 1983.

Molina, Juan Manuel. *La dialéctica de la identidad en la obra de Juan Carlos Onetti.* Frankfurt: Peter Lang, 1982.

Montes, Hugo, and Mario Rodríguez. *Nicanor Parra y la poesía de lo cotidiano.* Santiago de Chile: Pacífico, 1970.

Morales T., Leonidas. *La poesía de Nicanor Parra.* Santiago de Chile: Andrés Bello, 1970.

Moreno Aliste, Ximena. *Origen y sentido de la farsa en la obra de Juan Carlos Onetti.* Poitiers: Centre de recherches latino-américaines de l'Université de Poitiers, 1973.

Neyra, Joaquín. *Ernesto Sábato.* Buenos Aires: Ministerio de la Cultura y Educación, 1973.

Ortega, Julio, et al. *Guillermo Cabrera Infante.* Madrid: Fundamentos, 1974.

Oviedo, José Miguel. *Mario Vargas Llosa: la invención de una realidad.* Barcelona: Seix Barral, 1970.

Pacheco, J. E., et al. *Asedios a Vargas Llosa.* Santiago de Chile: Universitaria, 1973.

Pamies, Alberto N., and Dean Berry. *Carlos Fuentes y la dualidad integral mexicana.* Miami: Universal, 1969.

Pereda, Rosa María. *Guillermo Cabrera Infante.* Madrid: Edaf, 1979.

Petrea, Mariana Doina. *Ernesto Sábato: la nada y la metafísica de la esperanza.* Madrid: Turanzas, 1986.

Polar, Antonio Cornejo, ed. *José Donoso: la destrucción de un mundo.* Buenos Aires: Cambeira, 1975.

Premore, James R. *Un estudio crítico de las novelas de Ernesto Sábato.* Madrid: Turanzas, 1981.

Preso, Omar, and María Angélica Petit. *Juan Carlos Onetti, o la salvación por la escritura.* Madrid: Sociedad General Española de Librería, 1981.

Pujals Abascal, Josefina. *El bosque indomado—donde chilla "el obsceno pájaro de la noche": un estudio sobre la novela de José Donoso.* Miami: Universal, 1981.

Quinteros, Isis. *José Donoso: una insurrección contra la realidad.* Madrid: Hispanova, 1978.

Ramírez Mattei, Aida Elsa. *La narrativa de Carlos Fuentes: afán por la armonía en la multiplicidad antasónica del mundo.* Río Piedras: Editorial de la Universidad de Puerto Rico, 1983.

Rein, Mercedes. *Nicanor Parra y la antipoesía.* Montevideo: Universidad de la República, 1970.

Ríos, Julián, ed. *Severo Sarduy.* Madrid: Fundamentos, 1976.

Riquer, Martín de, and Mario Vargas Llosa. *El combate imaginario; las cartas de batalla de Joanot Martorell.* Barcelona: Seix Barral, 1972.

Rivero Potter, Alicia. "La estética mallarmana comparada con la teoría y práctica de la novela en Gómez de la Serna, Huidobro y Sarduy." *Dissertation Abstracts International* 44, no. 7 (1984): 2160A.

Rodríguez Lee, María Luisa. *Juegos sicológicos en la narrativa de Mario Vargas Llosa.* Miami: Universal, 1984.

Salvador Jofre, Alvaro. *Para una lectura de Nicanor Parra: el proyecto ideológico y el inconsciente.* Sevilla: Secretariado de Publicaciones de la Universidad de Sevilla, 1975.

Sánchez-Boudy, José. *La nueva novela hispanoamericana y "Tres tristes tigres."* Miami: Universal, 1971.

————. *La temática narrativa de Severo Sarduy.* Miami: Universal, 1985.

Sánchez Reyes, Carmen. *Carlos Fuentes y "La región más transparente."* Río Piedras: Universitaria, 1975.

Schopf, Federico. *Del vanguardismo a la antipoesía.* Roma: Bulzoni, 1986.

Solotorevsky, Myrna. *José Donoso: incursiones en su producción novelesca.* Valparaíso: Ediciones Universitarias de Valparaíso, 1983.

Stoopen, María. *"La muerte de Artemio Cruz": una novela de denuncia y traición.* Mexico: Universidad Nacional Autónoma de México, 1982.

Taggart, Kenneth M. *Yañez, Rulfo y Fuentes: el tema de la muerte en tres novelas mexicanas.* Madrid: Playor, 1983.

Urquidi Illanes, Julia. *Lo que Varguitas no dijo.* La Paz, Bolivia: Khana Cruz, 1983.

Uzal, Francisco Hipolito. *Nación, sionismo y masonería: rectificaciones a Ernesto Sábato.* Buenos Aires: Corregidor, 1980.

Verani, Hugo J. *Onetti: el ritual de la impostura.* Caracas: Monte Avila, 1981.

Vidal, Hernán. *José Donoso: surrealismo y rebelión de los instintos.* San Antonio de Calonge, Gerona: Aubi, 1972.

Wainerman, Luis. *Sábato y el misterio de los ciegos.* Buenos Aires: Castaneda, 1978.

Yamal, Ricardo. *Sistema y visión de la poesía de Nicanor Parra.* Valencia: Albatros, 1985.

B. In English

Adams, Michael Ian. *Three Authors of Alienation: Bombal, Onetti, Carpentier.* Austin: University of Texas Press, 1975.

Bacarisse, Salvador. *Contemporary Latin American Fiction: Carpentier, Sábato, Onetti, Roa, Donoso, García Márquez, Fuentes: Seven Essays.* Edinburgh: Scottish Academic Press, 1980.

Brody, Robert, and Charles Rossman, eds. *Carlos Fuentes: a Critical View.* Austin: University of Texas, 1982.

Claude Ollier / Carlos Fuentes Number. *Review of Contemporary Fiction* 8, no. 2 (Summer 1988): 147-291.

Díez, Luis Alfonso. *Mario Vargas Llosa's Pursuit of the Total Novel.* Cuernavaca, Mexico: Cidoc, 1970.

Durán, Gloria. *The Archetype of Carlos Fuentes: from Witch to Androgyne.* Hamden, CT: Archon, 1980.

Faris, Wendy B. *Carlos Fuentes.* New York: Ungar, 1983.

Feal Geisdorfer, Rosemary. *Novel Lives: The Fictional Autobiographies of Guillermo Cabrera Infante and Mario Vargas Llosa.* Chapel Hill: University of North Carolina Press, 1986.

Fenwick, M. J. *Dependency Theory and Literary Analysis: Reflections on Vargas Llosa's "The Green House."* Minneapolis: Institute for the Study of Ideologies and Literatures, 1981.

Foster, David W. *Currents in the Contemporary Argentine Novel: Arlt, Mallea, Sábato, and Cortázar.* Columbia: University of Missouri Press, 1975.

Gerdes, Dick. *Mario Vargas Llosa.* Boston: Twayne, 1985.

Grossman, Edith. *The Antipoetry of Nicanor Parra.* New York: New York University Press, 1975.

Guilbert, Rita. *Seven Voices: Pablo Neruda, Jorge Luis Borges, Miguel Angel Asturias, Octavio Paz, Julio Cortázar, Gabriel García Márquez, and Guillermo Cabrera Infante.* New York: Knopf, 1972.

Guzmán, Daniel de. *Carlos Fuentes.* New York: Twayne, 1972.

Hellerman, Myrna Kasey. *Myth and Mexican Identity in the Works of Carlos Fuentes.* Stanford: 1972.

Jones, Yvonne Perier. *The Formal Expression of Meaning in Juan Carlos Onetti's Narrative Art.* Cuernavaca, Mexico: Centro Intercultural de Documentación, 1971.

Kadir, Djelal. *Juan Carlos Onetti.* Boston: Twayne, 1977.

Kerr, Lucille. *Suspended Fictions: Reading Novels by Manuel Puig.* Urbana: University of Illinois Press, 1987.

Kushigian, Julia. "Three Versions of Orientalism in Contemporary Latin American Literature: Sarduy, Borges, and Paz." *Dissertation Abstracts International* 46, no. 4 (1985): 993A.

Lewis, Marvin A. *From Lima to Leticia: The Peruvian Novels of Mario Vargas Llosa.* Landham, MD: University Press of America, 1983.

Luisa Valenzuela Number. *Review of Contemporary Fiction* 6, no. 3 (Fall 1986).

McMurray, George R. *José Donoso.* Boston: Twayne, 1979.

Magnarelli, Sharon. *Reflections / Refractions: Reading Luisa Valenzuela.* New York: Peter Lang, 1988.

Merrim, Stephanie. *Logos and the Word: The Novel of Language and Linguistic Motivation in "Grande sertao, veredas" and "Tres tristes tigres."* New York: Peter Lang, 1983.

Millington, Mark. *Reading Onetti: Language, Narrative and the Subject.* Liverpool: Cairns, 1985.

Minc, Rose S., ed. *Literature and Popular Culture in the Hispanic World: a Symposium.* Gaithersburg, MD: Hispamérica, 1981.

Nelson, Ardis L. *Cabrera Infante in the Menippean Tradition.* Newark, DE: J. de la Cuesta, 1983.

Oberhelman, Harley D. *Ernesto Sábato.* New York: Twayne, 1970.

Paolini, Gilbert, ed. La Chispa. *Selected Proceedings, Feb. 26-28, 1981.* New Orleans: Tulane University, 1981.

Pokorny, Elba Doris. "The Theme of Alienation in Contemporary Spanish American Literature as Exemplified by Juan Carlos Onetti." *Dissertation Abstracts International* 47, no. 4 (1986): 1343A.

Quintana de Rubero, Hilda. "Myth and Politics in *The Passion according to Antígona Pérez* by Luis Rafael Sánchez." *Dissertation Abstracts International* 44, no. 9 (1984): 2760A.

Robbins, Stephanie Laird Malinoff. *Persona in the Poetry of César Vallejo, Jorge Guillén, and Nicanor Parra.* Austin: University of Texas Press, 1970.

Rossman, Charles, and Alan Warren Friedman, eds. *Mario Vargas Llosa: A Collection of Critical Essays.* Austin: University of Texas Press, 1978.

Salinas, Judy Kay Ferguson. *Social Reform in Selected Works of Carlos Fuentes.* Norman: University of Oklahoma Press, 1971.

Standish, Peter. *Vargas Llosa: "La ciudad y los perros."* London: Grant & Cutler, 1982.

Swanson, Philip. *José Donoso, the "boom" and beyond.* Liverpool: F. Cairns, 1988.